Prairie Fire

Prairie Fire
A Great Plains History

Julie Courtwright

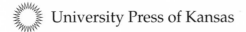 University Press of Kansas

Published by the University Press of Kansas (Lawrence, Kansas 66045), which was organized by the Kansas Board of Regents and is operated and funded by Emporia State University, Fort Hays State University, Kansas State University, Pittsburg State University, the University of Kansas, and Wichita State University

Library of Congress Cataloging-in-Publication Data

Courtwright, Julie.
Prairie fire : a Great Plains history / Julie Courtwright.
p. cm.
Includes bibliographical references and index.
ISBN 978-0-7006-1794-4 (cloth : alk. paper)
1. Grassland fires—Great Plains—History. 2. Grassland fires—Great Plains—Prevention and control—History. 3. Fires—Great Plains—History. 4. Prairies—Great Plains—History. 5. Prairie ecology—Great Plains—History. 6. Human ecology—Great Plains—History. 7. Indians of North America—Great Plains—History. 8. Great Plains—Environmental conditions. 9. Great Plains—History. I. Title.
SD421.5.C68   2011
633.2'08918—dc23
2011029126

British Library Cataloguing-in-Publication Data is available.

Printed in the United States of America

10 9 8 7 6 5 4 3 2 1

The paper used in this publication is recycled and contains 30 percent postconsumer waste. It is acid free and meets the minimum requirements of the American National Standard for Permanence of Paper for Printed Library Materials Z39.48-1992.

For my parents, Philip and Carol Courtwright,
with love and thanks for everything

Contents

Acknowledgments

For eight years now my friends and colleagues have teased me about my obsession with "smokin' grass." It's an addiction I freely admit. Indeed, I have become famous among my friends and acquaintances for my weird ability to connect virtually any topic under discussion to prairie fire—a skill that serves absolutely no purpose. Still, it was my passion for flaming grass and for the Great Plains that pushed this book to completion—plus a lot of help along the way.

That help came from numerous people, none of whom I can ever repay for their kindness, expertise, and good humor. First and foremost, Dr. Elliott West, Distinguished Professor of History at the University of Arkansas, spent countless hours over the years talking prairie fire with me and provided invaluable encouragement and advice over the breadth of the project. Elliott is a wonderfully insightful and quirky scholar, possessing more imagination than any other human I have ever met. I thank him for his confidence in me (when I didn't always have it myself), for his friendship, and for his uncanny knack for knowing just what to say.

I owe a tremendous debt to the Department of History at the University of Arkansas for financial assistance during my first few years of research and writing. In particular, Dr. Jeannie Whayne, professor and former department chair, showed me enormous kindness and encouragement. I thank her for her constant support and friendship as well as for not taking offense at a certain spirited "Well, how's *your* book going?" exchange in the hallway at the end of a frustrating day. Dr. Patrick Williams read an early draft of my manuscript and worked his usual magic with his editor's pencil. I thank him for his insight and for understanding why Kansas is so important. Patrick got a kick out of the "flaming jackrabbits" discussion in the book, and I think of him each time those critters hop through my mind.

Without generous research grants from Fulbright College at the University of Arkansas, the Kansas State Historical Society, and Iowa State University, this book would have far fewer footnotes. The support these institutions gave to me during the research and publication phases allowed me to drive the Plains in search of prairie fire, present my research at scholarly conferences, and locate photographs for the finished book.

Many individuals took the time to offer advice, research tips, or emotional support over the years. Dr. James Sherow at Kansas State University was a source for prairie ecology early in the research process. Dr. Geoff Cunfer at the University of Saskatchewan and Dr. James Hoy at Emporia State University each offered valuable advice and encouragement. Numerous archivists across the Great Plains helped in my search for material, very little of which was conveniently cataloged under "fire" in their computers. My friend Dr. Craig Miner at Wichita State University provided knowledge on Kansas history and kept his eyes open for prairie fire references. Craig always said that someday we'd exchange books—a copy of his latest for one of mine. He died a year before this book's publication, and I deeply regret that we will not be able to make that trade. I hope he knew that this book would not exist without his example and help.

Since arriving on campus in August 2009 I have received tremendous support from the Department of History at Iowa State University. Dr. Pamela Riney-Kehrberg, professor and chair, read my manuscript during several stages of the revision process and offered helpful critiques and edits. Dr. Charles Dobbs, Dr. Brian Behnken, and Dr. Kathleen Hilliard, as well as virtually every other member of the history faculty, have been a constant source of encouragement and generosity. I look forward to deepening friendships and collegial conversations in the years to come. Jennifer Rivera, department secretary, is the person who has taught me the most about Iowa State. Among the graduate students, Dr. Angie Gumm (a fellow proud Kansan!), Will Hunt, and Kelly Wenig have, in particular, contributed their opinions and lent me their ears. I value their questions, as they force me to think beyond the level to which I would push myself.

I have many good friends who have helped me either directly or indirectly with this project. Derek Everett and Jason Pierce (both fellow Westerners and "disciples" of West) each brought me a steady stream of prairie fire stories and citations they encountered along the way. Derek earned the title "King of Weird Prairie Fire References" when he found a cappuccino machine that used a brand of coffee called Prairie Fire at a gas station in Missouri, went to his car to retrieve his camera, and took pictures of it for me despite getting odd looks from the store attendants for his abnormal interest in their coffee maker!

Jason, Derek, and other friends—Aneilya Barnes, Matt Byron, Tammy Byron, James Finck, Scott Tarnowieckyi, and Gene Vinzant—all provided laughter, sympathy, and decidedly unintellectual discourse at countless lunches over the years. Without these folks, life for me would have been far less fun. Thanks to them, with hope that we will continue our discourse in the years to come.

During the last half-dozen years or so I have found many dog-training friends in Arkansas, Texas, and Iowa. Real dog people are the best people I know, so I'm honored to include myself among them. Back in 2005 Valerie Murphy, Ed Minar, Donna and Randy Phillips, and Mary Haney, among others at Canine Connection in Fayetteville, Arkansas, gave me something to talk about (dogs!) other than prairie fire. From 2007 to 2009 Eve Peacock, Jean Miller, and the rest of my Texas Aussie and agility friends made me feel at home in an unfamiliar place. Thanks for letting a funny Border Terrier and a wild Cavalier run with the Aussies. In Iowa Renee White and her devoted agility students and dogs at Canine Craze in Urbandale, as well as all my agility friends in Ames, provide a welcome respite from the pressures of academic life. My friends in the dog world, more than any other people in my life, will understand why I also must thank my dogs, Mabel and Pearl (even though they can't read this—at least I don't think they can . . .). If I didn't have them to take care of me, nothing else would matter.

Back home in Kansas my family and friends always provide unquestioning support for whatever I do. I do not often say so, but I rely on them very much. Thanks to my good Kansas friends—

Kristyn Eastman and the rest of the "A Group." They know who they are. My parents, Phil and Carol Courtwright, were always there for me and gave me the time to finally decide in which direction to take my life. I thank them for being who they are and for everything they taught (and continue to teach) me. The same goes for my grandparents and great-grandparents, all of whom are gone now except my Grandma Mary, but all of whom continue to inspire me.

My brother, sister, and I were lucky to grow up in a small Kansas town in which our family roots run deep. Recently I had occasion to spend more time in Augusta than I had in years. Every time I went to the grocery store or the public library, it seemed, I ran into someone who had known my family for a very long time. "I knew your grandmother," was a sentence I heard more than once. I do not take that connection lightly, for it was those roots that fostered in me a sense of place and a love for my home state and the rest of the Great Plains. Fundamentally, it is that connection that made me want to tell their story. Well . . . that and an obsession with "smokin' grass."

Julie Courtwright
April 11, 2011
Ames, Iowa

Prairie Fire

Burnt Prairie, Illinois, highway sign. Photograph by Derek Everett.

"Think of This"

Mr. Wheaton did his best, but he could not save his wife and son. Perhaps, as a newcomer, he simply did not know what to do. The fire came too suddenly and left no refuge. Surrounded by open prairie, Wheaton drove his oxen-drawn wagon, carrying his wife and two children, onto the piece of ground with the lightest grass cover. The inadequacy of the plan was magnified by the family's disastrous decision to get out of the wagon to wait for the fire. Soon it was upon them, and the oxen spooked. In the seconds that Wheaton took to calm the team, and then to grab his daughter and place her in the wagon, the prairie fire overtook his wife and son. Wheaton rushed to their aid, burning one hand so severely that he later lost it, but he could not save them. Mother and son died a few agonizing hours later, whereas Wheaton's daughter, the only person inside the wagon as the fire rushed by, was uninjured. The local newspaper editor in El Dorado, Kansas, appropriately shocked at the tragedy that had occurred just nine miles west of town, used the occasion to warn his readers of the dreaded prairie fires of the Plains and to shame any careless residents. "Think of this," the editor wrote, "you who willfully set fire to our almost limitless prairies."[1]

A second fire near El Dorado began by accident. Town officials and citizens heard the report that the prairie was on fire shortly after noon one dry and windy March day and spent the next five hours dealing with the emergency. People from El Dorado and the surrounding area, many of them volunteers, turned out to fight the fire, which, unlike the blaze that had killed the Wheatons, threatened property and even the town itself. As the flames spread over the grassland on the northwest end of town, spewing choking smoke into the air, teachers evacuated students as a precaution, and citizens whose homes were threatened rushed to save personal items or to help neighbors in trouble. In the end, ten thousand acres; one unoccupied house; and a few outbuildings, woodpiles, and other miscellaneous property burned, but no homes or lives were lost due to the efficient work of those fighting the fire. This time the local editor praised the efforts of the citizens and reflected that they had sidestepped a tragedy. "It Could Have Been a Nightmare," the editorial headline read.[2]

Although one fire took human life and the other only minimal property, the two were more alike than not. They shared a location, pushed across the same piece of prairie by the seemingly unceasing Kansas wind blowing from the southwest. Each fire was threatening, each feared, each misunderstood, and each, in its own way, a typical Great Plains prairie fire—part of a long history of fires in the region. Each, too, burned in my home county. Butler County, Kansas, where I was born and spent the first twenty-eight years of my life, is part of the North American tallgrass prairie. In fact, the Flint Hills of Kansas, where Butler County is located, constitute the largest section of unplowed tallgrass prairie in the world.[3] Fire is common in such a place, even vital, so the burning prairie is not new to me, although neither of the two fires in question burned while I was in the county. The first happened in October 1872, almost exactly one hundred years before I was born. The second occurred in March 2006, just as I was settling down to start this manuscript in Fayetteville, Arkansas. Although the two fires burned the grass 134 years apart and ultimately had different consequences, both were remarkably similar in the threat that they represented to nearby citizens and in the response that they generated from those citizens. Each fire was met with resistance, and each fire caused a community (the same community, in fact) to react.

Together the two fires indicate continuity in a region that has experienced rapid change over the years, particularly since the onset of Euro-American settlement in the mid–nineteenth century. In 2006 the technology used to fight the fire was more advanced, the groups of professionals and volunteers mobilized a bit more bureaucratically, and the prairies seemed not quite so limitless, but the grass burned just as it did in 1872, and the danger was just as real.

It is true that uncontrolled prairie fires are less frequent in the twenty-first century than they were in the nineteenth. Still, modern Plains people retain an awareness of the historical fires that helped shape their region, and occasional modern fires, such as that near El Dorado, help remind them. In 2006 fires scorched thousands of acres in Texas, Oklahoma, and Kansas, burning barns, fences, and homes that stood in the way. Hundreds of people were forced to evacuate as the fires threatened their towns.[4] The media, perhaps more accustomed to reporting on forest fires, replaced the historical term "prairie fire" with the more neutral "wildfire," or occasionally with "grass fire," but the name change did not alter the event. Prairie fires, both present and past, remain a presence on the Great Plains.

The fires are important because they affected (and continue to affect) the lives of Plains people. Yet their influence does not end there. Prairie fire is also a critical part of the environmental history of the region. In this role, fire connects stories such as Mr. Wheaton's to place and, on a large scale, helps to explain how people, acting on and within their environment, cause significant change to that environment. Prairie fire is as fundamental to the Great Plains as the sun, soil, wind, grazers, and grass. It influences grass composition; allows for more nutritious growth on which cattle can graze; and, when applied regularly, prevents trees from intruding into native prairie grasses. Furthermore, fire's *absence* is just as influential as its *presence*. When human beings suppress fire on the plains and prairies, it is just as significant as when they apply fire. Prairie fire's influence never goes away. Whether absent or present, it plays a pivotal role in the environmental history of the Plains.

A history of prairie fire, therefore, is an important addition to the American West and Great Plains environmental story—a piece of the puzzle that has been missing. Even before environmental history emerged as a distinct field of study in the 1970s, and before it was "academically cool," some historians connected the grassland environment to history. They paid attention to the Great Plains and to how Plains people interacted with the region. Walter Prescott Webb, in *The Great Plains* (1931), argued that the unique environmental characteristics of the prairie—space, lack of trees, and aridity—caused would-be settlers to adapt technologically as well as socially in order to flourish in a place so different than the East. James Malin, professor of history at the University of Kansas from 1921 to 1963, fused ecology and history. He believed that human ingenuity could overcome the obstacles or limits set by nature, even on the semiarid grasslands. Malin used this argument to counter claims, made by government representatives during the Dust Bowl, that the Plains should not have been plowed. In his 2005 book *On The Great Plains: Agriculture and Environment*, Geoff Cunfer offered an updated interpretation of Malin's theories when he argued that land use in the region has been remarkably stable and can be called, therefore, sustainable. Farmers learn how to utilize the Plains, then adapt as circumstances change.[5]

Much of historians' study of the Great Plains environment has focused on crisis. Donald Worster and Pamela Riney-Kehrberg, for example, examined the Dust Bowl on the Southern Plains. Worster argued that farmers, driven by capitalism, plowed too much of the soil. The plow-up caused the dust to fly in the 1930s and forced destitute farmers out of the region. Whereas Worster focused on the cause of the crisis and on those who left, Riney-Kehrberg studied those who stayed. She maintained that the great plow-up was a factor in the Dust Bowl but that the event was actually part of a much larger, recurring cycle of drought and dust on the Plains. Farmers and ranchers were not entirely to blame. Riney-Kehrberg presented a social as well as environmental history of southwestern Kansas and told the stories of the people who stayed in the state and worked through the crisis.[6]

In 1998 Elliott West also examined environmental crisis on the Plains. He argued, in *The Contested Plains: Indians, Goldseekers, and the Rush to Colorado*, that competing visions of the Plains held by peoples who both lived there and traveled through the region led to competing land-use practices; competition for resources; and unintended environmental consequences, including the destruction of key "microenvironments" that aided in the demise of the bison. Other scholars, such as Andrew Isenberg, Dan Flores, and James Sherow have also studied the complex circumstances surrounding the bison's decline.[7]

Perhaps attracted to the Plains because it is one of the most altered ecosystems on earth, these and other historians have expanded our knowledge about the interaction between human beings and

the grasslands. Environmental historians contend that human beings are not separate from their environment but are a part of it. The
environment is thus a full player in historical events. Richard White
compared the interaction between people and the nonhuman world
to a conversation—a continual exchange between participants. Engaged in this long conversation, neither human beings nor the environment are unchanged. Each continually influences the other.[8]
Although environmental and American West historians have documented significant parts of the ongoing human-grasslands conversation—most notably the introduction of large-scale monoculture,
the Dust Bowl, and the decline of the bison—they have not examined in any detail prairie fire and its environmental and social role
in the history of the Great Plains. Human beings, prairie fire, and the
Great Plains have been engaged in a conversation for centuries. It is
time for historians to sit up and take notice.

Fire history is not, of course, limited to the prairies and Plains.
Fire has played a universally significant role in landscapes and cultures throughout the world.[9] As such, its story extends far beyond
the boundaries of the vast Great Plains. The fire history of the Plains
is thus an addition to a developing literature that points us toward
a greater understanding of world fire history. Although numerous
historians, folklorists, and others have briefly noted the significance
of prairie fire in individual book chapters, articles, and essays, no
one has examined the topic thoroughly or made significant use
of the numerous primary accounts of fires that fill the archives.[10]
People who experienced prairie fire wanted, and perhaps needed,
to tell their stories. Historians should use these individual narra-
tives to help communicate the collective Great Plains fire story. Doing so will furnish a missing piece of fire history—examining North
American prairie fire on its own terms and not, as is often the case,
as a less significant "second cousin" of sorts to forest fire. Taking its
place amid other fire histories, the history of prairie fire on the Great
Plains thus extends beyond its regional focus.

The history of prairie fire is at once simple and complex. At its
most basic, yet vitally important, level, each fire that burned across
the prairies over hundreds of years is part of someone's personal
narrative. Even the small fires, absent from the records of history,
changed lives—became a story told to someone's children and their
grandchildren, destroyed someone's property, threatened some-

one's safety, made someone's breath catch because of a fire's astounding beauty.

For individual people, whose stories too often get left out of published histories in favor of larger (and supposedly more significant) historical issues, the experience of prairie fire was terrifying, exhilarating, devastating, mesmerizing. Perhaps above all, it was binding. Prairie fire—setting it, fighting it, watching it, fearing it—bound Plains people to each other and to the prairies themselves. It is a part of everyone who is or becomes native to the Great Plains.[11]

Certainly until the twentieth century Plains people—Native and Euro-American—were a prairie fire people. Some still are. Take, for example, South Dakota rancher and writer Linda Hasselstrom, who, in her book *No Place Like Home: Notes from a Western Life*, noted that beating out flaming grass with a wet gunnysack is part of her definition of "home."[12] Similarly, Oklahoman Ree Drummond (a.k.a. The Pioneer Woman), in her popular blog about life on a working ranch, described a prairie fire on her family's land in November 2010. Drummond worried about the safety of her husband and oldest son, who hurried to the front line as soon as they got word that an uncontrolled fire burned on a neighbor's land. Everything turned out fine, largely because neighbors rushed to help fight the fire. "Some are landowners, some are cowboys, some are wellmeaning friends from town," Drummond later wrote in her blog. "And they all rush to the scene in whatever water-holding vehicle they can find and work together. . . . When [the community effort] works—and it usually does work—it's a beautiful sight to behold." As Drummond's description illustrates, some of the most important things about fire have not changed in the centuries during which it has been a part of the prairies. Witnesses may blog and post digital pictures online to tell their stories rather than send letters by train or telegraph to relatives in the East, but the stories themselves are eerily similar. Just like women who lived on the Plains in decades and centuries past, Drummond worried about her family's safety; admired how a community worked together to meet the emergency; and, from a safe observation point, marveled at the beauty of the blaze. "Have you ever sat in a vehicle and observed a prairie fire from a distance?" she wondered. "I'd recommend it sometime." If not for her references to modern technology, Drummond's observations about prairie fire might be from 1870, or even 1670, rather than 2010.[13]

Drummond is one of the lucky modern Plains residents who get to experience prairie fire firsthand. For most Plains people, as well as for the curious who live outside the region, such opportunities are rare. When they do arise, the danger of the fires usually surpasses adventure and beauty. Most people, therefore, have to experience prairie fire through historical accounts and, much less seriously, through popular culture.

Prairie fires thrive as a part of the mythic past. Starting in the late nineteenth and early twentieth centuries, the famed showman Buffalo Bill Cody included a prairie fire scene in his Wild West shows. Even smaller shows, such as the Oklahoma-based Pawnee Bill's Historical Wild West, featured fires. Pawnee Bill's official program for 1905 advertised "The Burning of Trapper Tom's Cabin." Spectators were urged to "kindly remain seated until the end of this act, as it illustrates the Massacre of the White Settlers, Burning of the Cabin, Prairie Fire, [and] Rescue of the Daughter."[14]

Exciting and dangerous, the fires of the past have earned their place in present-day stories of the "Wild West." A "swift-running, sky-blackening prairie fire" made an orphan out of one of author Denver Bardwell's main characters in his 1940 "Gunfire Western Novel" titled *Prairie Fire*. More recently, Hank Mitchum's novel *Red Buffalo* (1989) highlights the adventures of a greenhorn who travels by stage to Dakota Territory in 1877 and is quickly educated in the dangers of the prairie.[15] A less traditional adventure story is Don Pendleton's *Mack Bolan: Prairie Fire* (1984), set in Kansas in the post–Vietnam War/Cold War era. Bolan, a.k.a. "The Executioner," runs from "The Cowboy," a man hired by enemies of America and the "American way." Bolan's mission is to protect America, and the author uses a prairie fire as a metaphor for his protagonist. Bolan, like a prairie fire, moves fast across Kansas, "purifying" the land with his actions. In this novel, prairie fire is a metaphor for conquest.[16] Don Coldsmith, in contrast to Pendleton's bellicose prose, has woven a thoughtful story of fictionalized Native peoples into the known historical context of the region in his Spanish Bit novel series and included the Native American experience with prairie fire and with purposeful burning.[17]

Even children's literature features prairie fire as a part of the West. Laura Ingalls Wilder recounted the most widely read description of prairie fire in her 1935 classic *Little House on the Prairie*.[18] The 1970s television show inspired by Wilder's books featured a prairie fire in the pilot episode and even launched a *Little House* board game, which required players to make their way through various prairie "dangers"—one of which was fire—to safety.[19] In the 1950s, London publishers eager to take advantage of the public's fascination with the American West issued *Gene Autry and the Prairie Fire*, a children's pop-up book featuring Autry and his battle with a gang of thieving bank robbers who set the prairie afire to distract the townspeople from their nefarious goal. Autry, who cleverly deduces the robbers' plan, abandons the prairie fire fight to hunt the bad guys down. The townspeople mistakenly believe Autry is afraid to fight the dangerous blaze and call him a coward until they learn the truth.[20] More recently, children's author Betty G. Birney published her children's adventure story *Tyrannosaurus Tex* (1994) about a dinosaur in the West who fills his "ten-thousand-gallon hat" with water to put out a prairie fire started by cattle rustlers. Tex succeeds in his efforts, but not before the cowboys, in an effort to teach the rustlers a lesson, throw a bag of corn into the fire, causing the dried kernels to start "popping like fireworks on the Fourth of July."[21]

Prairie fire also blazes through the pages of various romance novels. Authors use the fires as a symbol of passionate, wild, untamed lust. In Patricia Werner's 1988 bodice-ripper, *Prairie Fire*, a white woman on the ranchlands of Oklahoma Territory in 1887 falls in love with a Cherokee Indian named Raven Sky. The ensuing "encounters" between the two allow Werner plenty of opportunity to employ the hot prairie fire metaphor. Other romances, though not graced with terribly original titles (please do not judge historians with insistent editors and a sense of irony too harshly for a similar lack of creativity), run the gamut of experiences. *Prairie Fire* (1998) by Catherine Palmer is a "Christian historical romance novel"; *Prairie Fire* (2001) by Terri Branson is a paranormal romance; and *Prairie Fire* (2002) by L. J. Maas is a traditional Western romance featuring lesbian protagonists.[22]

Beyond the written word, prairie fire has been featured in movies such as the 1938 film *The Texans*; as the title and main event of a 1960s television episode of *Rawhide*; in country music songs such as

Marty Robbins's "Prairie Fire"; as a name for a blistering-hot red, yellow, and orange pepper plant; and even as an adult beverage, made by combining tequila or rum with Tabasco sauce and served in a shot glass. Ignite the shot with a match before serving at your own risk.[23]

Although such pop-culture references (and many others too numerous to mention—you never know what will appear on eBay) are tangential reminders of prairie fire's history on the Plains, the images presented in books, shows, songs, and the rest actually belong to the imagined West more than to the real Great Plains. They, like so many other manufactured symbols, are entertaining but ultimately are only caricatures of the fires they represent.

Real prairie fires, even controlled versions, are much more interesting and, of course, significant to the real Great Plains. Sometimes, on particular parts of the Plains, events more pleasant than the threat of evacuation serve as subtle nudges to link the legacy of fire with the consciousness of the region's people. Neither of the two El Dorado fires nor the recent wild blazes in Texas and Oklahoma, for example, were like those I am used to. I did not grow up on a farm or a ranch, but I nevertheless experienced, if only marginally, the annual controlled fires just to the north and east of my home, a more common type of modern grass fire than the threatening ones of 2006. The Flint Hills of Kansas are famous for the rock that inspired their name, for their treeless wide expanses, and for grass so magnificent that one native writer deemed it "green gold."[24] Fire can make no claim on the rock, but other characteristics of the area owe much to it. The ranchers of the Flint Hills burn the prairie almost annually. They do it to keep the prairie healthy, to burn away the old grass and make way for the new, to support their cattle. They do it because their fathers and grandfathers and great-grandfathers did it. They do it because the Indians who once dominated the region did it. They do it because fire is part of the prairie.

The tradition of springtime firing, known to locals as "burnin' pasture," therefore, is at once a necessary agricultural task and a traditional folk custom.[25] It provides a stunningly beautiful reminder of fire's role. The people of Wichita, many of whom have never set foot on a ranch, understand the cause of the burned-grass smell that drifts into the city from the northeast every April. Artists and photographers capture the magnificent images to preserve regional culture. Journalists dutifully note the legacy both of Indian and Euro-American burning but rarely dig more deeply into the historical record. Prairie fires, through remnant burns, art, literature, vernacular, and an intangible awareness that comes with roots in the region, are part of the identity of Plains people.

Despite the long history of fire use in the region and the continued presence of prairie fires on the Plains, both physical and symbolic, historians have, with a few exceptions, neglected the topic. They have allowed scientists to dominate the subject while their attention has rested on other matters, most notably the great plow-up of Plains soil that came with white settlement. This is an odd disjunction that needs correcting. The relationship between fire and humans has shaped Plains ecology and Plains history for centuries. The suppression of prairie fire, which began with Euro-American settlement, was one of the most significant events in Great Plains environmental history. Prairie fire's role on the Plains, its culturally driven use and suppression, and its enduring ties to regional identity make its story well worth our attention.

Historians' neglect of prairie fire reminds me of a story: In October 1878 rumors of an impending Indian attack swept through south-central Nebraska, sending the population into a panic. Someone had seen a war party in Phelps County, and neighbors urged neighbors to pack up and flee before the massacre began. One party constructed a fortress around a home in northwest Kearney County. Their actions seemed justified when a passing rider told them that he had witnessed the Indians on the prairie doing a war dance around a fire. Settlers spent a tense night waiting for an attack that never came, for, despite the rider's panicked report, Indians were not the threat. It was *the fire* that demanded attention. As residents fled the rumored Indian attack, a prairie fire was burning in southwestern Phelps County. The supposed war dance had actually been a group of settlers jumping around, yelling, and using wet gunnysacks to beat out the flames while the rider looked on from a distance and misinterpreted everything he saw.[26]

Despite differences of opinion on the details, virtually all prairie scientists acknowledge that fire has had at minimum an influence on the entire Great Plains, a considerable impact on the tallgrass prairies, and arguably a considerable impact on the entire region. It follows that the *suppression* of fire has had an equally important

Anonymous, "Fighting the [prairie] fire." *Harper's Weekly* (February 28, 1874).
Courtesy of the Library of Congress.

role on nearly all of the Plains. Yet historians have paid far more attention to the plow, which, according to Cunfer, has touched only
30 percent of the midgrass and shortgrass country.[27] Although certainly more than 30 percent of the tallgrass region has been plowed,
this country likewise is more affected by fire suppression than areas
farther west.

A key difference between plowing and fire suppression may
account for historians' tendency to overlook the latter. Plowing,
planting, and their accompanying changes brought something new
to the region—new activity, new flora and fauna, dramatic changes
in appearance. Changing the ancient fire regime, by contrast, involved the reduction of what was already there. The change was
far less obvious because its consequence was not something seen
but something missing, and from the perspective of a century in the
future, what was new and present naturally caught the historian's
eye more than what was gone. Yet when Euro-Americans sought to
remake the Plains by eliminating fires that had burned for millen-
nia, a task that proved difficult and was never fully accomplished,
the results were considerable. Like the Native peoples before them,
Euro-American settlers, driven by their own cultural traditions and

economic imperatives, manipulated fire on the Plains. Both the outcome of the manipulation and the action itself were important—one helping to form the landscape and the other contributing to the identity of the region's people. Like the panic-stricken rider in Nebraska, we have not recognized the fire that demands our attention.

In *Prairie Fire: A Great Plains History* I hope to open a wider discussion of prairie fire and to foster recognition of its environmental and social influence on the Great Plains, thereby broadening the larger history of fire and of the American West. In particular, my focus is on the transition from American Indian use of fire to Euro-American settlement of the Plains and the settlers' subsequent attempt to suppress fire.

The first chapters describe the ecological importance of fire on the plains and prairies and the role of the American Indians as the original source of human-ignited prairie fire. The presettlement era (ca. 1535 to 1870) provided Euro-American explorers with an opportunity to form early impressions of prairie fire and its worth in the region. The fires were otherworldly, strange and alien, yet mesmerizing. Permanent, sedentary Euro-American settlement of the Plains (beginning ca. 1850), however, forced a shift in perception and ultimately resulted in the settlers' campaign to suppress fire on the Great Plains. Eliminating the fires, however, was not easy. Even in the midst of suppression the new Plains people had to contend with frequent, threatening prairie fire. They prepared for it, feared it, watched it approach, and learned how to fight it. Then, after a fire had passed, they dealt with the consequences—the immediate ones of the burns themselves and, more subtly, those of their efforts to eliminate fire from the landscape.

The act of fighting fire, as well as the suffering the blazes caused, significantly contributed to the identity of Plains peoples. So, unexpectedly, did the beauty. The magnificence of the prairie ablaze drew people in despite their best efforts to eliminate the very sight they admired. Prairie fire helped make the grasslands distinct and special. The beauty, along with the knowledge of fire and how to fight it, cultivated a familiarity with the flaming grass at odds with earlier presettlement attitudes. The new familiarity emerged even as suppression continued. Despite a cautious admiration for the fires, Plains people nevertheless felt that they had to eliminate them in order to safeguard their way of life and their version of the transformed, imagined Plains. On the modern Great Plains, a well-developed infrastructure and a campaign to curb fire have done their work (ca. 1940 to the present). Fire still burns on parts of the landscape, but most of the Plains today is affected more by its absence than by its presence. The majority of residents, once a prairie fire people, see the sight again, just as in the presettlement era, as unfamiliar—otherworldly, strange and alien, but still mesmerizing.

In many ways the history of prairie fire has come full circle. American Indians first applied fire to the grasslands and, in the process, helped shape the landscape. Euro-Americans, at first unacquainted with prairie fire, became familiar with it but now, through suppression efforts, have largely lost the acquaintance again. Still, in the last few decades, burning grass has once again garnered favor, at least among those who work most closely with the land and the grass. Perhaps a new cycle of familiarity, at least in a modified form, is beginning. Stories from the past can help. Plains people experienced prairie fire and wrote about it. There is much we can learn from their combined accounts, but the individual stories themselves, and the telling of them, are equally important.

The "red buffalo," as American Indian peoples reportedly called the great prairie fires that spread across the land, consuming the grass as they went, connects all Great Plains peoples, past and present, to the region and to each other.[28] Its story belongs to the Native peoples, to Mr. Wheaton, and to me. It is a history well worth the telling.

Chapter One

"Mass of Grass"

In an instant everything changed. A gust of wind, a stray spark, and a peaceful night by the campfire turned to fear and chaos in the face of uncontrolled prairie fire. Dark turned to blazing light and grass to ash. John Irving witnessed it all on the Central Plains in 1833. "In an instant," he noted, "fifty little fires shot their forked tongues in the air, and seemed to flicker with a momentary struggle for existence. There was scarcely time to note their birth, before they were creeping up in a tall, taper blaze and leaping lightly along the tops of the scattering clumps of dry grass." The explorer watched, astounded, as the wind hurled flakes of burning grass into the air. The fire grew and swept across the prairie, carried by the same wind that had initiated the trouble. "Leap succeeded leap," Irving wrote of the fire's travels. Each new bound propelled it to more fuel—more dry grass to feed the expanding flames.

Eventually the fire moved on, and Irving went to bed. When he arose at sunrise the sight before him was almost as amazing as the fire itself. The prairie was bare. "Not a single weed—not a blade of grass, was left," just the remains of one charred grove of trees. The fire had burned to the roots of the tall grass. "The sun had set upon a prairie still clothed in its natural garb of herbage," Irving mused. "It rose upon a scene of desolation."[1]

Fortunately, in the case of Irving's blaze and on countless other occasions when fire rendered a lush piece of prairie desolate, the effect was only temporary. In fact, the "desolation" was mostly illusion. Prairie fires like Irving's burn only the grass on the surface. They remove old growth, freeing the grass roots, undamaged belowground, to produce new.[2] Fire, therefore, does not kill the grass.

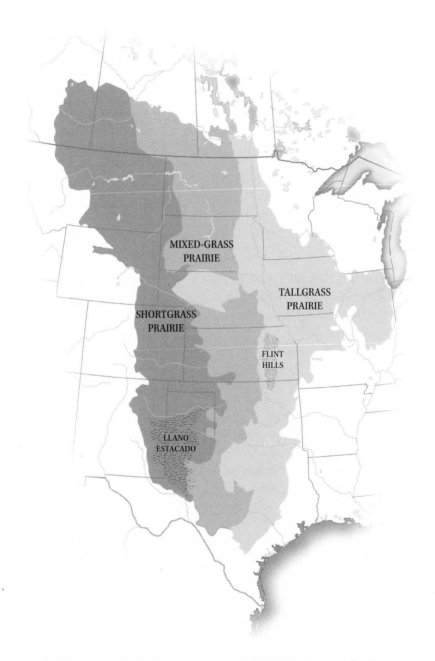

Great Plains map. Map by Lauren James and Darin Grauberger, the University of Kansas Cartographic Services.

Instead fire and grass sustain each other and, together, renew the prairie. Just as fire and grass are inexorably linked on the prairies and plains of North America, so too are their histories hopelessly intertwined.

Regrettably, written descriptions of the Plains stretch back only a few hundred years. "The first [Euro-American] arrivals to the Llano Estacado, or Staked Plains" of West Texas, one observer remembered, "found an almost unbroken stretch of dense, grass-matted table land, broken here and there only by dry lakes, creek beds and canyons."[3] Hundreds, perhaps thousands, of travelers described the Great Plains, which stretch 1,500 miles in length and between 400 and 700 miles in width across the center of the North American continent, as a great sea or ocean of grass.[4] Grass was the common link among varied written descriptions of the region dating from Francisco Vásquez de Coronado's journey across the Southern and Central Plains in 1541 until at least the 1920s, when roads and plowed fields became dominant over the once seemingly endless stretch of prairie. Even today, on parts of the Plains, grass still reigns supreme.

Despite observers' fascination with what one 1874 writer called the "mass of grass" that was the Great Plains, their understanding of it was minimal at best.[5] Coronado himself, disappointed by his failure to locate golden cities, noted that the Plains was "a wilderness in which nothing grew, except for very small plants." The discovery was not unpromising, however, because despite the dearth of larger vegetation, the land "nonetheless was teeming with millions upon millions of strange humpbacked cattle."[6] The "very small plants" were obviously nutritious and surprisingly hardy. Their diminutive and humble appearance was deceptive. Underneath the various types of grass and wildflowers lived a complex root network, which, combined with its more visible aboveground counterpart as well as hundreds of animal and insect species, created an environment that historian James Sherow compared to a "rich tapestry that seemed uncomplicated from a distance, but upon closer examination revealed an intricate binding of innumerable threads forming subtle patterns of color and design."[7]

Prairie naturalist writer Candace Savage called native grasses "the heart and soul of the prairie, the living link between the physical resources of the Great Plains—sunshine, rain and soil—and almost every other aspect of the ecosystem."[8] At least 140 grass species are native to the Great Plains, ranging in height from the 10-foot-high big bluestem to the ground-hugging blue grama. The plants, which many observers find unattractive and modest, are masters of their environment—highly evolved and able to flourish (far more efficiently than any human) in the cantankerous semiarid Great Plains climate.

Their main challenge is finding and keeping moisture. Aboveground the narrow leaves of the grasses provide a limited surface area for each plant, thus limiting moisture transpiration. During hot days the stomata, or valves, of the grasses close to minimize transpiration, then open up in the cooler nights to breathe in carbon dioxide without the risk of too much moisture loss. Beyond these safeguards, on some grasses ridges and hairs protect the plants from the wind, which, as it rushes over the grass, can draw out more moisture from smooth surfaces than from rough ones. Other plants roll their leaves during drought.[9]

The real action, however, takes place belowground, where 60 to 80 percent of the mass of grass is located. The 10-foot-high big bluestem's roots, for example, can stretch up to 12 more feet underground, whereas the blue grama, reaching only a few inches above the surface, has roots extending up to 6 feet underfoot. The extensive roots locate and utilize every available bit of moisture. The importance of the belowground action is obvious in drought conditions, when the grasses send vital sugars and proteins away from their stems and leaves and toward their roots. "Dead to the work above ground," Savage explained, "the plants live frugally below the surface." Despite the grasses' rather bleak appearance during times of scant rainfall, they are usually in fine shape underground. When the weather improves, even if only slightly, the resilient plants green up again. Blue grama, for example, requires only .2 inches of rainfall to "awaken" from dormancy. Taller eastern prairie plants need more moisture than shorter ones on the western High Plains, but, continued Savage, "all prairie grasses can contend with drought more successfully than can most deciduous trees—which is why the prairies are prairies instead of forests."[10]

Simplicity is just one common misperception about the grassland. Another is that the Plains never change. The so-called monotonous look of the prairies (for those not looking closely enough) and

the wide-open spaces inspired in observers a false sense of time-
lessness and inactivity. The observer from West Texas, for example,
after describing the unbroken expanse of dense, matted grassland,
noted that "the grass was unmolested except by roving herds of buffalo, antelope or wild horses." The first Euro-American settlers arrived on the prairies with the idea that they brought the potential
for change—what they thought of as "civilization"—with them. By
their terms the Plains before their arrival had been static. The Texan
and many others might have been surprised, in fact, to learn that
the same Llano Estacado Plains that supported all that magnificent
grass in the nineteenth century had hosted pine and spruce 14,000
years before and oak and juniper a mere 10,000 years ago.[11]

Even much more recently the Texan's statement could not with-
stand scrutiny. Disproving his "unmolested" claim with his own
words, the Texan next noted the influence of "that subtle, insidi-
ous enemy," both to the cattleman and to the grass, the prairie fire.
The Texan must have been well aware that human beings, both Native and Euro-American, were responsible for the majority of grassland fires. Still, he chose to describe prairie fire in one-dimensional
terms—as an enemy—and to ignore the fact that human beings,
through their use of fire, had a profound impact on the Plains environment before, during, and after Euro-American settlement. "The
ranker the growth on the grass-laden prairies the greater impetus
the fires assumed and the more furious they raged; consequently,
fires of the earlier days assumed enormous proportions," he continued. The blaze

> licked its fiery, flaming tongue in all directions seeking what it
> could devour. Its distressing roar and crackling . . . made the
> natives quake in horror, and it left a black and smouldering trail
> of desolation in its wake. It obscured the sun and darkened the
> sky. . . . At night it resembled a red river of fire extending in
> either direction as far as the eye could see. It illuminated the
> heavens. . . . It beggared all description.[12]

This sensual account betrayed a fundamental misunderstanding of fire's role. To this observer, and to many other "recent" (in the
past 500 years) arrivals to the Plains, prairie fire was an enemy to
the grass—a force that left only a desolate wasteland behind. Prairie

fires, in fact, played a critical role in prairie formation and mainte-nance. Clearing away old grass to make room for new was just the beginning. Fires also released nutrients back into the soil, limited the growth of woody intruders, influenced grass composition, and pro-moted grass variety and therefore richer forage.[13] Prairie fire even helped facilitate links between grasses and other life forms. Take, for example, the relationship between prairie grasses and mycorrhi-zae fungi. The many varieties of this fungus attach themselves to the outer root cells of prairie plants such as bluestem and buffalo grass. The plant supports the fungi, and the fungi help to convey needed phosphorus to the roots of the plants, thus improving growth. The heat of prairie fires increases the production of fungi spores, thereby ensuring that a hardy supply of mycorrhizae is present.[14]

Where there is grass, there is fire. The two are symbiotic. Prairie fire needed grass as a fuel source, but grass, as it developed on the Great Plains, also needed fire for its own health and to maintain its dominance over other forms of vegetation. When something or someone prevented the two from coming together, there was a de-cided impact. Take, for example, Flowerpot Mound in south-central Kansas. Covered at the top by sand and sage, this outpost stands above a surrounding sea of grass. Sherow noted the overhang of sandstone that forms the top of Flowerpot, protecting it from both fire and grazers. Meanwhile, for thousands of years, fire and grazers cropped, shaped, and altered the grassland around the mound, re-sulting in two distinct forms of vegetation on one piece of prairie.[15]

Over these thousands of years of evolution, grasses adapted to periodic burns. Unlike trees, which have growth points that are in-jured by fire and are sometimes left unable to produce new growth following a burn, grasses' growth points are under the soil and pro-duce new grass within two weeks after a spring burn. "Few species of trees can survive frequent, intense fires," one naturalist quipped. "Grasses, by contrast, are basically born to burn."[16]

The Great Plains is particularly friendly to fire. The region is a wet-dry landscape where, more than elsewhere, periods of pre-cipitation are often followed by drought.[17] Such a landscape is an ideal fire environment, unlike locations that are habitually either too soggy or too parched. Abundantly wet or dry environments rarely burn because of preventive moisture or lack of combustible fuel, re-spectively.[18] On the wet-dry Plains, however, grass grows profusely during the wet times, particularly in the eastern tallgrass prairies, where rainfall is more plentiful. Then a dry season withers the vegetation, making it flammable. Western and southerly winds easily push fire across the gently rolling landscape, with few obstacles to impede its progress.[19] In such an environment, noted one historian, "fire becomes not merely possible but also routine."[20]

Recurring fire in a fire-friendly place should not, however, imply simplicity. A multitude of environmental conditions, any number of which can and do affect a fire's path and intensity, ensure, as historian Stephen J. Pyne has suggested, that no single kind of prairie fire exists. Fires vary due to burn frequency, precipitation, topography, season, soil moisture, grass consistency, wind speed, and grazing history, among other factors. Diverse environmental conditions create diverse fires, which in turn produce diverse *results* from fires. Again a multitude of factors come into play. Even intentional "controlled" burns are not always controllable. During drought years there is often too little grass to burn, whereas other years are too wet. The unpredictable patterns of grazing animals also affect fuel loads, which affect burning patterns, which during the next season affect grazing once again. This constant dance among interdependent forces within the ecosystem—grass, grazers, climate, and fire—is not easily explained or predicted. "The choreography is complex," noted Pyne, "even chaotic, yet rhythms and regimes emerge."[21] Despite the complexity, one thing is clear. The grasses within the Great Plains of North America have long been influenced by, and in many ways are dependent on, fire.

It was only recently, however, that the Plains achieved the grass-dominated, treeless appearance that historical observers described. In the early Holocene (10,000 years ago), barely a blink in geologic time, the Great Plains of today was semiopen forest interspersed with grass. By the time Europeans viewed the Plains and recorded their observations, however, the area was an expanse of grass broken only occasionally by woody escarpments protected from fire.[22]

Scientists argue that a grassland initially formed in the region as a result of several factors. First, starting about 50 million years ago, the Rocky Mountains emerged, and rivers eroded debris eastward, eventually creating the flat landscape of the High Plains that remains familiar today. The mountains also formed a rain shadow, blocking most Pacific storm moisture from ever reaching beyond the eastern slope. Second, a significant shift in ocean currents elsewhere in the world resulted in an average global temperature reduction of 14 degrees Fahrenheit in only one million years. A corresponding decrease in moisture, both on the rain-shadowed Plains and world-wide, led to the demise of the then-dominant tropical forests. "But grasses don't require much moisture," Savage noted, "and this char-acteristic gave them a competitive edge. Over the next several mil-lion years . . . grasses gradually became the dominant plants across the Great Plains."[23] The evolution of this first grassland happened long before humans arrived on the scene.

Then came the Ice Age. Between three and two million years ago, a long winter of sorts settled in on the North American conti-nent. Ice sheets advanced and retreated several times, at one point extending as far south as present-day northeastern Kansas. The last big melt started 18,000 years ago and took many thousands of years to complete. In the meantime humans migrated into North America and, once again, the climate had changed—with consequences. The cooler, wetter weather during the Ice Age had allowed other veg-etation to supplant grasses, which, quite literally, had lost ground and dominance. Supported by lush, woody vegetation, broken only occasionally by remnant meadows, giant mammals such as woolly mammoths, bears, horses, cats, camels, and bison roamed what is now the Great Plains in the Pleistocene epoch.

Some 10,000 years ago came yet another dramatic reversal. The temperature of Earth rose significantly, and the giant mammals died out, either as a consequence of climate change or at the hands of human hunters or both. The animals were not the only life forms affected. Vegetation patterns also shifted. Forests faded in the wake of warmer, drier weather. "Spruce forests gave way to pines, then in places to open, mixed woodlands, and ultimately to grass," noted Savage. "In the blink of an eye (relatively speaking), a carpet of grasses spread out across the plains. . . . The prairies of historic times had finally been created."[24] This second coming of the grassland, argue some scientists, like the first, was a result of climate change. Although humans were present during the second transformation, they (and their use of fire), these scientists maintain, had little to do with the creation of the grasslands.[25]

"On the other hand," botanist Daniel Axelrod noted, "a con-siderable body of evidence has been assembled to indicate that fire has had a major role in the spread of grasslands."[26] In a paleoeco-logical study of ancient and current prairie and woodland sites in North Dakota, Minnesota, and Wisconsin, researchers found a wide fluctuation in prairie and woodland coverage area over the past several thousand years. Analysis of sediment produced evidence of increased burning 2,000 years ago, indicating that a moister cli-mate had produced more grass, thus providing a greater fuel load for fires, which extended the reach of the grassland at the expense of woodlands. The researchers demonstrated a clear partnership be-tween climate and fire for grassland formation and maintenance. "Across this prairie-forest transition we observe a range of sensitivi-ties and 'directions' of change, depending on vegetation, moisture, and fire," they concluded.[27]

Pyne drew similar conclusions, based in part on the accounts of historical observers, who noted fire's ability to stop tree and brush intrusion. Were prairie fires just an admittedly beautiful "ecological decoration" on the Plains, he asked, or were they instead a "flaming axe that hewed back the original forest"? Perhaps they were a little of each, but what is often overlooked in the midst of arguments re-garding fire's *formative* role on the grassland is its ability to *maintain*. "To argue over its might as a generative agent is to miss its greater power as a preserver; it could hold grasses against the woods, so long as weather allowed for dry spells and people wished to burn."[28]

The significance of fire in maintaining and extending the grass-lands suggests a greater human role than some scientists have al-lowed. Prairie fires come from two basic sources. Although the fre-quency of grass ignition from lightning is debated, it is clear that lightning does start prairie fires, most often during the summer thunderstorm season. One study of lightning-strike fires from 1940 to 1981 reported an average of between six and ninety-one fires each year per 10,000 kilometers^2 within several defined study areas in the Dakotas and Montana. The researchers found that 73 percent of those ignitions occurred in July and August, with other strike fires reported in April, May, June, and September.[29] Still, the importance of lightning as a source of ignition is limited. Only a small percent-age of lightning strikes kindle fire.[30] The strikes that do are usually accompanied by rain, which limits the size and scope of any fledg-ling burns. Also, because of the rain, the grass in summer on the Plains is often greener than at other times of year, which further limits burn potential.[31] The real fire season, as anyone who has lived on the Plains for any length of time could attest, begins not in the rainy period but in autumn, when the lush, rain-nourished summer growth dries, providing plenty of fuel. By that time of year lightning strikes are far less common.[32] Instead ignition comes from a second and much more volatile source.

Most scholars now argue that humans started many more fires on the Plains than lightning, but this opinion was not always so common.[33] Anthropologists, ethnographers, ecologists, and historians alike dismissed American Indian use of fire, and consequently the influence of human ignitions on prairie ecology, for the better part of the twentieth century.[34] Working mid–twentieth century, anthropologist Omer C. Stewart criticized scholars for ignoring American Indian burns and argued that Native peoples used fire to generate and maintain the grasslands. Stewart's work was a complete deviation from the opinions of established ecologists and anthropologists of the day. Many refused to believe that the Indians had either the technological knowledge to carry out large-scale burns or any awareness of the ecological consequences of burning. Since the 1950s, work in the biological sciences has supported Stewart's conclusions.[35] Still, some scholars remained skeptical. Thomas R. Vale, for example, arguing in favor of a continuum of human impact on the pre-European West concluded that Indian fires likely had more influence in some locations than in others but overall did not significantly affect the Great Plains environment.[36]

Pyne found the evidence of Indian burns so conclusive that he considered the scholarly debate over the issue to be "fantastic." The debate had more to do with the cultural context of Euro-Americans than with actual evidence, he concluded. In the early years of settlement Euro-Americans fully acknowledged that Indians purposefully set fire to the prairie. It would never have occurred to them to think otherwise. Over time, however, Euro-Americans' views of fire shifted, as did their characterization of Native peoples. By the mid–twentieth century Americans believed fire to be harmful to the environment and simultaneously viewed Indians as environmental stewards. Consequently, the idea of Indians applying fire to the prairie was unfathomable. "As a child of nature, the American Indian could not deliberately have damaged his environment, and by mid[–twentieth] century fire was generally considered an environmental evil," Pyne concluded. More recently, controlled burning has again gained favor. "Once again," Pyne quipped, "it has been discovered that, indeed, the Indian burned. . . . The evidence has not changed, but its cultural context has."[37]

Although grassland specialist Kenneth F. Higgins believed that climate played the largest role in forming the grasslands, he also maintained that Indian fires were decidedly important. In early historical times, he argued, Native peoples likely acquired their initial knowledge of the benefits of burning from observations of the land after a lightning strike and subsequently adapted prairie fire use to their own situation. In this way Indian peoples applied fire in whatever places and whatever seasons it could help them most.[38] Prairie fire in human hands thus became predictable and therefore useful. Pyne used eastern Plains topography to argue in favor of anthropogenic burning. "In the more densely rivered east," he noted, "the landscape fractured into smaller shards and slivers, each demanding its separate ignition, a density of fire that people alone could kindle."[39]

The importance of climate in creating and maintaining the Great Plains, particularly in the west, should not be underestimated. Still, humans played an important role as well. The dispute comes in determining the balance between climate and human activity and how much one might outweigh the other. Most scholars recognize that human-set fires had at least minimal impact and arguably more. Without extensive burning at the hands of Native peoples the Great Plains that Europeans encountered would have been significantly less "great," the vast expanse of grassland less vast.

The flood of Euro-Americans who migrated to the Plains following the Civil War caused dramatic change. They brought to the region a fundamentally different kind of settlement and with it a fundamentally different perception of fire. In spite of variations among Indian peoples and cultural change within the tribes, Indian fire use, in connection with other environmental factors, had effectively maintained the Great Plains as a grass-dominated region. Euro-American settlement, however, with its corresponding suppression of prairie fire, initiated a process that, over time, produced a fundamental shift away from grass in favor of trees and shrubs. Through their culturally driven use (and nonuse) of fire, therefore, Euro-American settlers brought significant environmental change to the region.

Changes in fire practices were part of a larger transformation of the Great Plains. Beginning in the 1850s and continuing through the remainder of the century, the population of the region rose sharply. In eastern Kansas, 8,637 souls inhabited Douglas County in 1860. A decade later that number had increased almost one and a half times. Farther west, Ford County, Kansas, entered the federal census in 1870 with a population of 427. Ten years later the county boasted 3,122 persons, an increase of over sevenfold. Nebraska's total population more than quadrupled between 1860 and 1870, tripled again before the next census, and doubled one more time before stabilizing at just over one million residents. Clearly the late nineteenth century was a time of enormous change on the Plains, if only in the dramatic increase in human numbers.[40]

The new residents were more than numbers, however. Each person recorded in the census brought to the Plains the desire to carve out a life there—a process that frequently involved significant alteration of the environment. Towns and cities quickly multiplied in number and expanse; livestock took the place of bison as the dominant grass-munching animal; roads and train rails crisscrossed the terrain; and, perhaps most notably, large-scale agriculture, involving some irrigation and extensive plowing, became the desired norm. Euro-Americans transformed the Great Plains into a place where, as historian Geoff Cunfer noted, "nearly all land [was] in agricultural use of one sort or another"—either farming or grazing.[41] These transformations have been widely studied by historians, with good reason. There is little doubt that the urbanizing, grazing, watering, and plowing of the Plains had a profound effect on the land and on the organisms that lived there.

But changes in fire use by Euro-Americans, in particular its suppression, had an effect comparable to that of plowing or planting because fire and the prairie are intimately linked. With repeated exposure to fire, grass species most adaptable to frequent burn-offs and intense heat became dominant within the prairie. Fire, then, argued biologist Richard J. Vogl, was a "force in the subsequent development of most grassland species."[42] The absence of fire, however, also caused change. Dick Rice, whose family settled in Oklahoma in 1908, remembered that change on his father's land. "There used to be big fires. . . . That was one thing that fooled my dad. He thought he was getting a prairie place more or less. After he started pasturing it . . . why the trees commenced to growing [and] in 8 or 10 years it all turned to brush. But when we first come here it all looked like prairie land almost."[43] As Rice learned, a prairie without fire was no longer a prairie at all.

Most prairie scientists agree with Rice. In 1899 Charles E. Bessey interviewed "old settlers" of Nebraska to verify his suspicion that trees were advancing onto the eastern Plains. One farmer noted that in 1872 "very few of the 'draws' (i.e. ravines) had any trees in them, but now [in 1899] where fire is kept out all are filled with timber. . . . The timber belt along the Nemaha River has widened from a hundred feet to half a mile and in some of the draws it has run up from half a mile to a mile."[44] More recent scientific studies support the farmer's observations. In 2002 a fifteen-year study of woody plant expansion noted that in some locations on the tallgrass prairie, land management changes—most notably fire suppression—have transformed native tallgrass prairie into closed-canopy forest in only thirty-five years. Fire application, the same study reported, prevents most woody intrusions into the tallgrass, but once frequent fires stop and woody plants intrude, there is no going back.[45] Another study from 1983 to 2003 found that "periods without fire are necessary" for shrub intrusion onto the prairie; "however, once established, shrub cover will increase regardless of fire frequency and even annual fire will not reduce shrub abundance."[46]

The impact of fire suppression on the tallgrass prairies is well documented—one writer even called prairie fires the "guardians of the tallgrass prairies."[47] Farther west, on the shortgrass plains, where rainfall is significantly less, the influence of suppression is more subtle. The shortgrass lies west of the "dry line" (approximately the 98th meridian), where average rainfall drops below 20 inches per year. Lack of moisture creates an environment more inhospitable to lush, tall grass and woody invaders.[48] Undoubtedly prairie fires played less of an ecological role there than in the East, although they occurred with enough frequency and intensity to alarm settlers. In July 1893 the Dodge City, Kansas, *Globe-Republican* reported that "Western Kansas is passing through the worst season it has ever experienced. All of the west central portion has suffered perhaps more than any other section. At no time this season has the grass been so green but what the fire would run over the prairies. This condition exists from Great Bend westward beyond Garden City."[49] On the shortgrass, the land transitioned from green to a postfire black to green again, or perhaps green to a withered, dry brown to black in times of drought. It was a "landscape mosaic," constantly changing in composition and thus affecting other organisms, such as grazers, that depended on the grass for survival.[50] Fire, even on the High Plains, played a role in the shifting mosaic.

A constant in this variable landscape, however, is the limited presence of trees. In the West fires helped maintain treelessness but were more significantly aided by drought and desiccating wind than in the wetter East. "Fire still played a role," noted historian Brian Allen Drake, "although its impact was limited due to the light fuel loads generated by [shortgrass] species. . . . Lack of water was the area's most significant ecological characteristic."[51] Because of the shortgrass region's semiarid climate, grassland scientist Daniel Licht called it an effectively "treeless ecosystem."[52] Still, botanist P. V. Wells noted that although broad-leaf deciduous trees were not common on the Western Plains, drought-resistant conifers did grow there. "Apparently," Wells concluded, "there is no range of climate in the . . . central plains of North America which can be described as too arid for all species of trees native to the region." Trees grow even on the Western Plains, Wells argued, when protected from fire by fragmented topography.[53]

Intruding trees and shrubs are one result of fire suppression, but the grasses too are affected. A study in the 1970s found that grasses "produce more biomass than can be decomposed." If not removed by grazing or by intermittent fires, the "productivity of grassland systems declines."[54] In a controlled comparison of burned and unburned grasslands from 1918 to 1921 in the midgrass region of Kansas, little bluestem dominated at the outset, with big bluestem second. At the end of the study, however, the composition had changed: "Little bluestem showed a decided increase on the burned area (48 percent) and a decrease (61 percent) on the unburned. Big bluestem decreased approximately 20 percent on the burned section and increased 75 percent in the unburned."[55] More recently a study on the effects of fire and topography on grass composition in the Konza Prairie, a tallgrass region in Kansas, found that grasses such as big bluestem, little bluestem, switchgrass, and Indian grass dominated in areas burned annually. In unburned prairie the composition changed. Overall grass cover declined in favor of flowering and woody plants. Of the remaining grass, big bluestem was most evident, but other varieties, such as Kentucky bluegrass, also flourished more than on the burned areas.[56] At what point the prairie without fire ceases to be prairie is a subjective determination, but, as Dick Rice indicated through his experience, that point exists.

The magnificent grass of the Great Plains is without a doubt the region's defining characteristic. Grasses survive. They are masters of efficiency in a volatile and difficult environment, a living conduit of the sun's energy, a tangible indicator that the Plains are the Plains and not a desert.[57] But to flourish, to be healthy, and to prevent woody intruders, grass depends on fire. "The history of the Plains is the history of the grasslands," Walter Prescott Webb, the dean of Great Plains history, wrote eighty years ago.[58] The history of the Plains, and of the grass on the Plains, is also a history of prairie fire. More than that, it is a history of the human application, management, and suppression of prairie fire. In 1871 former Confederate cavalry commander Thomas Rosser directed a survey for the Northern Pacific Railroad through Dakota Territory. Though Rosser's journal describing his experience is brief—spanning just two weeks in September—he focused much of his attention on the grass, the burned or burning prairie, and the origins of the fires he witnessed during his travels. In fact, Rosser seemed hardly able to discuss one topic without soon mentioning the others. On September 16 he noted that the Indians had left camp and had burned the prairie, perhaps by accident. The following day's entry: "There appears to be fire on the Prairie in our front & I fear that the Indians are burning off the grass." After another few days of travel: "Running through a fine country today. The prairie back from the river covered with good grass. . . . But the entire country is on fire and in future we will have trouble for grass." Grass, fire, and the human hands that put the two together were all on Rosser's mind as he journeyed across the rolling Dakota landscape.[59] So, too, are the three intertwined in history. As Rosser noted, it was the Native peoples who first put the grass to the torch. The history of human-ignited prairie fire on the Great Plains, therefore, begins with them.

Chapter Two

"Putting Out Fire"

That day the boys ran as fast as they could toward the river—toward cool safety. The fire, though, was simply too fast. Their only course of action, a frightening and nearly hopeless one, was to lie on the ground, press their faces into the earth, cover their bodies with their robes, and wait. The grass was high, the ground hot, and the boys should have been burned alive, but they were not. Miraculously, the children, who had wandered away from a hunting camp to shoot prairie dogs and birds, escaped the Great Prairie Fire during "the-people-were-burnt winter" of 1762–1763, each with a burn only on his right thigh. The fire destroyed the camp, killed several people, and burned others badly. The event was so significant and the boys' survival so amazing that their people thereafter called themselves Sican-zhu, or "the people with the burnt thigh." The French later corrupted the name, calling the people Brule, or "burned," Sioux.[1]

Certainly the Sioux, as well as other Plains peoples, had long been familiar with prairie fire—familiar enough, perhaps, for the fires to become part of their collective identity. "On all sides the Indians had burned off the prairie," one European noted while exploring the Platte River in 1823. They "know how to fire the prairie with great skill. They take advantage of a favorable wind. In spite of the fact that all around the village the grass was burned, the corn fields near the village were unharmed."[2]

Such skill developed over many generations, dating back to the earliest human presence on the Great Plains, as did other talents necessary for survival in the region. For Plains people, Stephen J. Pyne has noted, "knowledge of fire was a precondition to successful habitation." Thus, fire, in the hands of the Native peoples, became an important tool with which to manage the grasslands.[3] Historian James Sherow argued that Plains inhabitants and the grasslands actually coevolved, with the former applying (and, when beneficial, withholding) fire to shape the latter.[4] Although climate certainly played a fundamental role in grassland creation, the maintenance of that creation was largely due to burning. Indeed, when explorer Henry Y. Hind wrote in 1858 of the Northern Plains Indians "putting out fire," his meaning was the direct opposite of most Euro-American settlers' interpretation of the phrase just a few years later.[5] "Putting out fire," for the Plains Indians, did not mean extinguishing fire; it meant the intentional torching of the grass. The phrase encompassed a long history of fire management on the Plains, a history not without its accidents, miscalculations, and consequences but one that allowed people better to survive and even flourish within the grassland environment.

Evidence of a managed burning tradition is convincing. Geological scientist Matthew Boyd, examining mineral particles buried in the sandhills of southwestern Manitoba, found carbon inclusions within the material. The presence of carbon within the plant paleoecological record indicates that the particles, dating to the late Holocene some 5,000 years ago, had burned. Humans were present during the time period studied. Although Boyd acknowledged that it was impossible to know whether this specific plant material had burned because of natural or human causes, he argued that the historical record from later eras, combined with his own findings, was enough to convince him that hunter-gatherers in the late Holocene had intentionally burned the prairie. "The reconstruction of Holocene vegetation histories without reference to human agency is a naïve pursuit," he concluded.[6]

Human agency thus augmented natural burns, but typically the timing was different. Indian-set fires occurred primarily in the spring and fall, whereas lightning fires typically originated with summer thunderstorms.[7] This indicates that Native peoples did more than just react to nature.[8] They attempted to control when and where the fires happened, thereby choosing, based on seasonal conditions, how the fires affected their surroundings. Burns were not, for the most part, large or wide-ranging, but frequent local applications of fire caused widespread results.[9]

Historical accounts of prairie fires demonstrate the frequency and timing of Indian burns. In his 1972 study, geographer Conrad Taylor Moore read over 600 published diaries and memoirs describing the Great Plains between the years 1535 and 1890 and found 417 noted fire occurrences throughout the region. Of this number, the observers attributed 36 percent of the fires to Indians and 23 percent to Euro-Americans, whereas 41 percent of the fires' causes went unascribed. Only one fire was reported as having been caused by lightning. Moore noted the bias of his sources. Accounts written by white explorers, travelers, and settlers focused primarily on heavily traveled routes, with most sightings occurring in settled areas and around military posts, where white observers congregated over long periods of time. Although Moore argued that a large percentage of the unascribed fires likely were started by Indians, given their numbers and reported propensity for firing the prairie, there was also a probable racial bias in play that caused some Euro-American observers, when they had no firm knowledge of a fire's origins, to attribute the blaze to Indians based on a strong association of Native peoples with prairie fire. Nevertheless, according to Moore, at least twenty observers based their accounts of Indian fires on a "sound foundation," including eyewitness accounts and testimony from Native peoples themselves.

The seasonal distribution of the observed fires also indicated that they had human origins. Moore found that almost 40 percent of the recorded fires occurred in the fall. Summer fires accounted for 31 percent, almost 22 percent occurred in the spring, and just under 10 percent happened in winter. Almost three-fourths of observed fires, therefore, occurred at times when thunderstorms on the Plains were rare (fall and winter) or when the grass was normally too green to burn accidentally (spring). Most summer fires, Moore found, were signal fires used by Native peoples for communication. This fact, combined with the lack of lightning fires reported (only one out of 417 fires), suggests that the vast majority of the fires studied had anthropogenic origins. At the conclusion of his study, Moore remained convinced that most prairie fires across the Plains, purposeful and accidental, had originated with the Indians.[10]

Notations by weather observers at Fort Leavenworth, Kansas Territory, support this conclusion. In the two decades preceding settlement (the 1840s and 1850s), observers noted the frequent presence of prairie fires within sight of the fort in the fall, winter, and spring. Records of fires were notably absent, however, in the summer-thunderstorm months. Summer fires were rare because lightning did not frequently start them, the Indian peoples had little reason to burn purposefully in that season, and the grass was normally still too green for large-scale accidental fires.[11]

An overwhelming number of historical accounts describe Indian fire habits. Explorers, traders, and settlers clearly believed that the Indians frequently burned the prairie. The earliest Spanish explorers became angry when the grass around their camp burned, they assumed, due to Indian action. The fire deprived their horses of food. Edwin James, botanist on the Stephen Long Expedition of 1819, associated fires on the "Great American Desert," as well as fires within grassy regions around the world, with nomadic cultures. Finally, Euro-American travelers and explorers adopted Indian fire techniques to assist in hunting, ease of travel, development of pasturage, and fire prevention. Washington Irving's traveling party, for example, at first was confused about how to contend with an escaped campfire. They finally "attacked" it "in the Indian mode, beating down the edges of the fire with blankets and horseclothes, and endeavoring to prevent its spread among the grass."[12] In imitating Indian methods of fire use and prevention, early explorers implied a high degree of respect for the Natives' proficiency and knowledge of fire. Possession of such skills is a strong indication that the Indian peoples of the Plains used fire, and used it extensively.

Widespread fire use among Native peoples was an economic necessity. Without fire, Pyne argued, "most Indian economies [in the Americas] would have collapsed." On the Plains, peoples used fire to hunt and to manipulate the migration of the bison, thereby providing food, clothing, and other materials for their families. Whereas lightning fires often occurred at inopportune times, purposeful fires "added considerable degrees of predictability" to the environment. "The important question," one anthropologist noted, "is no longer why hunter-gatherers would have set the fires but, rather, why on earth they would not have done so."[13] Of course, added predictability did not ensure success, and sometimes the economic consequences of burning were not those that were expected or desired. In 1781 on the Northern Plains, for example, the Cree and Assiniboine attempted to use fire to advantage only to get "burned" when things went wrong. The peoples "put out" fire on the autumn prairies that surrounded the Hudson's Bay Company posts, intending to drive bison to the south and thereby deprive the traders of easy access to meat. Once the bison were diverted, the Indians planned to serve as middlemen, selling food to the post and acquiring a profit for themselves. The plan went astray, however, when the fires burned too far to the south, pushing the bison, in search of grass, out of a reasonable range. The miscalculation led to hard times, noted one historian, "and the Indian speculators found themselves indebted to the company for supplies to tide them over during the winter."[14]

Finally, the vastness of the Plains themselves, as well as their treeless appearance at the time of Euro-American settlement, supports the theory of widespread Indian burning. Many environmental historians have argued that Native American use of fire to manipulate the North American landscape was extensive and influential. Grassland, or possibly open forest, was likely the prevailing form of vegetation over much of North America at the time of European contact. "The role of fire in sustaining these landscapes is incontestable," noted Pyne. "When broadcast burning was suppressed as a result of European settlement, the land spontaneously reverted to forest."[15] Fire is so influential within an environment that a fairly small number of humans who use it can have an unusually large impact. "Fire can create," concluded Pyne, "but even more powerfully, it can sustain. Intelligent beings armed with fire can apply it at critical times for maximum spread and effect."[16] Anthropologist Omer Stewart argued that fire was the "essential ecological ingredient for the formation and maintenance of grasslands. Without a fairly intense fire, woody growth of some type takes over." Stewart concluded that the great grasslands of the North American continent owe their very existence to the Indians. Climate, extreme elevations, and poor soil conditions do create grasslands, but usually these areas are small in size and number and are due to very narrow, specialized environmental conditions. The Great Plains, Stewart claimed, are different. The soil is deep and rich, the area vast (spanning several climate zones), the elevation not extreme. "The uniformity making the area a unit was its grassy nature, its slight topographic variation, and the fact that it was periodically subjected to fire," the anthropologist noted. In short, Stewart argued that a variety of factors, such as climate, soil quality, and topography, came together on the Plains to create a perfect place for grass to flourish. Without human-induced fire, however, the grass could not have maintained its hold on the region. Anthropogenic fire gave the grass the edge it needed to dominate the Plains at the expense of other forms of vegetation.[17]

The sheer number of human beings on the Plains affected fire frequency. Many explorers noted an increase in fire occurrence on the prairies and in nearby wooded areas in the late eighteenth century, extending into the nineteenth.[18] This purported rise in fire use, not coincidentally, corresponded with a large migration of Indian peoples into the region during the same period. "The plains had never seen such movement and displacement of people in such a blink of time," observed historian Elliott West. The new arrivals brought with them material goods and animals plus their own cultural traditions, knowledge, and practices—all of which proceeded to transform the region.[19] Culturally driven fire practices, proliferated by increasing populations, were one of the "transformational forces" that West indicated. More bodies living in the region, in short, meant more sources of ignition and more potential for prairie fire.

Although fire use was virtually universal among humans, not all Plains peoples managed fire in the same way. Nor were Native fire practices static. Over the centuries, tribes experienced tremendous change, including migrations, internal political upheaval, population fluctuation, shifts in the availability of bison, and changes in technology, among others. With these changes came modifications in land management, including, almost certainly, changes in fire use. Eastern tribes that relocated onto the Plains as a result of the Euro-American push west, for example, brought with them fire practices from other regions. Such customs doubtless had to be rethought in the new, and often quite different, environment. Reliance on extensive agriculture required burning practices different from those used in primarily hunting economies. Fire use and cultural traditions, therefore, are wholly intertwined. The result is a complex history of fire—one in which culturally driven human action and fire, a so-called natural environmental force, cannot be separated.[20]

Because tribes were culturally distinct, fire use was neither "uniform in intent" nor "homogeneous in technique" across the Plains. American Indians used fire for a variety of purposes—to clear out old grass and to promote new growth; in hunting and war; for communication, celebrations, and revenge; and even for pleasure. Accidental fires were not uncommon. Particularly during years in which a wet spring and summer were followed by a dry autumn, a spark from a campfire or a poorly planned controlled burn might ignite a massive conflagration that would consume thousands of acres.[21]

Certain peoples appear to have used fire more extensively than others, and for different reasons. In Moore's study of 600 Plains accounts, 31 percent of fires attributed to a specific tribe were linked with the Sioux. The Blackfeet and the Crows used fires extensively on the Northwest Plains, whereas the Osages were the heaviest fire users on the Central Plains and the Apaches in the South.[22] Overall, communication was the most commonly cited reason for Indian burning, with war, hunting, pasturage improvement, accident, and horse stealing also regularly mentioned. Although the bias of his sources is a concern, Moore concluded from numerous fire accounts that some peoples, such as the Sioux and the Apache, were far more likely than others, such as the Assiniboine, Osage, or Comanche, to use fire in warfare.[23]

Immersed in their ethnocentrism, many observers imagined that when the Indians burned, they did so primarily in reaction to the Euro-American presence on the Plains and not for reasons of their own. "The Indians now set fire to the prairies and woods all around us," Charles Murray noted during his journey in the 1830s. "These malicious neighbors were determined to drive us from the district; they evidently watched our every motion. . . . They pursued this plan so effectually, as not only to spoil our hunting, but on two occasions to oblige me to provide hastily for my personal safety."[24] Likewise, Thomas Rosser, while surveying for the Northern Pacific Railroad in Dakota, noted that the Indians were burning the prairie in advance of the survey party. With no thought of the many other reasons that might be behind the burn, Rosser implied that the fire was the Indians' reaction to his party's advance into the country. Faced with the situation, the Indians had decided to "give up the Country themselves & will not be there to fight us."[25] Indeed, Indian peoples did use fire to harass and intimidate opponents, but

George Catlin, *Prairie Meadows Burning*, 1832. Smithsonian American Art Museum, Gift of Mrs. Joseph Harrison, Jr.

such practices, as well as numerous other fire traditions, did not commence when Europeans arrived on the Plains. It was the Euro-Americans, in fact, who wandered into an already well-established Plains system of "putting out fire." This fire regime continued to exist amid the wanderers' explorations and tentative settlements.

Putting out fire for communication was common among the Plains Indians, who lived in a region of few trees and wide horizons, a perfect environment for smoke-signal communications at long distances. Richard Dodge, traveling on the Central Plains in the 1860s, noted that a "single smoke" was frequently used to signify approaching strangers. To distinguish the signal from a campfire, Natives started small fires in locations not ideal for camps, such as on top of a hill or on a wide plain away from water. Once the smoke rose, the fire was quickly extinguished.[26] John Sherburne, traveling across the Southern Plains in 1853, witnessed "quite a quantity of Indian signs."[27] Although many of the signals might have had little to do with his exploring party specifically, travelers such as Sherburne often interpreted smoke signals as Indian communications regarding the Euro-American presence on the Plains.[28]

Native peoples, however, had good reasons for signaling with fire that had nothing to do with Europeans. Signal fires were part of a larger system of long-distance telegraphing, which included the placement of horses on hills to communicate information and the use of mirrors and blankets to send messages across an expanse much too large for the human voice.[29] In this way open space and treelessness were not obstacles but advantages. Fires were used in celebration; in emergencies; and for mundane, practical matters. In May 1680 Father Louis Hennepin, prisoner of the Santee Sioux, witnessed his captors setting fire to the grass "to give notice to their people of their return."[30] A Sioux war party in 1804 fired the prairies to indicate victory in battle. Signals could also be used when the situation was reversed. Alexander Ross reported that a group of Ojibwa warriors had attacked twenty Sioux on the Cheyenne River in July 1840. "At the same moment," Ross explained, "three smokes were seen to rise as a signal to the Sioux camp, signifying what had happened; at the camp the signal was repeated to warn another at a still greater distance. . . . The Sioux had set the plains on fire in various directions."[31] Finally, Indians used signal fires to communicate the onset of prearranged events during which coordinated timing was important. While traveling with the Osage in 1840 Victor Tixier noted that two bands that had camped separately that summer wanted to travel together later in the year. Arrangements were made for one of the groups to fire the prairie when it began to fold lodges so that the two groups could rendezvous. A few days after the signal was received, Tixier's adopted band reciprocated, firing the prairie to communicate that it too was ready to travel.[32]

Indians used fire more forcefully as a tool in war. On the Central Plains in the 1590s the Wichita Indians reportedly burned a group of Spanish explorers to death, surrounding them with fire in a way reminiscent of a bison hunt. There was one survivor, injured but still living with the Wichita in 1601. Percival Lowe, camped with his army unit near Council Grove, Kansas, in 1853, experienced a similar type of "surround" fire, which he interpreted as an act of war. "We had finished dinner, about two hours before sunset when, as if by one act, fire broke out in a circle all around us not more than a mile from camp," Lowe recalled. "A stiff gale was blowing from the south, and when we noticed it the fire in the tall grass was roaring furiously." The soldiers set a backfire—a controlled fire set, allowed to burn, and then extinguished, thereby providing a fuel-free zone of protection from the oncoming wildfire—and used blankets to beat out the flames. Lowe believed he knew the source of the dangerous blaze. "Undoubtedly the Kaws had set the fire to burn us out," he claimed, "and while they did not quite succeed, if they had seen us they should have been fairly satisfied." Although not devastated by the fire, the men walked away from it with blistered hands and faces. While visiting the nearby Kansa camp the next day, Lowe found that his odd appearance incited laughter among the men of the village. "Doubtless the scoundrels who had set fire to the grass were before me," Lowe claimed.[33] Prairie fires set near camps, though not always a serious threat, were at minimum an effective method of harassment against an annoying neighbor or an enemy too strong to attack directly.[34] They were also a way to drive the enemy out of cover. In 1820 Edwin James witnessed a party of Sioux using this technique to flush out a small group of Omaha who were hiding in tall grass.[35] The Blackfeet also used the strategy in the spring of 1835 against a party of trappers. The group was saved when the grass and brush in which it was hiding inexplicably did not catch.[36]

Prairie fire was usually too unpredictable for the Native peoples to use extensively as an offensive weapon. Too many variables were involved, including grass cover, topography, and wind. The fire might not burn if the grass was too green or too sparse. Poor planning or a sudden unexpected gust of wind could send the volatile fire line in a different direction than planned or even cause it to turn against those who had originally started the fire, doing more harm than good in the midst of a chaotic battle. Reliance on fire as a weapon to harm the enemy, therefore, was risky.

More often Indian peoples used fire defensively. Well-placed prairie fires could confuse the enemy, hide the movement of warriors, disguise the number of men and their location, and hinder pursuers. In his diary Captain John G. Bourke related a story told by General John Gibbon about the Nez Percé and their use of prairie fire to confuse the enemy in battle. One summer, while traveling to the headwaters of the Yellowstone, the Nez Percé stopped at Fort Shaw, Montana, where Gibbon was stationed. That night the warriors "offered to give a sham fight for the amusement of the garrison." One of the "peculiarities of the exhibition was the burning of a quantity of hay to represent a prairie fire." Using the smoke to confuse and disguise their movements, the Nez Percé charged the imaginary enemy. "Little did I then think," Gibbon continued, "that these very Indians should, within less than a year, repeat the very same strategy upon me . . . and had not the grass been too green and the wind adverse, their tactics would have succeeded completely."[37]

Another harassment technique, employed at a greater distance, was to use fire to destroy forage. Moore argued that the practice was commonly used by the Sioux and the Crow. In July 1865 a commander warned his soldiers, who were pursuing the Sioux in eastern Montana, of the Natives' strategy, noting that the pursuers could do nothing to prevent such an occurrence.[38] Eugene Bandel remarked on a similar situation with the Sioux ten years earlier. "The Indians kept well out of our way," he remembered, "but everywhere set fire to the prairies in front of us, so that our horses and mules should not find anything to eat. However, there were places where the grass was not dry enough to burn well, so that we always managed to find a place to camp."[39] Fires set to impede the progress of the enemy also had the effect of eliminating the traces that those being pursued left behind, thus making tracking much more difficult. Father Hennepin, in 1680, noted yet another use of prairie fire on the march—to force prisoners of war to pick up the pace. "To hasten us," Hennepin, a captive of the Santee Sioux, noted, "they sometimes set fire to the dry grass in the meadows through which we passed; so that our choice was march or burn."[40]

Indian peoples also had fire used against them. In January 1865 the U.S. military used prairie fire as a widespread weapon of war against the Plains Indians with the intention of making the prairie "a lean place for them" through the widespread destruction of grass. Captain Eugene Ware witnessed the planning and execution of the fire, which originated from his commanding officer's frustration and inability to "catch the Indians" that winter. On the morning of January 27, Ware reported, the general awoke and deemed the brisk northwest wind perfect for the burn. He telegraphed instructions to posts across the north-central Plains that "at sundown the prairies be simultaneously fired from Fort Kearney [Nebraska Territory] west to Denver. . . . Each was to use its own method to accomplish the purpose, but the whole country was to be set in a blaze at sunset." The posts carried out their instructions, and a fire started across 300 miles "rolled on and on, leaving in its train only blackness and desolation. All night the sky was lighted up. The fire swept the country clean; three days afterwards it was burning along the banks of the Arkansas River, far to the south." There were further reports that the fire jumped the Arkansas in a few places and traveled all the way into the Texas panhandle. The Native peoples lit backfires to save themselves from injury, although some people were nevertheless burned, scarred, and blinded by the massive fire. The most widespread damage, however, was the destruction of forage, which not only left horses hungry but also drove game out of the area, forcing the peoples to either move north of the Platte River or south of the Arkansas for the season. The general believed that he had punished the Indians adequately. He showed them "plainly that they were in great danger," Ware concluded, "and that if they did not make peace they must move."[41]

Both Natives and Euro-Americans used prairie fire extensively in the American Civil War. One rider on a running horse could fire the prairie numerous times with little time, effort, or risk. Perhaps the most serious conflict in which prairie fire played a role occurred in 1864 and involved a refugee wagon train of Union soldiers moving out of Indian Territory toward Kansas. Captain Christian Isely of the 2nd Kansas Cavalry later heard the story: "Heart sickening intelligence reached our ears that the rebels attacked the refugee train and fired the prairie all around them, and the whole train was burned up," he wrote to his family. "The guerrillas charged out of the brush and timber with yells and shrieks setting the prairie on fire [and] enveloping the train with a dense volume of smoke, thus screening the strength of their number, the engagement soon became hot right and left. It is not known how many were killed yet."[42]

Such incidents were relatively rare, however. In the Civil War, as in any other conflict, prairie fire was usually too unpredictable to be used offensively. Most of the documented uses of prairie fire, therefore, are defensive, as the Native tradition had been for centuries on the Plains. In November 1861, for example, Douglas H. Cooper, in command of a Confederate Indian regiment, attempted to chase Opoethleyohola, a chief of the Creeks, out of Indian Territory. Opoethleyohola and 5,000 of his people had attempted to isolate themselves from the war but had attracted the attention of Cooper, who decided that the group was a threat to the Confederacy and needed to be pushed out of Indian Territory. Cooper's 2,000 troops joined with the 9th Texas Cavalry in pursuit of Opoethleyohola. The fleeing Indians burned the prairie as they traveled to deprive the Confederates of forage and to slow their progress. On November 19, however, the pursuers finally encountered Opoethleyohola's pickets, who "fired the prairie as they went and led the Confederates into a timber-lined, horse-shoe shaped prairie where they received a welcome of hot lead and flying arrows. Surprise, smoke, and darkness added to the confusion of battle."[43]

While most soldiers found that a prairie fire indeed added confusion to an already chaotic experience, a few noted increased visibility during nighttime battles. "The Choctaws had been formed on our left and rather in advance of us. By the light of the prairie burning some half mile in front of us we could see their passing," remembered one Texas cavalry officer. Another Texan noted a case in which troops intentionally set fire to the prairie "in half a dozen places affording the men light to fight by."[44]

Just as in war, American Indians' skilled application of fire aided in the hunt. Fire was a critical tool, both for the act of hunting itself and for the improvement of pasturage, used to lure game to desired locations. Euro-American observers could be skeptical about the success of such practices (one soldier in Kansas scoffed that he did not think that the buffalo were "very aware" of human efforts to cultivate lush pastures).[45] Undoubtedly misjudgments and poor fire placement sometimes led to undesired consequences. The short-grass prairie, certainly, presented a particularly difficult set of challenges due to sparse vegetation and aridity. For these reasons Indian peoples did not burn as regularly on the High Plains for hunting purposes. Even farther to the east, mistakes were occasionally made, as when the Crees and Assiniboines attempted to manipulate the bison at the expense of the Hudson's Bay post in 1781. In general, however, the Indian peoples developed sophisticated hunting techniques that used fire and smoke to their ultimate advantage.[46]

One strategy in hunting with fire was the surround, in which hunters encircled a group of animals and then torched the grass in order to trap the bison with the flames. One of the earliest Euro-American references to native fire use mentioned this technique. The Spanish explorer Álvar Nuñez Cabeza de Vaca, in south Texas in 1535, noted that the Indians "go about with a firebrand, setting fire to the plains and timber . . . to get lizards and similar things which they eat, to come out of the soil. In the same manner they kill deer, encircling them with fire."[47] Father Hennepin, in 1679, witnessed an alternative version of the surround technique in which the Natives fired the prairie on only three sides, forming a horseshoe around a herd of bison. With only one path of escape, the bison moved toward the fire-free area, only to be met by hunters who shot the animals as they came through the bottlenecked opening. Hennepin asserted that the Indians could kill 120 bison a day using this method, but other observers placed the number much higher, mentioning as many as 1,500 to 2,000 bison killed with the assistance of a surround fire.[48]

A less direct method in which fire was used for the hunt involved strategic burning to create smoke, which would then drive the bison herd to a desired location. Alexander Henry, a hunter and trader on the Northern Plains, noted that in 1808 the Assiniboine sent several young men out to begin the process of driving the bison, "a tedious task which requires great patience, for the herd must be started by slow degrees. This is done by setting fire to dung or grass. Three young men will bring in a herd of several hundred from a great distance. When the wind is aft it is most favorable, as they can then direct the buffalo with great ease."[49] In August of 1833 Prince Maximilian witnessed a ceremony at a Blackfoot camp that demonstrated the importance of fire to the hunt. In the dance women imitated the movements of the bison cows, and men represented the bulls. At first the women drove the men back, but the movement of the dance changed with the introduction of fire. "A fire is kindled to the windward," Maximilian reported, "and the women, or buffalo cows, as soon as they smell the smoke, retreat into the medicine lodge which concludes the festival."[50] The dance not only reflected the usefulness of fire in the hunt but also indicated that prairie fire was important enough to Blackfoot culture and economy for it to warrant ceremonial distinction.

Finally, Indian peoples used seasonal burns to improve pasturage, which in turn affected the hunt.[51] By manipulating forage conditions, Natives attempted to influence the migration of the bison and other animals to a specific location by luring them with the young, tender, green (and apparently tastier) grass that grew on burned-over prairie. Coaxing the bison into a new-growth area required a fall or early-spring burn, timed so that the new grass would come in as the animals migrated through the area. William Clark noted, for example, that the Hidatsa had set fires in early March 1805 "for an early crop of grass, as an inducement for the buffalo to feed on."[52]

An alternative method of manipulating bison migration through use of fire, however, could be employed at other times of year. Here the object was not to lure the bison by *providing* new grass on the burned area but to burn particular parts of the prairie in order to *deprive* the animals of pasture, thereby funneling them onto grassy areas purposefully left unburned (and into the path of waiting hunters). Using this method, Native peoples could better anticipate where the herds might graze. Henry Hind, for example, noted in July 1858 that the Crees had burned with the purpose of "turning the buffalo" from their eastern course to the south. In this way the herd would "feed for a time on the Grand Coteau before they pursued their way . . . in the country of the Sioux, south of the 49th parallel."[53] Unintentional fires also had an effect on bison migration. If an extensive fire occurred in the fall, hunters attempting to locate the main herds the next spring followed the fire's path, even if that path was outside the scope of traditional bison migration patterns.[54]

Although pasturage manipulation continued, prairie fire's usefulness as a hunting tool almost certainly lessened when Native peoples acquired the horse. In fact, the transition to a more nomadic lifestyle, made possible by the horse, likely resulted in the most significant change in fire practices on the Great Plains until Euro-Americans settled in the region during the late nineteenth century. The horse, introduced to the American Southwest in the late sixteenth century by the Spanish, brought dramatic change to Plains Indian cultures and economies. The "horse frontier" moved onto the Plains, expanding from southwest to northeast, throughout the seventeenth and eighteenth centuries. The animals changed everything. They gave rise to the great and much-romanticized Plains horse cultures. They made war, trade, hunting, and travel easier. However, as historian Pekka Hämäläinen has shown, they also changed social and political hierarchies; redefined wealth; altered economies; transformed power relationships among tribes; accelerated competition for grass, water, and timber; and, over time, depleted the grassland environment.[55]

Horses, in short, set off a revolution that engendered both positive and negative change extensively, if not uniformly, across the region. Equestrianism was more prevalent on the Southern Plains than in the North. The northern climate was difficult for horses to endure, and forage was scarce during part of the year. As a result, it was the tribes in the South that fully adopted mounted hunting. By the 1760s, Hämäläinen noted, the Comanche had entered an era of "full-blown equestrianism that was marked by highly efficient mounted bison chases, extensive reliance on bison for subsistence, and intensive nomadism."[56]

Adoption of such a lifestyle had an impact on fire practices. Now on horseback, hunters could run down, circle, and contain the animals much more efficiently than they could on foot. The fire-surround method had once been a tremendous tool for directing and confusing the herds while hunters on foot moved into position for the kill. After horses made hunters more mobile, the need to use the technique likely diminished significantly.[57]

The shift to nomadism also changed the Indians' needs regarding the prairie grass, which, because grass and fire are inexorably linked, also altered fire practices. The more mobile a people were, the fewer possessions they owned, the less they were tied to a particular place, the less likely they were to be devastated by prairie fire—through loss of either property or human life. Greater mobility thus theoretically freed the tribes, at least under the right conditions, to make even greater use of fire in war and to thwart their enemies. In addition, more people traveling on the Plains simply meant more ignition sources from a greater variety of locations. However, the accumulation of large horse herds warranted extreme caution. Horses needed grass to graze, and they needed it year-round. A single Comanche or Kiowa family owned thirty-five horses by the late nineteenth century.[58] Such numbers meant that access to extensive grazing was critical. A large autumn or winter prairie fire had the potential to destroy vast amounts of needed forage. Such a loss might devastate a tribe economically, or at minimum force it to seek grass elsewhere—not always an easy task. Horse ownership (particularly of very large herds), therefore, dictated a particular need for caution.

Still, fire remained a critical tool, even as the need for reliable forage increased. As horses, along with other incentives such as participation in the fur trade and the need to outrun European diseases, carried Indians onto the open grassland, the peoples became more dependent on the bison and consequently more dependent on fire. Horse-driven nomadism linked the survival of the tribes with the survival of the bison. For many tribes, this change decreased economic diversity and placed too much emphasis on one resource—a resource, it turned out, that was dangerously susceptible to unseen pressures. As early as the 1840s the number of bison on the Plains dropped due to increased hunting, competition for key riparian environments, disease, and drought. At the time, however, the cause of the decline was unknown. Use of prairie fire was one way to at least *attempt* to take control over that all-important resource, the bison. Well-timed spring burns cleared the land and encouraged early new growth, which attracted the herds.[59] Applied prairie fire was thus one of the ways in which nomadic tribes such as the Comanche and Cheyenne could actively manipulate their environment and the bison amid—at least by the mid–nineteenth century—the crisis of the animals' increasing scarcity.

On the Northern Plains, horses did not encourage such a dramatic shift to nomadism. The dissemination of the animals in the north was irregular and protracted. Horses did not arrive in large numbers until the mid–eighteenth century. Even then, herds were typically much smaller than they were in the south because of the climate, which kept northern peoples from transitioning completely to a mobile existence. Northern tribes, therefore, used hunting techniques that did not require as many horses as the bison chase.[60] Hunters set fire to the prairies to drive game into wooded areas because it was easier to hunt on foot in such an environment, whereas hunters on horseback, when they did use fire, preferred the open grasslands.[61] Mounted hunters chased the bison, but northern peoples often brought their prey to them—luring the animals to specific locations using minimal numbers of riders.[62] Fire thus likely remained a critical tool to move the bison in preparation for the hunt, as it had been for centuries, and for longer on the Northern Plains than in the South.

Despite evolution of lifestyle and therefore of fire use, American Indians continued to use fire extensively for communication, war, hunting, and pasturage manipulation well into the Euro-American settlement period. They also used prairie fire for less essential or purposeful reasons. Indians occasionally torched the prairie simply for the pleasure of watching it burn. Already noted is the Nez Percé use of fire to entertain soldiers at Fort Shaw.[63] Francesco Arese and his Sioux guides, in August 1837, set the prairie on fire "every night for our diversion," despite the danger of attracting the attention of an enemy war party.[64]

Other prairie fires were not intentional but started by accident or as a result of carelessness. An 1810 fire in Saskatchewan, witnessed by Alexander Henry, was reportedly started by the Gros Ventre Indians as they prepared to leave camp. Henry also noted an instance, ten years earlier, in which a band of Ojibwa had accidentally set the grass on fire, thereby alarming Henry and his companions, who, at a distance from the camp, misinterpreted the blaze as a signal of an attack by the Sioux.[65] Accidental prairie fires, started by escaped campfires and by controlled burns run amuck, were common, particularly in tall, dry grass. Euro-American and Indian travelers alike frequently left campfires burning with the assumption that they would simply go out on their own. Caught by the wind, however, a peaceful cooking fire could spark a massive prairie conflagration in very little time. Josiah Gregg, traveling in Kansas in the 1830s, noted deserted but still burning campfires of the Pawnee and Kiowa-Comanche. On the Southern Plains, another expedition found an abandoned village, reportedly Comanche, in which eight campfires were still burning.[66]

Despite such incidents of carelessness, Indian peoples were skillful managers of fire. The techniques and strategies used by these longtime inhabitants of the Plains to put out fire (in both meanings of the phrase) and to protect property and human life were later adopted by Euro-American newcomers. Ranchers in the Flint Hills of Kansas, for example, still use a version of the native "ball drag," a way to start a controlled burn. Natives wove a ball of dead grass, set it on fire, and dragged it, either on horseback or on foot, across the prairie where they wanted the burn to begin. Today ranchers substitute a bale of hay, a burlap bag soaked in kerosene, or a used tire for the ball of grass, and sometimes a pickup truck or an all-terrain vehicle for the horse, but the concept is the same.[67] A witness to an Indian peoples' attempt to extinguish a fire on the Northern Plains noted that as soon as the alarm was raised, "everyone rushed forth to fight the fire with whatever happened to be at hand." People grabbed blankets or robes to beat the fire while others used their feet to trample it, and several women even used large pieces of dried meat to beat at the flames, which were "soon extinguished by these combined and vigorous exertions."[68] Such resourceful and communal action would be repeated by Euro-American firefighters in later years.

Fanny Kelly, a captive of the Oglala Sioux in October 1864, witnessed one Native group's reaction to a threatening fire that swept across the dry prairie grass and toward their camp. As the fire advanced, pushed by a strong wind, the prevailing emotion in the camp was panic. Kelly thought they were doomed as the fire completely encircled them. A lull in the wind, however, temporarily stalled the fire's momentum, and the people, given a reprieve, set aside their fear and focused on the task at hand. "The Indians," Kelly remembered, "old and young, male and female, began to pull up the grass by the roots all around the camp, then lassoed the horses and hobbled them in the center, and, in a few moments, a large space was cleared, where the . . . grass had been pulled up with the feverish rapidity which all display in the fear of death." The people then piled the dislodged grass around the newly created earthen circle and started a backfire to widen the fuel-deficient area. Then the camp waited as the two fires came together. "It was a moment of intense and awful anxiety," Kelly wrote, but "by degrees the flames became less fierce, the air purer; the smoke dispersed, the roaring diminished. . . . A sigh of relief burst from every heart. Our camp was saved!"[69]

The scene Kelly described was similar to those experienced by numerous peoples throughout Plains history. Although cultural groups used fire differently and assigned it various meanings, the experience of fighting a prairie fire was a universal one that bridged divisions between people rather than causing them. In the most intense moments of the prairie firefight, Fanny Kelly was not dwelling on her captivity or other concerns. Instead she joined in combating the common threat and rejoiced with her fellow firefighters when their efforts were successful.

The practice of "putting out fire," then, used by Indian peoples over centuries of settlement, had significant consequences for the grassland environment. In the hands of the Indians, fire helped keep the prairies free of brush and woody intruders, thus maintaining the

Plains' unique treeless appearance. Cultural practices drove fire use as the various peoples burned for communication, war, pleasure, and economy. The first Euro-American explorers in the region made note of the numerous fire practices and traditions, even adopting some for their own use. As with many other aspects of life on the Plains, however, the increasing Euro-American presence meant a great change in fire's role. The shift was gradual but persistent. "Putting out fire" eventually came to mean something entirely different to the newest arrivals to the Great Plains.

In the mid-1860s a white soldier on the Plains described a group of Indians, whom he did not identify by tribal name, gathered around a fire at night, dancing, drinking, and shouting. "Suddenly," the soldier noted, "the fire began to grow brighter, and greater. . . . We soon saw that the fire had spread to the prairie-grass, and that the Indians were not trying to put it out." There was no wind that night, and the grass burned slowly, although relentlessly, across the ground. Finally, when the fire had "spread until it lit up the whole country," the soldier could not see the Indians any longer through the smoke. "At the corners of the fort several sentinels were placed to watch carefully," he reported, "and still the prairie-fire spread."[70]

Although only one incident, the true meaning of which is masked by the witness's ignorance and misinterpretation, the telling of the story is revealing and is an indicator of things to come. The soldier, clearly mystified by the sight before him, was bothered by the Indians' inaction, their apparent indifference to the fire that burned around them. Runaway prairie fires, the soldier thought— even those burning very slowly and posing no threat—should be extinguished. As Euro-American exploration and settlement of the Plains continued, many others like this soldier would begin to "put out" fire, but by their own definitions and terms.

Chapter Three

"Master of the Prairie"

Despite the long day's march in the heat, supper and rest would have to wait. That August afternoon John Sherburne, a junior member of the scientific corps that accompanied the 1853 Pacific Railroad survey across the Southern Plains, had just pitched his tent, attended to his horse, and settled down with a pipe to wait for the evening meal when the cry swept over the camp. "The prairie is on fire," someone yelled, and the men, including Sherburne, jumped to their tired feet and ran for blankets and branches to combat the blaze. "There was a general rush of Surveyors, Computers, Teamsters, Herdsmen, Cooks, Servants, etc. to the scene of the conflict," Sherburne reported. Everyone helped because the fire, a campfire run amuck, could not be allowed to reach the tents and wagons.[1]

The immediate threat was contained, but later that night another, larger fire, one the survey party believed had been started by Indians, appeared on a nearby ridge. The men once again gathered and this time started a backfire to safeguard the camp. Sherburne was ecstatic. "It was then about dark," he later wrote. "In half an hour the prairie was on fire for miles & for the first time I saw for myself that which I've long desired to see—a *prairie on fire.* I can truly say I was not disappointed. The flames rolled up for 6 or 8 ft., perhaps more—10 ft., & the heavy columns of smoke for 50 ft. It was a magnificent sight." A full moon rose over the fire, and Sherburne, a native of New Hampshire on his first trip to the Plains, marveled at the beauty. All in all it was quite a day, and the Easterner chuckled at the memory. "It was a very amusing sight to see the fellows rush into the fire," he wrote. "They seemed in a moment to forget their 20 miles march & became quite excited."[2] John Sherburne's first experience with a prairie fire was all that he had hoped—beautiful, exciting, and full of adventure.

Lieutenant Amiel Weeks Whipple, the commander of the survey expedition, which ultimately traveled from Fort Smith, Arkansas, to Los Angeles, California, witnessed the same fire but did not share Sherburne's unadulterated pleasure. With leadership came responsibility, causing Whipple to see the blaze as a possible impediment to the expedition and a threat to the safety of his party. Sherburne, who happened to be Whipple's brother-in-law, discussed the situation with the lieutenant. "Whipple was concerned that this prairie fire, and subsequent fires, were set deliberately [by the Indians] to impede the wagon train's progress," he wrote, "but he also was aware that Indians set fires in order to prepare fresh grass for buffalo herds."[3] Whipple himself, in his diary entry for August 22, 1853, described the fire and the backfire that the men started in order to curb its advance: "The fire which had been kindled threatened camp, and we were obliged to burn a wide space around us for protection. At night its appearance was sublime. Huge waves of flame, with a roaring sound like that of the ocean, were rolling over the rank grass, and rushing onward with fearful rapidity."[4] Although he gave this brief nod to beauty, Whipple was most concerned with the threat. He had none of Sherburne's sense of adventure. Writing out of greater experience and concern with his mission, Whipple ended with a lesson: "In camping upon the dry prairie, it requires constant vigilance to avoid the catastrophe of a conflagration. Many a party has, by carelessness in this respect, been reduced to a destitute condition."[5]

A third reaction was anything but dispassionate. Heinrich Baldwin Mollhausen, a German immigrant and artist for the Whipple expedition, also witnessed the August 22 fire. Mollhausen was across a ravine as the fire approached, allowing him a safer view than either Sherburne or Whipple. Perhaps the distance and his assured personal safety affected his description, or perhaps the artist's eye was one for detail, but Mollhausen's record of the fire itself is far more comprehensive and dramatic than its counterparts. As night fell, he noted, "the vivid colour of the flames made the sky appear of the most intense black, while they shed a glowing red illumination on the grey clouds of smoke that were rolling away, and changing their hue every moment as the fire was driven before stronger gusts of wind, or nourished by more or less luxuriant vegetation." The artist called the sight "awe-inspiring" and also referred to the sound of the fire's approach, the behavior of animals running before the flames, and the emotions that the fire inspired in those who witnessed it.[6] Mollhausen was drawn to the fire in a way that neither Sherburne nor Whipple was. All the men recognized the splendor of the sight, but only Mollhausen detailed the changeful nature of the beauty and the triggers behind that change. The scope of the fire impressed Sherburne, who was drawn to the adventure more than anything. Whipple was far too practical to give anything but logistics much thought. Mollhausen appreciated the prairie fire on its own terms, independent from issues of practicality or human exploit.

As the members of the Whipple expedition demonstrated, European explorers' first view of prairie fire on the Great Plains was an event—an experience simultaneously anticipated and feared, treasured and dreaded. Much of each observer's reaction depended on practical considerations—the circumstances surrounding the fire and the potential for danger inherent in the flames. More importantly, however, visitors in the presettlement era (ca. 1535–1870, depending on location) came into the grassland with their own preconceived notions of what they would find there—notions that included prairie fire. To borrow William Goetzmann's phrase, each visitor to the Plains had been "programmed" by his own personal history and circumstance.[7] Each had a particular agenda or point of view based on individual background, future goals, occupation, personality, and all the other countless experiences and influences that shape a life. Although most are unrecorded, each of the witnesses to Sherburne, Whipple, and Mollhausen's blaze saw a different fire. Each internalized the experience, made the fire his own, and used it to help shape his impression of the Plains past, present, and future.

Such variance of outlook was typical in the years before permanent Euro-American settlement. The presettlement era was one of great transition and uncertainty. Newcomers tentatively got to know the area, but exploration, as Goetzmann argued, is never neutral.[8] As explorers wandered onto the Great Plains, they entered a foreign environment—one dominated by grass and impossibly long horizons. Immediately they began to assign meaning and possibility to the landscape. Prairie fire, it was clear, meant something in the place. It was beautiful and exciting, but it also, perhaps, had the ability to alter, to shape. What that meant for the future of the region was the question, and the answer depended heavily on each person's individual vision of the Plains. Although visitors arrived with their own preconceived notions of the grassland and of prairie fire, once there, having seen the blazes for themselves, they re-formed judgments about fire and its role in the region.

Impressions formed by explorers, surveyors, hunters, artists, overlanders, adventure seekers, and soldiers were jumbled and confused and were also colored by their overall purpose. Presettlement visitors did not call the grassland home. They were temporary travelers and as such did not experience prairie fire in the same way that the American Indians did or Euro-American settlers soon would. Permanent settlers on the Plains necessarily saw prairie fire as a threat to property, a problem that was less significant for explorers. Fire sometimes threatened the gear that travelers carried with them, but their homes—their farms, houses, and families—were safe somewhere in the East. Still, presettlement visitors experienced prairie fire, assigned it meaning, and took that meaning back East with them to influence future immigrants. They were the first Euro-Americans to imagine prairie fire's role on the Great Plains. In many ways, their observations, speculations, and concerns anticipated what would emerge, in full form, later in the settlement era.

Before explorers could assign meaning to prairie fire, they first had to get over the shock of it. The sheer scope and magnitude of the fires astonished Plains visitors. Even the residue of an old fire impressed Henry Hind, who explored the Canadian prairies in the 1850s. "What a magnificent spectacle this vast prairie must have furnished when the fire ran over it before the strong west wind!" Hind remarked as he viewed land that had burned the previous autumn. The explorer continued:

> From beyond the South Branch of the Saskatchewan to Red River all the prairies were burned . . . a vast conflagration extended for one thousand miles in length and several hundreds in breadth. The Rev. Henry Budd, a native missionary . . . told me that in whatever direction he turned in September last, the country seemed to be in a blaze; we traced the fire from the 49th parallel

to the 53rd, and from the 98th to the 108th degree of longitude. It extended, no doubt, to the Rocky Mountains.[9]

Hind undoubtedly could see the blaze in his mind and wished he had seen the real thing. Philippe de Trobriand, however, did witness "an immense fire in the prairies" and was just as impressed as Hind had been with his imaginary view. De Trobriand, a commanding army officer stationed in Dakota Territory, noted that in November 1868 he and his men "watched with disquietude" as the wind drove the fire toward their encampment. He wrote:

The wind increased from moment to moment and it was very difficult to determine just how far away the fire was. One thing, nevertheless, was very evident; whatever the distance might be that separated us, the extent of the conflagration was very great. Indeed, on the horizon, beyond the bluffs, whenever a gust of wind raised or tore the vast curtain of smoke which commenced to obscure the sun, one saw distinctly twisting columns rise, white, red, brown, in a long line, under the feet of the wind.

Later that night the sight got even more impressive. "Almost immediately, with a rapidity of which no one could have any idea without having seen fire driven across the prairies . . . the flames ran over the crest of the ridge and all the line of the hills was crowned with a splendid illumination, so much more splendid since night had already fallen."[10]

Even the earliest explorers returned from the Plains with descriptions of vast fires that spread over the landscape. In 1601 Don Juan de Oñate, for example, related a tale of the Wichita Indians' use of fire in war.[11] The English explorer David Thompson, in 1798, commented on the extraordinary renewal of the grass after a prairie fire.[12] Meriwether Lewis and William Clark noted incidents of fire on the prairie many times on their famed expedition, indicating that blazes were frequent and widespread.[13] John Irving was awestruck by an 1833 fire on the Central Plains:

For several hours the blaze continued to rage, and the whole horizon became girdled with a belt of living fire. As the circle extended, the flames appeared smaller and smaller until they looked like a slight golden thread drawn around the hills. They then must have been nearly ten miles distant. At length the blaze disappeared, although the purple light, that for hours illumined the night sky, told that the element was extending into other regions of the prairie.[14]

Some of the early reports on both the magnificence and the danger of the fires were published and read by others preparing for their own journeys. Diarist Susan Magoffin, for example, while describing a prairie fire, mentioned that the "scene reminded me of one described by Mr. Gregg." Josiah Gregg's *Commerce of the Prairies*, which included a description of a prairie fire along the Santa Fe Trail, had been published in 1844, three years before Magoffin's own trip along the same route.[15] In 1859, at the request of the U.S. War Department, Randolph B. Marcy published a handbook for pioneers, including instructions on how to deal with a prairie fire, to help overlanders in their trips to the far West.[16] Such reports helped prepare later visitors for the sight and fostered the intense anticipation (equal parts excitement and anxiety) that Hind, de Trobriand, and countless others carried with them into the region.

Fueled by what they had heard and read, Plains visitors were simply curious about prairie fires. The fires were a unique feature in a mysterious and unfamiliar landscape, the sight of which could not be ignored. Soldiers stationed at the various military forts on the Plains, for example, frequently included observations of prairie fires in their daily weather records. Weather ledgers, such as those kept at Fort Leavenworth, Kansas Territory, contained no specific place to record fire observations, as they did for precipitation, wind, and temperature, but over the years many soldiers who recorded the more mundane weather statistics chose also to note, in the daily "comments" section, their observation of fires. The soldiers' comments were limited by space available on their official form, and they were perhaps inhibited by an expectation that they would be matter-of-fact in recording regular weather observations. Still, the men could not help but remark on the fires. In November 1848 a Fort Leavenworth observer recorded on the 21st of the month, "Prairies Burning in the distance. South and West." On the 25th the report read, "Prairies burning all around." The next day, perhaps inspired by the beauty of the night sky, the observer was more descriptive: "Aurora Borealis of a very deep red—perhaps occasioned by the reflection through smoke from the Prairies."[17]

Over the next few years of weather observations at Fort Leavenworth, a pattern of prairie fire observation emerged. Soldiers normally made seasonal notations of the fires from October to March, give or take a month on either side, depending on weather conditions and the resulting condition of the grass. Because recording observations of fires was strictly voluntary and spontaneous, it is significant that the fire notations were consistent in the early years of the fort's occupation, an indication of the frequency of the fires as well as the soldiers' interest in them. Normally entries were short and to the point ("Prairies on fire" or "Prairies still burning"), but occasionally an observer broke from the pattern to note the ubiquity of the fires. After several months of "Prairies on fire" in 1851–1852, an observer wrote on February 14, "Prairies constantly burning."[18]

At Fort Riley, also in Kansas Territory, the pattern of observations in the 1860s was similar. In January 1863, however, the government changed the format of the weather observation form. Thereafter weather observers were asked to record the appearance of "Casual Phenomena" near the fort, including thunderstorms, lightning at a distance, meteors, shooting stars, solar and lunar halos, depth of ground frozen, and even earthquakes. Prairie fires were notably absent from the list of required observations. The soldiers included them anyway. Prairie fires were observed and noted at Fort Riley in thirteen separate months (often on several days within each month) between October 1863 and February 1866. The observations were typically brief. "Prairie Fires in every direction tonight," one of the longer entries read.[19]

Such curiosity and interest were not limited to soldiers. S. N. Carvalho, an artist who accompanied the Fremont expedition of 1853, let his curiosity get the better of him one night around midnight. He wrote:

I was in a great state of excitement. I mounted my horse and rode out in the direction of the Kansas [River], to see if the fire had actually crossed; I suppose I must have advanced within half a mile, before I discovered that the prairie was on fire on this side of it. I turned round, and galloped as I thought, in the direction of camp, but I could not descry it.

Carvalho, disoriented by and fearful of the fire, wandered three hours before finally finding his camp.[20]

Perhaps curiosity contributed to a generally casual attitude that many presettlement travelers had toward fire. As transients, most travelers were not immediately concerned with the possible damage that a fire might do—until, that is, the fire turned on the travelers' own camp or threatened their personal safety. Such temporary circumstances, combined with an intense desire to see the prairies ablaze, often led to careless and dangerous behavior. As more travelers came to the Plains, the situation, according to one witness, became more serious. When employees of the Hudson's Bay Company were the only party on the Northern Plains, the witness argued, they carried spades and were careful to cover their campfires with dirt. As miners, traders, and tourists entered the country, however, "there has been a very different state of affairs." The traders, in particular, purposefully set fire to the grass around their camps to ensure better growth (and better feed) when they returned the next autumn.[21] Also, overlanders and other campers, out of apathy or in an attempt to mislead Indians concerning their location, frequently did not bother to put out smoldering or even burning campfires as they resumed their journey each morning. A gust of wind and a stray spark from one of these abandoned fires might torch a much larger expanse of prairie.[22] It took very little fire to touch off the dried grass. Eugene Ware, while traveling with the military near Fort Kearney, Nebraska Territory, witnessed his captain light a cigar. "This was a great feat for any one to do, in such a wind, on horseback. But the Captain from his former service in the army claimed that he could light a cigar in a tornado." Apparently the reports of the captain's skill were accurate, as he achieved his goal and threw down the used match, thinking it was out. Although only short buffalo grass, the vegetation was dry and very flammable, and the wind was strong. "The flame went with the speed of a railroad train," Ware remembered, "enlarging as it went. Towards the river the blaze widened and the fire went with a hoarse rumble. In the track ahead of this fire were some cattle grazing. They immediately took flight, and fled towards the river in front of the fire." The cattle escaped, but several were injured running down the riverbank. The owner of the cattle approached the captain and demanded payment for the injured beasts. After apologies and an exchange of whiskey, the captain arranged to purchase the cattle, thus providing fresh beef for his men as a result of his accidental prairie fire.[23]

Not all fires that started because of ignorance or carelessness turned out so well, and not all Plains visitors were as calm and collected as the captain. It was easy, when unfamiliar with grass fires and the methods for extinguishing them, for travelers to become flustered and highly agitated during an accidental fire. Some of the most panicked firefights (and resulting comical descriptions of them) occurred when inexperienced men first set the prairie on fire and then attempted to stop the fire from reaching gunpowder or ammunition carried with their supplies. Not an uncommon occurrence, the threat of blasting ammunition inspired chaos like no other circumstance. An unidentified hunter noted that a carelessly started cooking fire "came very near causing the death of the whole party." The grass was dry and the wind brisk. "The flames almost surrounded us before we could comprehend our situation." The men tried to fight it, but the fire seemed always to have the advantage.

> The prairie and meadow behind us now appeared like a great, rolling wave of hissing, rushing, roaring flame. Shortly the fire curled up around the wagons. . . . At this juncture, one of the hunters exclaimed: "Look out for the powder!" and the fright and confusion that followed can not well be described. . . . One of the men, having more presence of mind than the rest of us, turned the horses, with some difficulty, and drove them back on to the burned district, where we were comparatively safe.[24]

Not everyone reached safety before the ammunition blew. Richard Dodge, a young officer in command of twenty cavalrymen stationed on the Plains, encountered a situation that he, "not [having] the first dawning of an idea of the details of plains life," had not experienced. While fishing at the river, Dodge heard a commotion at camp and ran back to find the prairie aflame. Dodge recalled,

I plunged with the others into the flames to save, if possible, the arms and equipments. We had hardly got to work before the carbines (laid across the saddles on the ground) began to go off with the heat; and this fire, added to the other, and an occasional explosion of a cartridgebox, made it so hot that we were all obliged to get out of the camp and take cover. Some of the horses broke their lariat ropes and stampeded; and in five minutes from the first alarm we were reduced from a well-armed, well-mounted aggressive force, to an apparently half-armed, half-mounted, singed, and dilapidated party.[25]

In Indian Territory, the soldier Oliver McNary helped fight another escaped cooking fire that rushed through camp, catching one company's tent, clothing, blankets, saddles, guns, and cartridge belts as it passed. "The cartridge belts were full of cartridges," McNary explained in a letter to his father, "and the reports of the bursting of the cartridges was like a fourth of July celebration."[26]

Explosions or not, prairie fires caused great anxiety when they drew close to early travelers. Even finding a place of safety did not ease all fears. "The sight was awful, indeed," hunter Alexander Henry noted of a fire on the Northern Plains in 1801, "but as the wind was from us . . . we had nothing to dread." Henry could not rest easy, however. He continued, "If the fire spreads all over the country, we shall be hard up for provisions, as there will be no buffalo."[27] The hunter's fears of having nothing to hunt were different from those of McNary, whose attentions following the accidental Fourth of July celebration (in March) shifted from worries over property to worries over personal safety. Unable to stop the runaway campfire, McNary's company set backfires to protect their camp in case the wind shifted direction and sent the fire back toward them. Even so, they "slept in fear of fire all night long, and the Officer of the day . . . never slept at all." The next night pickets were posted, until a 4:00 A.M. rain set in, to keep watch in case the fire threatened again.[28]

Depending on circumstances and personal temperament, what one traveler considered dangerous another found simply adventurous, and some observers handled the threat of danger better than others. Herman Lueg, jumpy from an experience with an accidental fire, imagined a few nights later that the prairies around his camp

Arthur Fitzwilliam Tait (1819–1905); Published by Currier & Ives. *Life on the Prairie. The Trapper's Defence [sic] "Fire Fight Fire."* Toned lithograph with applied watercolor, 1862, 18 3/8 × 27 3/16 inches (46.6 × 69 cm). Amon Carter Museum of American Art, Fort Worth, Texas.

were burning yet again. The "smoke" that night turned out to be dust.[29] Another hunter, however, caught by a real prairie fire, managed to think quickly and save himself from a horrible death. Jack Bickerdyke, buffalo hunting on Beaver Creek in the 1870s, had just killed a bison cow and had begun to skin the carcass when he noticed a prairie fire heading straight toward him, moving between two forks of the creek where he had shot the bison. Bickerdyke's horse fled for its own life, and the fire moved so quickly that it blocked the hunter's path to the water. He found himself surrounded by fire, with few options. Desperate to find shelter, a dead animal and knife his only resource, Bickerdyke quickly gutted the buffalo, dragged the entrails out, and crawled inside the carcass to wait until the fire passed. He emerged "nearly smothered and badly scared," but healthy enough to find his hunting companions and curse at one of them for carelessly throwing a match down and nearly "cooking me alive."[30]

Although often preoccupied with their personal safety, many presettlement observers also recognized that fire affected the vegetation on the prairies, which in turn had economic and aesthetic consequences. Early visitors to the Plains, mesmerized and sometimes dismayed by the lack of trees in the region, blamed the hardship (because of a lack of wood) and aesthetic "flaw" in part on prairie fires. Some also blamed the Indians for causing the fires, leading to the dearth of trees. "There will be no forest, as long as the Indians possess these regions," John Irving speculated in the 1830s, "for every year, when the season of hunting arrives, they set fire to the long dry grass."[31] Such comments pointed toward the future, as later settlers argued that Indians' use of fire was evidence of their "incorrect" use of the land, a failing that white "civilization" would correct.

Less interested in the lack of trees than in the existing vegetation, overlanders and hunters noted the effect that prairie fire had on the grass supply, especially if a fire burned in fall or winter, when the spring and new growth were weeks or months away. John Kerr, on his way home from Colorado in November 1859, noted as he traveled near the Little Arkansas River in Kansas Territory that "we d[r] ove in the knight—it was vary cold—the prary is burnt over So we cant get grass for our Catle."[32] Although Kerr was not a gifted speller, his complaint was a valid one. Other travelers remarked that their horses were "almost starved" at times for want of grass.[33] Traveling along the Platte in 1850, Thomas Christy even had difficulty finding grass in the spring because of a recent fire. "Started early this morning to get where the cattle can get some grass," he wrote. "Looks very discouraging the prairie has been burnt over late." After walking for fifteen miles, Christy finally found grazing for his animals.[34]

Christy would not be the only one discouraged by destruction of pasture. Permanent settlers, a few years later, suffered economic hardship due to unexpected prairie fires that destroyed pastures appropriated as feed. There was, however, another point of view. David Thompson, an early hunter and explorer in the Northern Plains, for example, noted that although the fires that swept the prairie halted the production of trees, the grass was only temporarily waylaid. "The mercy of Providence has given a productive power to the roots of the grass of the Plains . . . on which the fire has no effect," Thompson observed. "The fire passes in flame and smoke, what [was] a lovely green is now a deep black; the Rains descend, and this odious colour disappears, and is replaced by a still brighter green." Thompson believed that the grass flourished *in spite* of the fire.[35] American Indians and later ranchers who settled on the Plains knew that the grass flourished, in part, *because* of the fire. Still, Thompson's observation, made a number of years before Euro-American settlement, pointed toward the future and the debate that would emerge in the settlement era between farmers and ranchers concerning the pros and cons of fire on the prairies. Thompson, a hunter looking for bison in 1798, could already see a connection between fire and green, healthy grasses. Other observations on the effects of fire were less accurate. H. M. Brackenridge, for example, hypothesized that fire did great damage to the prairie soil and kept the ground "in an impoverished state."[36] Josiah Gregg, on the other hand, argued that prairie fires often caused "a refreshing shower of rain." His observations, Gregg believed, supported the theories of meteorologist James Pollard Espy, who, in his *Philosophy of Storms* (1841), argued that large fires caused a heating of the atmosphere, which in turn caused rainstorms.[37]

Visitors' conclusions on the effects of prairie fire were not always correct, but the fact that they were thinking about the issue was itself significant. Prairie fires, presettlement observers began to realize, were more than burning grass. They were an identifying feature of the Great Plains, and, even more importantly, they affected such things as animal migration, grazing availability, personal safety, and property security. If prairie fires really changed the soil or generated rain, how in turn might they affect the potential for agriculture in the region?

The debate over the pluses and minuses of burning would continue in the settlement era. In the meantime, fires had the potential to cause a number of economic hardships, particularly for those who were not just traveling through the region but earned their living on the Plains. Hunters remarked on the number of bison burned to death by prairie fire as well as the consequences of an interrupted migration. Not only did a poorly timed fire push the herds elsewhere, which made hide hunting difficult, but in dry years the consequences of the fires put undue stress on the Indian peoples, sometimes pushing them toward starvation. In such a condition Native peoples were not well equipped for extensive trade.[38]

Still, with the exception of a few hunters and traders, fears of economic collapse caused by prairie fire were not constantly at the fore of Euro-Americans' minds in the presettlement era, although that concern would soon become primary. Wonder and awe at the sight of a large fire usually surpassed practical concerns (assuming personal safety was assured), and virtually all who witnessed a fire acknowledged that it was a terrific and distinct force on the prairie.

The terror of a fire's power was juxtaposed with appreciation of its extreme beauty. The two visions, seemingly contradictory, actually were almost indistinguishable. It was difficult for observers to separate the emotions that the fires inspired—thrilling excitement, awestruck wonder, shock and dread, and ultimately feelings of their own powerlessness in the face of such intense beauty and potential for devastation. All of these feelings were present, rolled into one.

The effect of such emotional turmoil was for observers to view the scene as foreign, almost otherworldly. Siegmund Rothhammer was hospital steward to the 6th Iowa Volunteer Cavalry during an Indian expedition in Dakota Territory. On July 10, 1863, while the company was camped near Fort Pierre, someone in it set fire to the prairie. The camp, and especially the pasturage for the horses, was in jeopardy. Commanding officers considered moving the camp and simply letting the fire burn, but ultimately they decided to set a backfire and try to combat the blaze. Rothhammer was both fascinated and appalled by what he saw as darkness fell. The fire, he wrote, "resembling a Monster Snake [as] it coils its destroying folds around Hills and over them . . . presents to the Eie a fearfully grand Scene, as everything else is completely hidden in a perfect . . . darkness." Thirty men, he explained, backfired to stave off the uncontrolled blaze. Rothhammer continued,

> What a strange spectacle the Camp now presents! Encompassed by lurid Flames both near and at a distance everything assumes an eerie aspect. The uncertain and flickering reflections of light thrown on the tents . . . makes them appear like so many miniature Piramydes from whose base now and then emerges a man looking more a fleeting Ghost than a reality.[39]

If Rothhammer's description was a bit fantastic, he should be excused, as most observers agreed it was next to impossible to describe such a sight. Rufus Sage said that the tallgrass aflame "resembled [more] a cotillion of demons among their native flames" than anything earthly. It was, Sage concluded, "a stupendous scene, grand

and imposing beyond description, and terrible in its beauty!"[40] For presettlement observers, then, prairie fires were still unusual, still something so amazing that they often seemed not of this world. Such attitudes were never stronger than in this era. In contrast, permanent settlers gradually developed a familiarity with the fires that, while not completely overpowering their astonishment at the sight of prairies ablaze, at least tempered their reactions.

Adventure seekers of the presettlement era, however, thrived on the dangerous beauty of the fires. One of the most enthusiastic was dime-novel publisher Erastus Beadle, who crossed into Nebraska Territory in 1857. Traveling over rolling hills, Beadle decided to get off the wagon and walk the last 4 miles to camp. He was drunk with the sight before him: "The prairie was on fire in all dirictions, and presented a most Magnificent sight." It marched relentlessly like soldiers, Beadle claimed. It moved like the sea. "We Could see fires in all directions and as far as the eye could extend." Even this was not enough for Beadle, who wanted to participate in the action. He bragged:

> I took a Match and set a fresh fire where the grass was long and dry, [and] before we were out of sight it covered acres. It is a splendid sight in a cloudy night to stand on a high bluff and see the prarie on fire in all directions. . . . I ran on ahead of the coach near half a mile to a high bluff where I counted twenty different fires.

Noting the appearance of his fellow passengers, who were also walking behind and ahead of the coach, Beadle concluded, "The glare from the burning prairie gave [the humans] an unearthly look which was wild and romantic in the extreme. I enjoyed it as but few can."[41]

Beadle's enthusiasm was almost childlike, both in his recklessness and in his unbridled joy. Frederick Law Olmsted, the famed landscape architect, experienced similar feelings during his encounter but exhibited a more mature, measured perspective. Perhaps more than any other presettlement observer, Olmsted captured the total prairie fire experience—the terror, danger, beauty, and power— in his observations. The landscaper traveled to the Texas prairies in the 1850s with his brother, Dr. J. H. Olmsted. One evening the two stopped to make camp near a stream and a small grove of trees. The grass was plentiful, and "the Doctor," as Olmsted referred to his brother, attempted to burn off a small section to clear a space for their cooking fire. In spite of his planning and care, a sudden gust of wind caught his "controlled" burn and set the prairie at large on fire. The brothers tried to smother the flames with corn sacks, but the blaze quickly escaped them. "In another moment," Olmsted wrote, "the fire was *leaping* along the top of the grass before the wind, and we saw that in this direction it was master of the prairie."[42]

The brothers' first objective was to protect their supplies, particularly their ammunition. Then, concerned about the damage to others far away, the Olmsteds began to contain the fire as best they could. Perhaps employing his innate genius for understanding landscapes, Frederick Olmsted observed that the fire line moved irregularly on rough, uphill topography and picked up speed as it traveled over the level prairie. The brothers went in separate directions, using their corn sacks, lulls in the wind, and favorable ground to try to drive the fire lines to spots where the conditions for burning were not ideal, thereby slowing the fire's movement. As night fell the wind died considerably, and Dr. Olmsted began backfiring to burn up the remaining fuel load. Three hours after the stray spark started the blaze the brothers found themselves quite a distance from their camp but successful in turning the fire back upon itself and stopping its progress. They had created a very large circle of fire. The prairie still burned within the circle, but with backfiring (and a continued moderate wind) the brothers were confident that they had "restricted its damages to a matter of small consequence. If it had reached the prairie beyond the gully or over the hill," Olmsted concluded, "it might have extended to Canada or California for all we could do."[43]

The danger passed, and the brothers reflected on the experience. "There is something peculiarly exciting in combating with a fierce fire," Olmsted admitted. "It calls out the energies and the strength of a man like actual war. We had been hotly engaged for more than three hours, and it may be imagined we returned to our tent, after patrolling together our whole outer lines, greatly exulting and fatigued." The brothers watched the beauty of the dying fire and "amused ourselves with each other's appearance, our faces, red with heat, being painted in a very bizarre fashion, like Indian warriors, with streaks and spots, and clouds of soot and coal." As he sat up watching the fire, Olmsted claimed, he "recalled, in the leisure of imagination, some of the scenic effects of the flame and smoke hurrying up the face of the hill, that had passed with but momentary perception while we were in the heat of our exertions."

Olmsted's response to the emergency both reflected typical presettlement attitudes toward prairie fire and pointed toward the future—toward the settlement era. He stood, both literally (in the 1850s) and figuratively, on the cusp of a significant shift in how the newly arrived Euro-Americans perceived prairie fire. His story is typical of thousands of experiences to come. Even when people were extremely careful, prairie fires were a fact of life on the Plains. They were difficult to stop and could be quite dangerous. Yet the experience of fighting fire, as brutal as it was, brought people together, just as it did the Olmsted brothers. It was a communal experience shared by all on the Plains, and it was an experience that Easterners did not share. For the Olmsteds, as for many others to come, fighting fire was both terrifying and thrilling—and ultimately incredibly satisfying. When Olmsted began his ordeal, the fire was "master of the prairie." Three hours and a lot of sweat later, Olmsted and his brother emerged victorious against a fierce enemy. Euro-Americans who settled the Plains adopted this mentality on a larger scale. The settlers' role, as they saw it, was to subdue the "master" and make the Plains their own. Many settlers, however, would, again like Olmsted, carry with them the memory of the fire experience—the beauty of the grass ablaze. Olmsted recalled:

> The grandest and most remarkable picture that had painted itself on my memory had presented itself at the time when I came up the hill in the rear of the fire. The ground under me, and above the level of the eyes before me, was black as the darkness of the darkest night. I could see nothing, and knew not on what to place my foot. . . . It seemed to me I was groping in a sea of darkness, when just over me there was an atmosphere of light. My eyes, looking upward, were dazzled. The tide of fire was moving on, in one grand, clean sweep . . . the outline of the hill itself against the dark, distant sky.[44]

In Olmsted, just as in settlers who came after him, two competing ideas or emotions struggled to coexist—a marveling at the beauty of the fire and a need to conquer the fire threat. While exploring these ideas and how to resolve them, early visitors drew key conclusions about the role of fire on the Great Plains. These conclusions would be expanded later, leading to a reformation of attitudes toward prairie fire among permanent Euro-American settlers. Whether they were aware of it or not, settlers' drive to suppress fire had begun. "Everyone," noted one observer of a fire on the Northern Plains, "had their eyes fixed on this new enemy."[45]

Chapter Four

"One First Grand Cause"

George Munger loved trees. He loved them more than grass, more than fat cattle that fed on grass. In fact, George Munger settled in Greenwood County, at the foot of the Kansas Flint Hills, specifically to plant trees. Already a wealthy man in 1885, Munger left his flourishing Chicago business and dedicated his life to "improving" his Kansas land. He built his own lake, complete with dam and pumping house to irrigate his crops, and planted thousands of catalpa and fruit trees on his 2,000 acres. Munger raised cattle and devoted some acreage to hay and alfalfa production. He became active in state politics and served as regent of the State Agricultural College. Trees, however, were Munger's passion.[1]

Certainly George Munger loved trees more than prairie fires. Whereas the former "improved" his land, the latter threatened those improvements and forced Munger to send all his hands to combat the blaze. "The event of the day was a prairie fire that started S.E. or S. of this farm," Munger noted in his April 5, 1887, diary entry. The fire jumped all fireguards and roads and ultimately burned three-quarters of a section before the men stopped it. "A high S.W. wind made it burn rapidly—Lost remnants of 2 stacks of old hay that was still good and my last years hay crop was short—we may have to buy," Munger concluded. On several other occasions prairie fires threatened Catalpa Knob Farm. All were watched carefully by George Munger, whose trees were at stake. "Prairie fires plenty tonight in all directions," he remarked in the spring of 1890.[2]

Many a settler shared Munger's point of view. Euro-American settlement of the Great Plains began just before the Civil War and accelerated rapidly after the conflict ended in 1865. Railroads extended into the mass of grass, carrying farmers to the region and their crops back out. People founded towns, purchased or homesteaded land, and established permanent homes in the region. For the new residents, plentiful prairie fires were a problem and a constant source of worry. Not only did they threaten human safety and property, they also threatened to negate all the progress that Munger and other settlers like him had made toward remaking the Great Plains into what was, in their view, a more aesthetically pleasing and prosperous place. Despite the beauty of the fires and the reported benefits of burning, ultimately, settlers believed, prairie fires were a menace. They needed to be stopped.

The task would not be an easy one, as the fires were a regular sight on the prairies. Even early settlers expected an "annual visit" by the blazes and knew something of the seasonal timing of the fires, even if they could be fooled now and again. "The prairies commenced burning much sooner than was anticipated, and thus some were taken unawares," the *Kanzas News* in Emporia reported in early October 1858.[3] Despite such irregularities, people expected the fires throughout the early years of settlement, with widespread burning reported every autumn. Tapering rains along with a wind to dry out prolific summer grasses made October the pinnacle of prairie fire season. October fires, predominantly, are those referred to as the "annual visits." Sometimes the arrival of the fires was reported matter-of-factly, as one might report that the sun had risen once again. "The prairie fire is again a familiar sight in Kansas," noted the *Colorado Springs Gazette* in October 1875.[4] Other observers anticipated the fires based on familiar environmental cues, such as hot winds that dried the grass. After a week of such conditions, noted one editor, "we may look for prairie fires soon."[5]

Autumn, however, was not the only season in which prairie fires were routinely observed. In January 1871 the *Walnut Valley Times* in Kansas reported that "prairie fires may occasionally be seen from our office window," and again in March the editor noted succinctly that "prairie fires [are] every evening near town."[6]

The frequency of fires did not negate the terror they inspired in many settlers. Ann Anderson called prairie fires the "daily dread," while another woman remembered the constant worry that the threat inflicted on early Plains families.[7] Residents also acknowledged the inevitability of the "terror of the settler." Cornelia Bayly, who settled in Kansas in 1871, counted the "dreaded prairie fire" as "one of the experiences which came to each early settler."[8] Prairie fires, both benign and terrible, were a fact of life on the Great Plains.

The size, scope, and intensity of the fires depended on several environmental factors, the most important of which was grass. The earliest settlers on the tallgrass prairies had never seen such grass. In 1870 the editor of a southern Kansas newspaper reported:

> We were out hunting Prairie chickens . . . a few days since and in pursuit of the game, our hunting companion and ourself passed through a parcel of wild grass of the . . . blue stem variety. Following close upon the heels of our companion, we found ourselves considerably inconvenienced by the tall heads of grass flying back and striking us on the eyeballs, and consequently were compelled to fall further to the rear. The grass was as thick on the ground as the Jungles of India, and not a good year for grass in Kansas either.[9]

Even in a bad year grass was thick on the Plains, and a particularly good year often meant an active one for prairie fires. Heavy rains in the spring and summer provided the growth, which dried out in the fall. In such conditions the tiniest spark, as from a horseshoe striking a stone, "might start a fire which ended only when everything ahead of it was burned."[10] Settler after settler confirmed the fire risk that accompanied heavy growth, even on the western High Plains, where after one wet season an observer described the short buffalo grass in Logan County, Kansas, as "rank" and "dry as powder."[11] In such conditions the absence of prairie fire, not its presence, was news. In November 1881 the *Vermillion Republican* in Dakota Territory reported that "Dakota has been remarkably fortunate this year in its prairie fires. . . . The immense growth of grass led many to apprehend great destruction when the fires began to run, but opportune rains have frequently beaten out the flames altogether, and have left the grass generally so damp that back and guard fires have been comparatively safe and easy to manage."[12]

Wind, as well as rain, affected the fires' scope and intensity. A fire in dry grass, pushed by a strong wind, stated the quarterly report of the Kansas State Board of Agriculture in 1894, could travel one hundred miles in less than twenty-four hours.[13] Conversely, both horses and humans could easily step over a fire line that did not have a wind behind it. It was the wind-driven prairie fire, rather than the fire alone, that terrorized early Plains settlers. In addition to driving fires, the prairie winds also dried out the grasses in the days and weeks before the fires made their appearance, thus contributing to the intensity of the burns. Byron Stone, a Dakota settler, remembered the summer of 1882, when "a hot wind came up which dried up the prairie in one day—from a lovely green country-side to a parched brown one. Horses nearly perished and everyone who could climbed into their cellars to find relief. Prairie fires did much damage in the next few weeks until rain came."[14]

Issues of grass, precipitation, and wind on the Plains were nothing new. The Native peoples, through experience, understood how environmental factors could have a profound impact on the frequency, course, and intensity of the fires in any given season or year. The earliest Euro-Americans on the Plains, in fact, learned and adopted burning practices from the Indians. Conscious of their own ignorance, explorers such as S. N. Carvalho, an artist who accompanied one of John C. Fremont's expeditions, acknowledged that the Indians, who have "annually set the high rank grass on fire," knew from experience what fire might do on the prairie.[15] In fact, the Euro-American tendency to associate Indians with prairie fire was very common—even constant—throughout the history of Great Plains exploration and settlement. Both the Indians and the fires were identifying characteristics of the region, seen first as a curiosity, then as a threat, and finally as a nostalgic part of the past. Early Euro-American observers regularly assumed that the Native peoples possessed certain skills in the control and management of prairie fire. It came as a surprise, therefore, when the fires actually harmed those who were so experienced in the mysteries of the conflagrations. On October 7, 1867, for example, a terrific prairie fire swept through the newly established Fort Ransom in Dakota Territory. Captain George H. Crossman was in command of the post and sent letters east to tell of the tragedy, which resulted in multiple deaths of primarily Native peoples who had been camped near the fort. Crossman, who apparently assumed that Indians were more knowledgeable of and therefore less vulnerable to prairie fire, used the multiple deaths to crudely gauge the intensity of the fire:

To give you an idea of this fire, I need only say that in a camp of half-breeds about a mile from the post, there were some twenty or more burned so badly that they died. We had these poor wretches brought in and laid in our hospital (which was of course the first building erected [at the fort]). They died like flies. . . . Now when half-breeds are caught in a prairie fire it must be an exceptionally bad one.[16]

Everyone on the Plains, in fact, was susceptible to a fast-burning, hot, and unpredictable prairie fire. Indians, however, were far more experienced than the Euro-American newcomers, and settlers learned not only how to avoid the fires but techniques for management, such as the grass-ball method of "putting out fire," by watching the Natives. Such methods allowed control over purposefully set blazes, such as those Elisha Mardin, a rancher in the Flint Hills of Kansas, recorded in the spring of 1863, just six years after the first white settlers had arrived. Mardin and his neighbors, newcomers in a foreign environment, continued the Native practice of burning off the old grass in the spring to make way for the new.[17] A journalist in 1878, commenting on prairie fires along the Platte River, remarked that the burning would "do no harm but possibly good, as it leaves the soil clean for the new pasturage."[18] Controlled burns such as these were essentially a continuity of methods between Native and white varieties of pastoralism, even amid the transition on the Central Plains from nomadic Indian dominance to Euro-American permanent settlement. Both Native peoples and white ranchers needed good grass for their animals.[19] Both groups used fire to ensure that grass was available.

Despite some continuity of fire use, Euro-Americans were vulnerable to fires as other Plains residents had never been, for they brought with them the concept of landownership, the intent of permanent sedentary settlement, and a more extensive infrastructure than the Plains had ever known. Whereas most previous Indian settlements on the Plains had been confined to the banks of streams and rivers, Euro-Americans, in a dramatic departure, placed towns and farms away from the riparian areas, thereby forsaking uneven, fire-protected ground in favor of land perfectly suited for fast-moving, grass-hungry prairie fires.[20] This change, with the settlers' determination to build permanent homes, made the new residents far more susceptible to economic devastation by fire than any peoples before them. After fighting a prairie fire all day with his father and uncle, desperate to protect their house and barn, young Orland Esval of North Dakota gazed at a group of blazing haystacks on the horizon. He remarked that the scene was "kind of pretty" but immediately regretted the statement as he endured a disapproving stare from his father. "'Don't you know, son?'" the elder Esval replied. "'Nothing that awful could be beautiful. It is like war. Besides, those were our haystacks.'"[21]

The elder Esval said it all. How could settlers tolerate a force that destroyed their property? Prairie fires might burn for days, destroying crops, houses, and occasionally towns that stood in their way. Some fires were strong enough to jump rivers, and the Plains wind was notorious for reenlivening a fire thought dead and sending it to wreak havoc in unexpected directions.

The settlement period on the Plains, therefore, was one in which transplanted Easterners were particularly vulnerable to prairie fire. Settlers had to expend considerable time, money, and effort to try to protect themselves from the fires, sometimes to no avail.

The placement of settlers away from riparian areas had at most a minimal effect on fire frequency and no effect on fire intensity. Alternations in settlement patterns simply made the new Plains residents sitting ducks on the open prairie. Yet it is highly likely that prairie fires nonetheless did increase in frequency and intensity during the late nineteenth century—a period that roughly corresponded to the settlement era on much of the Great Plains. Although increases in frequency and intensity were related to the Euro-American presence and the simple increase in population, other environmental changes in the region were also contributing factors. Specifically, the frequency and intensity of prairie fires were augmented by the decline and near extinction of the bison.

The decline of the bison is a story of the Plains that has been well told.[22] Indian peoples' adoption of the horse culture, hunting and trading pressures, competition for grazing and water, bovine diseases, and many other factors caused a dramatic drop in the bison population, once twenty-eight to thirty million strong, in the first half of the nineteenth century. By 1850 the situation on the Southern Plains was so dire that many tribes were hungry, even starving, as the bison became a less reliable presence in the region. The arrival of the white hide hunters in the 1870s was only the final chapter in the complex, interwoven story of environmental, economic, and political change that led to the bison's near extinction.[23]

The timing of the bison's demise, as well as the near-simultaneous events that displaced many Native peoples from the Plains, is important when considering the consequences for prairie fires. With both the bison and many Indian peoples displaced by the 1860s and 1870s as a result of changing environmental conditions and actions taken by the U.S. military, the Great Plains became a region in transition. "Between 1865 and 1880 Americans disrupted the ecology of the plains, as one culture replaced another and as domestic cattle replaced wild bison," noted historian Geoff Cunfer. New settlers to the Plains did bring grazing cattle with them, but they did so only gradually. In fact, Cunfer noted, from 1868 to 1878 there was a

> gap in human occupation of the grasslands, [creating an] ecological and cultural vacuum that many rushed to fill. During those ten years bison numbers plummeted, but ranchers were yet to bring many cattle to the plains. As late as 1880 there were just over 2 million cattle in the region, on land that had supported some 28 million bison.[24]

Of course the land had not quite supported that many bison for a few years. Among many other factors, competition for grazing among the bison, Indian horses, and Euro-Americans' trail animals had limited the grass supply in critical riparian areas where bison, horses, and humans went for shelter and water.[25] Beyond these areas, although droughts stunted grass growth in particular places and years, the grass kept growing. The reduction of the bison population, including the great slaughter of the last 10 million of the animals by white hide hunters over just a few years, further reduced grazing on the Plains.[26] Furthermore, the displacement of thousands of Indian peoples in the 1860s and 1870s also presumably displaced many of the horses that had competed with the bison for grazing in the middle of the century. The result of the gap of human and animal populations from 1868 to 1878, argued Cunfer, was that "for a decade grass biomass increased dramatically across the plains. Without bison to hold them in check, midsize and tall grasses overtook short grasses, and a lush expanse of free grass beckoned enterprising people around the edge of the Great Plains."[27]

Euro-Americans answered this siren call and moved onto the Plains, bringing their cattle, sheep, and horses with them. Still, the new grazers were not as numerous as the old ones and could not thoroughly reduce the mass of grass that had grown up in the previous decade. There were 2.4 million cattle on the Plains in 1880 and 7.5 million in 1885 at the height of the cattle boom. When these numbers are compared to the number of bison that the grassland had previously supported, argued Cunfer, the Plains were "relatively understocked" even in 1885. The cattle population grew to 12.6 million between 1890 and 1900 but still did not reach the number of grass-munching bison that had previously been supported by the Plains. Contrary to popular assumptions, Cunfer concluded, the Great Plains at the height of the cattle boom was not, in general, overgrazed. By the early 1880s some of the land was worn down, but over the entire region there should have been more than enough grass to go around.[28]

The increased growth and smaller number of grazers was significant for prairie fires and for the settlers who moved into the paths of the fires. The increase in grass coverage was, from the perspective of the fires, an increase in fuel. A dense fuel source in turn almost certainly led to more intense and dangerous prairie fires. Significantly, the amount of fuel on the Plains increased dramatically just prior to and during the major settlement era in the region. "There was so much tall, old, grass then," Robert Maxwell remembered of the settlement days in Nebraska. Nellie Halverson moved to Nebraska in 1878 when her father rented a farm in Boone County. "The worst that we had to contend with the first years were prairie fires," Halverson recalled. "The country not being heavily grazed was covered with tall grass, and when fire started [it] was a job to put out."[29]

Early Plains settlers, then, determined to create a life for themselves, came to the region, bringing with them their traditions of permanent sedentary property ownership, and set themselves on the open, grassy prairie away from the natural fire protection of creek and riverbed topography. They did all this at a time when, due to historical events that altered the Plains environment, the open prairie was more loaded with fuel for prairie fires than ever before. "Never, since we have been in Kansas have we seen so big a growth of grass

as there has been this past summer and without the use of every precaution by our citizens, much property . . . [will] be destroyed during
the fall and winter," the *Emporia News* reported in 1861.[30]

The new ranchers on the Plains loved the lush growth of grass
because it created good grazing conditions for their cattle. When
the animals grazed on recently burned prairie they gained weight
faster than when they ate on long-unburned sections.[31] Thus, ranchers such as Elisha Mardin of Kansas adopted the controlled burning
practices of the Indians to keep the grass healthy and nutritious.
Mardin and others timed the burns carefully to achieve optimum
results. At the Espuela Land and Cattle Company in the Texas Panhandle, ranch managers knew the grass and how burning affected
its quality. Sedge, or red grass, for example, was good grazing when
it was young, but the quality declined as the grass aged. The ranch
manager therefore instructed the hands to burn sedge pastures as
soon as possible so that the area could be used for early-spring grazing. "[The grass] comes very fast with the least bit of mild weather,
especially when the ground is as moist as that place was this spring,"
noted the 1903 manager. "Usually in a favorable week after burning
there will be good picking for cattle over the burnt district and in
two weeks they can get filled up every day."[32]

Ranchers, whose livelihood depended on the grass, recognized
the wisdom in a frequent firing of the prairie, but their success with
fire depended largely on the timing of the controlled burns, which
were set in the spring. Burns in autumn and winter destroyed pasturage that would not renew itself until the following spring, leaving
ranchers looking for alternative grazing for their cattle. Therefore,
although Plains cattlemen used fire extensively, they did so carefully and were scornful of anyone who was not appropriately cautious. In 1903 the manager of the Espuela ranch in west Texas, for
example, reported his concerns about a proposed reduction in manpower to the representative of the London-based corporate owners.
The Texan explained to an Englishman probably unacquainted with
the Panhandle:

There is, however, one very important point that I think has
never struck you, and which I always have before me, and
[that] is the danger of fire in the range. The grass . . . just now
is very good, and has got to be as dry as tinder; were a fire

to break out with a wind behind it immense damage might be done. In any case it would take a number of men to cope with it and the settlers cannot be counted upon. This is a matter worth remembering.[33]

Plains ranchers, more than any other group of Euro-American settlers, learned about prairie fire—both its benefits and its dangers—and came closest to adopting the Indian method of "putting out" fire. Ranchers' use of fire and their general economic dependence on the grass, however, frequently conflicted with other land-use practices. Farmers and other settlers who were less directly invested in the grass for their livelihoods adamantly opposed controlled burns, arguing that the tradition was not only unnecessary but harmful to the land and its new inhabitants. Ranchers in turn complained about travelers' carelessness with fire and farmers' unyielding hostility to even appropriately timed burns. Alan Cheales, out on a hunting trip in the Cherokee Outlet one November day, noted in his journal that his companion had set the grass on fire (seemingly for no purpose other than boredom) as they walked across the prairie searching for game. "When we were cooking dinner," Cheales continued, "we suddenly became aware of a party of five or six cowboys riding towards us. They came up and the leader instantly began haranguing us, and asking us what the [illegible] we meant by setting the prairie fires." Cheales's companion denied having set them and blamed the incident on ashes from his pipe. "The cattle owner calmed down a bit" after the lie, but Cheales, if not his companion, understood that the cowmen considered reckless fire use to be a serious offense.[34]

As farmers began to move into predominantly ranched areas, conflicts over fires and controlled burns only became more intense. At the Espuela ranch, for example, the presence of farmers changed the once open range on the Texas Plains, where cattle had wandered freely to graze, to a closed, fenced range. Fences limited the cattle's reach, which made prairie fires an even greater economic threat. On an open range it was relatively easy to move cattle (or let them move themselves) to an unburned pasture even if a surprise prairie fire destroyed a portion of the range. After the fences went up, however, it was difficult for large-scale ranchers to find adequate grazing if a fire happened to destroy their pastures. Ranchers frequently had to drive their cattle long distances to find adequate forage, which required extra manpower and expense. Sometimes, no matter how far they traveled, not enough grass could be located to sustain the herds.[35] Even prairie fires as far away as Montana affected business. In 1904 a group of heifers, noted the Espuela ranch manager, were "as good as sold," but he "had a letter from the prospective purchaser this morning in which he tells me that his range in Montana has been burned off and in consequence he can not handle any more cattle."[36]

Ranch managers and owners also believed that the farmers responsible for fencing the land, thereby closing the range, did not participate aggressively in prairie firefights if the range alone was threatened.[37] Removed from complete dependence on the grass, farmers did not feel the urgency of a prairie fire unless their buildings, animals, or crops were in its path. Protecting the grass was not their priority. In response to news about a prairie fire in 1906, the London-based representative of the Espuela ranch thought it fortunate that the fire had done little damage before being extinguished. Using the derogatory name that ranchers had for farmers, he continued: "It is lucky also that [the fire] turned up in the Nester's Territory. It will make them very careful in the future. In a season like the present it is doubtless quite wise to let the fencing outfit feed a horse a piece."[38] Clearly this ranchman hoped that the Panhandle farmers might recognize the damage that uncontrolled prairie fires could do, not only to buildings and crops but to the grass itself. Feeding livestock became difficult and expensive when the grass was gone.

Occasionally farmers and ranchers used prairie fire as a weapon in their ongoing disagreement over how best to use the Plains. In 1908 the Espuela outfit contemplated prosecuting a local man named Gus West for intentionally starting a prairie fire but ultimately decided that the evidence was not conclusive enough for a conviction and that West's friends and relatives might make trouble if he was arrested. The ranch manager noted with relief:

We have had no fires for the past two weeks, and I shall be very glad to prosecute vigorously any case that gives any hope of conviction. . . . In the meantime our camp men and pasture riders are looking out for anything that looks suspicious, and I don't expect much trouble from incendiary sources. This one fire supposed to have been started by West is the only one we have reasons to strongly suspect of this nature, although we have had two or three more some weeks back—the origin of which could not be traced.[39]

On the Cherokee Strip in the 1890s, prairie fire again played a role in the ongoing struggle between ranchers and farmers. "A dispatch from Guthrie, OK, says that the Cherokee strip is ablaze tonight in innumerable places," the *Norman Transcript* reported in August 1891. "The prairie fires were started by homeseekers to drive off the cattlemen and their herds." Travelers just off the train reported that the prairie between Arkansas City, Kansas, and Guthrie, Oklahoma, was a "sea of flame." The alarmed cattlemen were said to be moving their cattle to keep them safe from the fire.[40]

Two years later, in the 1893 Cherokee Strip land rush in present-day Oklahoma, individual cowboys had the advantage over homesteaders traveling on cumbersome wagons or on foot. At the sound of the signal gun, the cowboys on their fast ponies easily took the lead in the rush. "They had gone but a short distance," the *Silverton Standard* noted, "when they spread out over the prairie and, dismounting, set fire to the thick prairie grass, hoping thus to turn aside those who were following." Although the wind was not ideal, the strategy nevertheless paid off as many racers were slowed and some even turned back because their horses refused to go near the fire. Later that night carelessly built campfires "set the parched prairies blazing" and "in other places unscrupulous men started the fire in the hope of driving some timorous claimant off a valuable tract." Boomers eager to start their new life in the region, in other words, spent their first night there engaged in a typical Plains activity— fighting prairie fire.[41]

The conflict over fire emphasizes the new agriculture's radical break with past land usage of the Plains. Ranchers largely maintained the seasonal burning practices of the Indians but despised prairie fires that burned the range at the wrong time of year. Farmers had far less tolerance for the fires in any season. Thus, the shift in fire regimes or systems on the Great Plains was not just a simple break between Indian and Euro-American land management techniques. The shift came when those intent on long-term property ownership and land use that was not dependent on the grass supplanted those whose livelihoods were more mobile and grass-based. The latter group included both American Indians and, to a lesser degree, Euro-American ranchers. Ranchers were never as mobile as Indians, but occupied a relatively fire-friendly land-use middle ground somewhere between nomadism and sedentary agriculture. Over time, however, ranchers were forced to moderate their use of fire. A steady immigration of Euro-Americans—particularly farmers—to the Great Plains created a physical and social environment in which prairie fires, whatever their aesthetic allure, were increasingly considered the enemy. "The supposed benefits derived from the burning are not worth three cents an acre to any farmer," one editor commented in 1871, "even if he could fire the prairie without firing his cornfields, his hay stacks, fences, and the roof which shelters his wife and children."[42]

Townspeople joined the farmers in their general opposition to prairie fires, which seemed to them a threat to life and property. Newspaper editors, as the voices of the newly established Plains towns, led the way in the fledgling efforts to suppress the fires, portraying the blazes as unnecessary and dangerous, the result of unneighborly carelessness with fire. Most editors argued that even purposeful burns were foolhardy, as the populace was incapable of adequately controlling them, especially during the dry autumn. "Prairies should not be burned, except for special reasons and then in small quantities," the editor of the *Bismarck Tribune* stated in 1874.[43] Three years later, the same newspaper reported on a prairie fire that had caused much property damage and severely burned a local man's face: "Some one unknown set the grass on fire about ten miles above Bismarck, on Monday, thinking, of course, to control it, but it got the best of the party and spread frantically down the river."[44]

Early in the settlement period newspaper editors recognized that their towns, situated on the open prairie, were vulnerable to destruction by prairie fire, and they repeatedly warned readers to prepare for the fire danger or face the consequences. "Who that has ever seen the prairie on fire does not at once see the danger of Junction [City] from this source?" a Kansas editor questioned in 1862. "Past dangers should admonish us to look out for the future."[45]

Editors became less patient as settlement continued. Frustrated by the continued menace, newspapermen frequently scolded or

Men fight fire near Darlington in central Oklahoma. Fire-fighting tools included buckets filled with water and blankets or gunny sacks to beat out the flames. Note the heavy growth of grass providing plenty of fuel for the flames. Photograph courtesy of the Frederick Samuel Barde Collection, Research Division of the Oklahoma Historical Society.

even admonished townspeople and rural settlers alike for their inability to prevent the fires. "One would suppose that with two or three years experience in this country people would have learned to be more cautious about firing the dead grass of the prairie, and instead of doing so when the wind is blowing a perfect gale, would select a calm day, and then make it their business to confine the fire to their own premises," the *Emporia News* editor huffed in 1860.[46] Settlers could not use the newcomer excuse for long, as survival on the Plains meant learning how to manage fire. "Any one who has lived in a prairie country fifteen minutes ought to know that everything they possess is subject to prairie fires," the *Jamestown Alert* in Dakota Territory noted after a damaging fire in 1879.[47] As reminders about the danger of carelessness and improper fireguard maintenance, fires that caused injury or death were especially effective. "Last Thursday, about noon, a most furious prairie fire came upon us from the West," a Kansas editor wrote. "Ed Laurenson lost all his hay and some fence. His house narrowly escaped. Sorry for Ed, but we hope his loss may be a warning to others."[48] Similarly, the editor of the *Walnut Valley Times* in Kansas used the tragic fire of 1872 that killed two members of the Wheaton family to shame his readers who were careless with fire.[49]

Although townspeople and farmers could be careless, they generally wanted to eliminate the fire threat. To do so was to preserve their new homes, to preserve "civilization." A newspaper editor functioned as a community's conscience and unifier and organized the public in its drive to suppress fires. In this way, town newspapers played a critical role. Ranchers who favored a controlled use of fire similar to the Indian methods had no such voice on their side. Newspaper writers used forceful prose and tragedy to push a fire-suppression agenda on settlers. "Prairie fires are the crying evils—the curses—of our State, and there must be protection against them," the *Emporia News* declared in the 1860s. "We consider that the evil effects of prairie fires . . . are greater than all the drouths, hailstorms, and hurricanes that ever have or ever will visit us."[50]

Despite a fascination with the beauty of the fires, most settlers embraced the suppression agenda willingly. Prairie fires were a significant danger to people who often were teetering on the edge of financial ruin anyway. In 1880 a writer from Kansas reported family after family whose economic lives had been virtually obliterated by an intense prairie fire that swept over Jewell County. "I hope that none are left in a more sad condition than we are," the writer concluded. "I fear men, women and children will suffer for the want of proper food. I, for one, have just sown all the wheat I had . . . I am not the only one in that condition."[51] Sometimes the economic calamity was simply the loss of what prairie fire consumed best—grass. When the family of Charles Loomis returned to their farm one evening they found the sod house intact but the prairie all around blackened for miles. Loomis recalled his parents making "quite a few naughty remarks against the SOB that set the prairie afire" because they were planning on feeding the livestock that season with native grass.[52] Often the losses were heartbreakingly complete: "Mr. Henderson," a journalist noted succinctly, "lost all he had."[53]

Fire threatened lives as well. In 1893 Baker Tomlinson, his wife, and their two children took up residence 6 miles west of Enid, Oklahoma. Tomlinson left his family and wagon on the prairie while he went into town to file his claim. While he was gone a prairie fire destroyed the wagon, loaded with his worldly possessions, and burned his wife and children so severely that two of the three later died.[54] At Mulberry, Kansas, in 1880, the *Lincoln Register* reported, "One of the most terrible prairie fires passed through here. Mr. James Wademan, an old settler, was burned to a crisp."[55]

In response, settlers campaigned against fires with a blend of practical, cultural, and aesthetic considerations. On one level, settlers' drive to suppress prairie fire was simply a way to protect themselves and their families from personal and economic injury. It's clear, however, that on a deeper level the drive to suppress meant more. In many ways the elimination of prairie fire was more about the cultural baggage that Euro-Americans brought with them onto the Plains than it was about the fires themselves. The campaign against prairie fire was part of a larger campaign to remake the Plains into a "civilized" place, into an *imagined* Plains. When settlers immigrated to the region, they brought the plans for the new Plains with them just as certainly as they carried the physical stuff with which to build their new lives.[56] Both the desire to protect the developing physical infrastructure and the mental imaginings of a newly structured region prompted calls for the near-total suppression of prairie fire.

As the desire to suppress fire strengthened, settlers' initial curiosity about prairie fire shifted to fear and dread. The change also brought a shift in the perceived connection between Native peoples and prairie fire. The two remained entrenched as identifying factors of the Plains. However, because prairie fire was increasingly seen as a menace rather than a tool, the Indians' historical fire use and expertise was called into question, and the association became a negative one.

To justify suppression, Euro-Americans had to neutralize the Indian rationale for firing the prairie and portray the Natives' motives for burning as trivial or vindictive. Whereas Elisha Mardin had purposefully copied the practices of the Natives to bring in healthy grass, as settlement progressed more people adopted the viewpoint of J. Palliser, who, while exploring the Plains of Canada, argued that "the Indians are very careless about the consequences of [fire] . . . [and] fire the prairie for the most trivial reasons; frequently for signals to telegraph to one another concerning a successful horse-stealing exploit, or in order to proclaim the safe return of a war party."[57] In other words, the perception was that the Native peoples used fire only to brag about episodes of thievery or violence—not for any useful environmental purposes. C. J. Jones, whose Western adventure book appeared in 1899, described a fire set by Indians to drive out settlers that also severely burned a herd of antelope. Jones "put an end to [the] suffering [of the antelope] at once" and noted that the "awful fire was in all probability set out by a band of Kiowa Indians who had been hunting in that vicinity, and was no doubt enjoyed by them as much as dreaded by the citizens."[58] The implication was that whereas Indians used fire as a tool to cause needless suffering, not only to white settlers but to animals as well, suppression by settlers was civilized behavior. Some argued further that Indian use of fire was harmful to the Plains environment and that it was ignorance that caused the Native peoples to believe otherwise.

It followed that white settlers would have to "correct," with a civilizing influence, the Native propensity for large-scale fire. One 1871 writer for the Kansas *Fort Scott Monitor* made a passionate argument against burning: "If it is true that the 'grass starts earlier' where the prairie has been burned that would be small return for the damage caused in every neighborhood every year by those destructive fires. But it is not true that fire is a beneficent agency." As proof the writer offered the lessons of civilization:

We who burn over the prairie every autumn are no wiser than these pagans. Is it the best way to raise grass? Then why do not the great haymakers of this and other countries—men whose sole income is derived from their hay crop—burn over their fields every year? They would no more think of adopting such a barbarous custom than they would of scalping their wives, tattooing their children, painting their faces sky blue, [or] wearing brass rings in their nostrils.[59]

A people "savage" enough to paint their faces blue and wear nose rings obviously would have no respect for trees—yet another hallmark of civilization that was missing from the Plains, courtesy of Indian prairie fires. The same Fort Scott writer noted that "our most rapidly growing tree is the cottonwood. It is the best tree to start prairie forests with. . . . The Indians could not let it grow. Every year they fired the prairie and destroyed these springing trees."[60] Dakota Territory, just after the Civil War, was not known for its abundant timber supply, but, noted one writer, at one location along the James River there were four groves of trees, the largest of which was known as "Big Grove." An early settler, W. G. Santee, staked his claim there but soon became frustrated by the Indians who hunted in the area, using fire to drive game into the open. Santee, fearful for the trees' safety, "came closest to having trouble with the Indians through his efforts to save . . . [the] groves." Santee reasoned with the hunters and "finally conveyed to them his own respect for trees."[61]

On the settlers' imagined Plains, trees spread across the landscape. Wayne Fields has noted that as Euro-Americans came out of the Eastern woods to settle the prairies, "they found it more difficult to see what the [new] landscape contained than what it lacked." The "centuries of forests in their heads" exerted considerable power over their perceptions of the treeless prairie.[62] Born in Indiana, six-year-old George Goff traveled west with his parents in the 1870s, stopping briefly in Illinois before ultimately settling in Nebraska. More than sixty years later Goff's impressions of the trip were telling: "About all I remember about Indiana was the trees. It was a great timber country." The same could not be said of Nebraska. Goff recalled using twisted hay, cornstalks, sunflowers, and cow chips for fuel in the absence of timber. In fact, it likely was the lack of trees in Nebraska that kept the Indiana foliage so prominent in his memory. "We had lots of prarrie fires then too," he remembered.[63] Abbie Bright, visiting Kansas in the early 1870s, wrote of a wagon ride across a 20-mile stretch of open prairie in which she saw "not a building of any kind—and only one lone tree. How that had escaped the fires that in times past had burned over the prairie—was a mystery."[64] Note Bright's intriguing use of the phrase "in times past." Southern Kansas in 1870 had only begun to be settled by Euro-Americans, but Bright betrayed her sense of the coming change through her phrasing. Although unaware of the future implications of her word choice, the young woman nonetheless encapsulated the way in which the new Plains settlers would come to view prairie fire. The great fires were a remarkable part of the Plains past but did not belong in the region's future.

Plains people understood that fires and treelessness were related, although the connections they drew could be fanciful. One editor speculated that the trees might "have been frightened out of existence by the fires of the Indians."[65] Serious observers, however, simply used common sense and observation to determine the effects of Indian-set and natural fires. They knew that trees would grow on the prairies, but typically only along streams and rivers where water was available and where the topography had protected the once-young saplings from fire. A Nebraska man remembered traveling 10 miles from his home to get wood, which could be found only on small islands in the middle of rivers where the prairie fires could not reach.[66] After noting the abundance of timber along the Walnut River in south-central Kansas, the editor of the *Walnut Valley Times* argued that "if the fires are kept out, the area of timber would be increased very rapidly."[67]

To the new settlers, who included trees as part of the "new and improved" vision of the Great Plains, the possibility of cultivating growth by eliminating prairie fires was tempting.[68] On the same day that a writer for the *Emporia News* reported a widespread prairie fire in the area, he urged residents to plant trees "to add beauty to the nakedness of their prairie habitations." If Kansans would only do their part, he thought, the territory would compare favorably to Illinois or Iowa.[69] In the early years of settlement Plains people were unceasingly harangued by the press and by politicians to plant more and more trees.

Frequently the need to suppress prairie fire followed the pleas for planting. The success of one effort, it seemed to settlers, depended on the other. Organizers of the Nebraska National Forest, one of the most ambitious attempts at tree-planting on the Plains, discovered this firsthand as, in 1910, a major prairie fire swept through the young man-made forest in central Nebraska and killed most of the trees. Planners had to rework their fire plan, plowing large fireguards, paradoxically, to protect the "forest" from the fire of the prairie.[70] In 1873 Margaret Hafford of Rosalia, Kansas, wrote to her local newspaper with a request that her fellow citizens expend as much energy planting trees as they did in a prairie firefight. To convince her neighbors to comply, Hafford recalled their Eastern roots and looked toward their future in the West:

Then by the memory of all you loved in the past—by your hopes and comfort in the future, plant and cultivate trees. If you would leave inheritance to your children which will be worth possessing, plant and cultivate trees. The best monument you can erect to your memory will be a grove of trees. . . . Let the same energy and perseverance be exercised in the planting of trees that is exercised in extinguishing a prairie fire.[71]

The *Kanzas News*, as early as 1858, had voiced similar opinions: "Bleak, cheerless, treeless, and uninviting, the fertile prairies stretch away beyond the homeseekers' vision," the editor lamented. Luckily he had the cure for such difficult circumstances: "The first thing to be observed in growing timber on the prairies is to prevent the annual visit of fire, so common in autumn and early spring."[72]

Aesthetic "improvements" typically were linked to economics. Two months before the Emporia, Kansas, newspaper encouraged its readers to cultivate trees, its editor had lamented land values in the vicinity: "Timber land ranges in value above that of prairie here . . . but the two will approximate more closely in time, as the quantity of the one is increased by being protected from fires."[73] George Munger, in his tree-planting fervor, certainly supported this vision of the future as he noted in his diary (in large print, underlined twice) his celebration of "ARBOR DAY" in 1886.[74] The previous year in Aberdeen, Dakota Territory, the occasion had warranted a bank holiday.[75]

Scientists (in addition to bankers) supported settlers' efforts to transform the Plains environment with trees. Some even argued, in a theory related to "rain follows the plow" (and only slightly more based in science than the "trees frightened out of existence" argument), that trees would transform the semiarid climate of the Plains. The incorrect but commonly believed "rain follows the plow" theory asserted that plowing the soil would release moisture into the atmosphere, causing a permanent increase in average rainfall across the region. Thus, one of the foremost activities inherent in Plains settlement—plowing—was actually a way to "civilize" the environment. Planting trees and safeguarding them from fire was yet another scientific civilizing strategy.[76] "In this enlightened day it is well understood that the presence of trees exercises a very beneficial influence in the way of increasing the humidity of the atmosphere," the [Hugo, Colorado] *Range Ledger* assured its readers.[77] A Kansan from Fort Scott took a wildly optimistic view of fire suppression and its impact on the environment. After ten fire-free years, he argued, forest growth would dominate a pasture. Trees would then keep the moisture in the soil, "cause springs to break forth, supply wells with never-failing water, and make the creeks flow all the year round."[78] Thus, the semiarid Great Plains would be a virtual water theme park if not for the fires set by the Indians and those settlers who tried to copy the practice. Scientists from the leading agricultural college in Kansas backed this opinion in the 1910s. Under the headline "Indian to Blame for Tree Famine?" a reporter noted that "experts . . . at last have found the 'true' reason why the prairies of Kansas are treeless. It is not on account of the soil or the climate. The blame is laid upon prairie fires during the time the Indians inhabited the plains." With the fires relegated to the past, forests would come to dominate the region.[79] "Shall we thus allow Nature to irrigate every farm and make drought and famine an impossibility," the Fort Scott editor concluded, "or shall we be savages and apply the burning torch to every blade of grass?"[80]

While some argued that suppressing fires would bring trees, and through them a wetter climate, still others claimed a direct connection between prairie fire, drought, and the horrific Rocky Mountain locust plagues that had devastated the Central Plains in the 1870s. Prairie fires, the argument went, caused droughts, thus creating the perfect arid air environment for a speedy and devastating locust flight, as locusts did not fly well in a moist atmosphere. Take away the prairie fire that caused the drought and the locusts would not flourish in the region. Charles V. Riley, chief of the U.S. Entomological Commission, noted in 1877 the tendency to attribute various calamities to the fires.[81] One Kansas writer argued that "the unbroken succession of curses [in Kansas] . . . all spring from the one first grand cause, the burning of the prairie grasses. . . . It matters not whether the country is an original desert, or whether it is made so by the action of our western prairie fires. For all present purposes the two are reduced to a common level and produce a common result—drouth, hot winds and locusts."[82] Riley, the leading locust scientist of the nineteenth century, declared the theory false. Fires, he noted, did not precede drought but followed it, and the locusts' permanent home was not the Plains but the Rocky Mountain region. The visiting insect's periodic "descent into the plains to the east where it can not permanently thrive," Riley concluded, "can not well be affected by the burning of the grass on those plains."[83]

Despite Riley's scientific denial, the theorized link between two great calamities of the settlement period—drought and locusts—and the third calamity of prairie fire was tantalizing. If the theory were true, a Great Plains utopia—a locust-free, watered, and wealthy region—hinged on the suppression of fire. This, the settlers thought, they could do. Despite the acknowledged benefits of burning—acknowledged at least by those who stood to profit—and the long tradition of burning established by the Indians, wide-scale prairie fires, to most Euro-American settlers, were increasingly seen as the enemy, a threat not only to property and human life but also to settlers' vision of a "new and improved" Great Plains. "Just think, less than 15 years ago this was all a desolate, unblest extent of buffalo grass," Emily Combes observed of central Kansas in 1871. The change, however, was evident: "The farmers have planted rows of trees. . . . It is a thrifty neighborhood, and a perfect Eden."[84]

If plowing, tree-planting, and the suppression of prairie fire could result in the "civilized" place that Emily Combes described, the transition was not an easy one. Despite efforts at suppression, homes, farms, and towns across the Plains were destroyed every year by prairie fire. "By one swoop, and the work of only a few minutes, the labor and money put in the farms, in fact the toil of six or seven years was swallowed up and leaves the farmer who was burned out just where he was when he first came here," noted one observer.[85] Eliza Crawford of Vermont, who in 1884 received a letter from her nephew describing a dangerous prairie fire that had threatened the Crawford home in Dakota, replied that she would "have one more thing to worry about now. I have always been afraid you would get blown away in a cyclone or blizzard, but hadn't thought of you getting burned up."[86]

Despite the continuing dangers, Plains residents believed that "civilization" was nevertheless progressing into the region and that the suppression of prairie fire was an important part of that process. More than just a by-product of settlement, the act of controlling fire was one that settlers believed placed them in control of this newly settled region. One Kansan, in 1886, remembered the earlier days of settlement when "our menfolks" did not know enough to plow fireguards around their hay supply, but just a few years later "we can not help but note the marked change that a thrifty and energetic people has wrought in so short a time."[87]

Again settlers compared themselves and their "correct" use of the land with the previous Plains peoples and their supposed misuse of it. "Hostile Indians had many times put the torch to prairie and timber alike to destroy the landmarks of civilization and the approach of the white man," Nathanial Ayers remarked.[88] No more would this be allowed to happen. An 1871 editor commented, "When we copied the burning of the prairie grass from the Indians we were perpetuating one of the most distructive barbarisms of that race. The prairie is to them a hunting ground. To us it is the treasury from which we call forth the finest wheat, teeming acres of corn, and fruits so rare as to win admiration and gain prizes wherever they are exhibited."[89] Proper, or civilized, land use included trees to change the climate, plowed land to nurture crops, and farmhouses dotting the countryside. It did not include the Indian-inspired prairie fires that prevented all these things from flourishing and, in addition, brought drought and locusts. "When we set the prairie on fire we are playing the savage," the editor concluded.[90]

What, exactly, would be the result of "playing the savage"? The suppression enthusiasts carefully explained the consequences for the environment, but what about the people who lived on the Plains? If settlers wanted to know what might happen, they needed only to look at the Indian example. The Indians had burned, and the result, according to Palliser, was to bring "starvation and misery to the Indian tribes themselves by spoiling their hunting grounds."[91] Another explorer, Joseph Nicollet, was more direct in his assertion that purposeful burning was harmful to Indian peoples. "It is evident that the destruction of the woods by the nations who burn the prairie is the very cause of the destruction of those same nations," he mused in 1838 while wandering in Dakota. "I will have time later to develop this thesis."[92]

Nicollet did not, in fact, ever expand on his theory. That some Plains explorers and settlers might connect the "destroying element" with the so-called demise of the Indians, however, is logical considering their culturally myopic perspective. If a "savage" people created this foreign, hostile environment with fire, then a more "civilized" people could correct the savagery by suppressing fire. Protect the land from fire, they reasoned, and the land would reward its protectors—as it had not rewarded (from the Euro-American perspective) the Indian peoples who lived there without "improving" their situation. Prairie fires would now be a thing of the past, just as the peoples that had allowed them to flourish, the peoples who had largely caused the environmental struggle in which the settlers were now engaged, were also fading away. The connection between Native peoples and prairie fire would remain, but only as part of the nostalgic past. "We may thank the Indians that the Kansas settler comes armed with a plow and a mowing machine instead of an axe and a stump machine," one writer concluded, "but we need not longer perpetuate his destructive dynasty. We need a turf to keep the moisture in the mowing fields and we need kindly forests all over the farm. They come spontaneously where fire is kept away."[93]

Plains settlers who advocated the suppression of fire, therefore, based their argument on a variety of factors ranging from protection of human life to a racially based theory of proper land use. Other, less prominent arguments also fueled the suppression agenda, most of which were based on faulty assumptions about the Plains climate. In an 1894 address before the Kansas State Agricultural Association, John L. Finley stated that the elimination of prairie fires, in keeping a heavy mat of grass on the ground, would allow the land to retain moisture better, thus improving crops in Kansas. Finley was not bothered by logical cause-and-effect relationships, instead choosing to blame all the farmers' hardships on prairie fires no matter what other factors, such as climate, might have been involved. Finley remained convinced that all prairie fires could be prevented (despite the extreme quantity of dry, dead grass covering the ground) if only settlers were vigilant in their prevention strategies.[94] Others maintained that prairie fires caused hot winds to blow across the Plains and that the grass in the spring following a prairie fire actually came in later, rather than earlier, as was once believed. Finally, if the prairie had to be fired, pleaded one editor, at least settlers should time the burns so as to kill the young grasshoppers with the flames.[95]

Not all settlers heeded the repeated pleas for caution and restraint in their dealings with fire. Within the developing social climate that supported suppression, however, individuals and even communities took action to punish or forcefully restrain those who did not take the prairie fire threat seriously. A Nebraska man placed a reward notice in the newspaper, offering $20 for the name of the person who had recently set the prairie on fire.[96] Occasionally groups within Plains communities even turned toward vigilantism or, at a minimum, threats of vigilantism. A Chase County, Kansas, resident remembered in 1940 that two men had passed through the area some fifty years before and carelessly started a fire. A neighborhood committee followed the men, questioned them, and hanged one.[97] Although this memory is unsubstantiated, at the least it indicates a lingering tradition of the importance of suppression. In 1896 an Oklahoma newspaper reported that prairie fires had destroyed a large amount of hay and several houses near Perry. "A man named Jones was arrested for disobeying prairie fire laws," the reporter continued, "and there was some talk of lynching him."[98] Fires flourished in the drought-plagued 1890s, and some Kansas residents, quite literally, were almost at the end of their rope. In April 1893 the *Ness County Sentinel* denied, almost with a wink and a nod, any desire to advocate extreme measures to prevent prairie fires but nevertheless warned those who were reckless with fire that a rope, and a potential "necktie sociable," might help them remember to be more careful.[99] Lynching threats demonstrate settlers' willingness to use social control to stop prairie fire.

Most Great Plains residents advocated less extreme, state-sanctioned efforts. Many states passed laws to regulate controlled burns and defined punishments for their citizens who were reckless with fire. The *Bismarck Tribune* stated:

> The man who deliberately, wantonly, or carelessly sets out a fire on the prairie, except for necessary protection of human life, and permits it to run, ought to suffer the greatest permissible penalty. Human laws hang a man who wantonly shoots into a crowd and kills a man, but a man who sets out a fire . . . [and destroys] property, leaves hundreds of poor pioneers homeless and burns many to death is deemed an innocent and sometimes an energetic man.[100]

In Lincoln County, Colorado, the Board of County Commissioners offered a $100 reward for information concerning maliciously set prairie fires.[101] One early Kansas resident, who signed his letter to the *Leavenworth Conservative* "A Practical Farmer," argued that the state would be one of the richest in the nation if only it were protected by good anti–prairie fire legislation. The writer suggested that legislation would be an effective and "practical mode" to eliminate the destructive force.[102] Prairie fires, nonetheless, refused to be legislated out of existence. The best lawmakers could hope for was to push more farmers into plowing and maintaining firebreaks during fire-prone times of year.

Plains states did use the law to encourage fire suppression. Kansas, for example, required every overseer within each road district to make certain that the ground on either side of traveled roads was plowed annually, thus increasing the effectiveness of roads as firebreaks. The Dakotas later copied the Kansas law, but residents continued to call for more stringent punishments.[103] "The present law makes any one who willfully or negligently starts a prairie fire liable to payment for damages sustained by others," the *Jamestown Weekly Alert* noted of North Dakota in 1886, "but [it] imposes no fine or imprisonment."[104] In the 1890s Oklahoma boasted strict laws concerning prairie fire. If a settler planned a controlled burn, he was required to warn all adjacent landowners at least twelve hours ahead of the scheduled time and place of the burn. He also had to plow a 20-foot fireguard around the planned burn area. If the fire damaged his neighbors' property, the settler was liable for those costs and could be convicted of a misdemeanor, with a fine and a possible six-month prison sentence as penalty.[105]

Many legal issues regarding fire involved the railroads, as sparks from locomotives were a primary cause of prairie fire. One Oklahoma woman whose family lived only a half mile from railroad tracks spent a good portion of her childhood fighting fire. "Whenever we saw some smoke coming up after the . . . train went by we knew there was a fire to be put out in one of the fields somewhere," she remembered.[106] The Colorado state legislature, in the 1870s, passed a law that required railroads running in the territory to plow fireguards at least 6 feet wide on both sides of the rails.[107] Companies installed spark-arresters on their locomotives and even used a particular type of coal to try to limit the number of sparks that escaped from the engines.[108] Still, such techniques did not stop all the fires.

Railroads' tendency to ignite prairie fires is ironic, given what the machines symbolized on the Great Plains. In the nineteenth century railroad companies, along with the federal government, promoted settlement. Rail lines connected farmers with markets, thereby making agriculture possible in the region. It was the "whistle of the locomotive," noted historian Craig Miner, that accompanied the "agricultural explosion" on the Plains. Symbolically, railroads came to represent the coming of "civilization," the end of the old era and the beginning of the new.[109] In contrast, prairie fire, according to suppression enthusiasts, was part of the old prairie and had no place in the future. Yet the very symbol of the new Plains, the technological instrument that made large-scale agriculture possible, became one of the most common ignition sources to perpetuate fire's presence in the newly "civilized" landscape.

Settlers who suffered property damage as the result of a stray train spark used mediators to resolve claims against railroads.[110] Occasionally claims could be quite large. In 1884 two sheep-raisers in Texas, for example, hired attorneys to sue the Southern Pacific Railroad for $25,000 in damages. They claimed that an engine had set the grass on fire in late February, burning 20,000 acres of grazing land, killing several hundred sheep, and forcing the ranchers to expend considerable time and money to find new grazing for their remaining sheep. The fire was so large that it took four days to fight it. The *Texas Live Stock Journal*, which reported on the suit, approved of the ranchers' aggressive stance. If the railroad companies were held responsible for all the fires they started, the writer believed, then the financial burden would force them to be more vigilant in fire prevention. "There is no justice or right in permitting railroad companies . . . to be the cause of great damage to citizens. It is also detrimental to the business interests of the country to destroy its ranges, and the railroads are in the end themselves injured."[111]

Although Plains people bore the primary burden of fighting railroad fires, the companies sometimes sent employees to protect threatened private property. One Sunday afternoon in March 1892 a Union Pacific engine started a prairie fire in Trego County, Kansas, near the farm of Eli McCollum. Railroad workers rushed to the scene and extinguished the fire, except for two haystacks, which were left smoldering throughout Sunday night. The next morning a high wind blew into the stacks, ignited sparks from the previous day, and carried them to unburned prairie grass. Off and running again, the fire then traveled to McCollum's farm, causing $700 in damages. Despite the Union Pacific's protestations that it could not control the wind, both the Trego County district court and the Kansas Court of Appeals ruled in favor of McCollum and forced the railroad company to pay for the fire's destruction on the grounds that the railroad had been responsible for extinguishing the fire the day it started and had failed to adequately do so.[112]

In the 1890s the Kansas legislature passed a law that levied a "fire tax"' on property owners west of the 99th meridian. The funds were to be used to hire out the plowing of fireguards, controlled burning, and mowing, particularly along roads and railroad tracks. The tax was controversial, however, on all sides. An editorial in one Kansas paper argued that the legislature had passed the law "under disguise of protecting the farmer" but that it really protected the railroads. The railroads were the primary instigator of the fires, the writer argued. With the new law in place the railroads could argue that the counties, and not their locomotives, were responsible for damages because the counties were under obligation (and receiving tax money) to create adequate firebreaks.[113] Meanwhile, the Atchison, Topeka, and Santa Fe Railroad balked at paying the Kansas tax. Railroad representatives argued in court that the company should not be compelled to pay a tax that did not protect its own property. The Santa Fe, they argued, "derived no benefit whatever from the [fire]guards." The Dodge City *Globe-Republican* disagreed. "The Santa Fe railway is much benefited by the fireguards as individual citizens," the editor argued. "The protection afforded by fire guards is a saving to the railway in litigation and payment of losses by prairie fires." The district court sided with the Santa Fe and declared the law unconstitutional.[114]

The infrastructure that included fireguards and the bureaucracy that created fire taxes and prairie fire laws were all part of the newly "civilized" Great Plains that emerged in the late nineteenth century. Prairie fires were not a part of *this* Great Plains and in fact were a threat to its success. Therefore, prairie fires had to be suppressed. George Munger, who created his personal vision of the imagined Plains on his tree farm in Greenwood County, Kansas, used fire sparingly and, in general, believed prairie fires to be a significant obstacle to his creation. On Saturday, April 7, 1888, Munger hitched up the team and drove his wife and two Eastern visitors out to a back pasture to watch the grass burn while he checked the fireguards. For the visitors it was a tourist attraction of sorts—"their first chance to see a Prairie fire." Four days later, Munger reported, the visitors, "after celebrating their visit by planting some trees . . .

started for home."[115] This isolated incident, forgotten except for two short journal entries, was repeated in theory and in practice countless times over the years of settlement. Settlers acknowledged the beauty of prairie fires and their past role in the region, determined them to be a threat, invented a plan to stop the fires, and ultimately continued with their creation of the imagined Plains—a home with no place for prairie fire.

"Stop the prairie fire!" the *Walnut Valley Times* pleaded in a fit of passion. "In the name of all that is good, stop the prairie fires at once! . . . Stop the prairie fire and Kansas is a Garden of Eden. Continue them and it will ever continue to be an American desert. For Heaven's sake, stop the prairie fire."[116]

Chapter Five

"Fight Fire When Necessary, Fight Together, and Fight It Out"

As it turned out, the January 1904 fire was only the warm-up. It destroyed some hay, fence, and pasture. John Thomas, who lived west of town and lost much of his feed, likely thought it very significant. Most citizens, however, probably did not. If the January blaze was easily forgotten—just one of many commonplace fire incidents on the Plains—the March 3 fire soon got everyone's attention. The prairie fire that raged that early-spring night was not one to forget and not one to ignore. The residents of Lawton, Oklahoma, had never seen anything like it.

Everything started innocently. "Last evening until nine o'clock the land of Oklahoma never witnessed a prettier sight," reported the local newspaper. "The moon shone with unusual brilliancy and the gentle breeze made those who had been cooped up all winter wish they could spend the [evening] out of doors. Parties living in the western part of the city, on going home last evening noticed a prairie fire raging a few miles west of the city limits. The scene was beautiful, and as the wind swept the fire northward many exclamations of admiration and awe were heard."[1]

The tranquil scene ended about 10:00, when "a fearful gale swept down from the north with the velocity of a hurricane."[2] Suddenly, "as if by magic," the *Lawton Enterprise* observed, dust clouds and burning grass filled the air, and the fire began to descend on Lawton at a rapid rate, terrifying the population.[3] It "came up so suddenly we did not know what to do," attorney and farmer R. E. Trosper recalled: "I looked out the door, and as I live, you never saw a storm where the snow flakes fell faster around you than the sparks did about my place. My wife, the children, and myself made a run for the plowed ground where we were forced to spend the night." From there Trosper watched as flames engulfed his house and barn. "Everything on the place was ablaze and I was helpless," he lamented. The storm cellar, used as storage space, "was a total wreck and everything inside of it was burned. How it could possibly have caught I know not, but it seemed that the fire would simply burn through the earth."[4]

Meanwhile, the citizens of Lawton did their best to combat the blaze. What the newspaper later described as "an army of men" moved to the northern edge of town. The wind was the fire's great ally—so strong at times that it was difficult for the men to walk, let alone fight the blaze. Seeing the problems the men faced and the need to get them to the fire scene quickly, the owner of the O.K. Cab & Bus Company in Lawton asked his employees to hitch up the horses and carry men to the fire in cabs. The drivers then used their carriages to haul barrels of water to the fire line.[5]

The cab drivers' actions were only part of a communitywide effort to keep the fire from destroying the town. Every available man, as well as some boys and women, desperately tried to curb the fire with gunnysacks and water. After hours of work the firefighters "came trooping in tired and worn but victorious for with only few exceptions the city of Lawton had escaped the ravages of [the] flames."[6] Nearby farms, however, were not so fortunate. Hundreds of homes and barns, thousands of range acres, and several lives were lost across Comanche County.[7] Besides the advantage of the fire brigade, the assistant chief of police in Lawton argued that, ironically, it was the extremely high wind that had saved the town. It "blew the burning cinders clean through the city. Had the wind been less strong," the officer remarked, "it would have given the cinders a chance to lodge in crevices and thus ignite the buildings."[8] Farms such as Trosper's, surrounded by crops and grass to feed the flames, suffered the full brunt of the fire.

Once the fire had passed, people began to take stock, bury the dead, and tell their stories. The local newspaper published the "horribly sickening details" of the death and funeral of Dock Harmon, who, along with his brother, had been burned over by the fire. Zora Hull's family soon moved the badly injured child to a hospital in

Kansas City. Many residents commented on the good work of the firefighters, thanking them publicly in the *Enterprise*. As opposed to the rural devastation, only a few Lawton citizens told of property lost. Most townspeople contended only with singed eyebrows and mind-numbing exhaustion, and they thanked God and each other that things had not been worse. Asked by a reporter for his reaction, Frank Wright summed it up for many: "I lost a hat, my house caught fire, and I'm tired."[9]

In more than one way, Wright was lucky. His loss might have been much greater, and his ordeal, although exhausting, had not been suffered alone. When fighting a prairie fire, much depended on circumstances—the condition of the grass, topography and location, prefire preparation, access to water, manpower, and wind speed, among others. Often split-second decisions carried great weight and meant the difference between success and failure, an intact house or charred wood, a family uninjured and safe or a funeral to plan. A lot also depended on luck and preparation. The fires always came, and those who were ready faced them with more confidence than those who were not.

An anticipated part of Plains life, the act of fighting prairie fire became a distinctive experience for the region's people. The settlers were joined together in their efforts and bound by the knowledge and techniques to which all who came to the Plains were privy; how they coped with the threat of prairie fire became part of the culture of the place, part of the identity of the people. Newcomers, who initially did not share this knowledge, were humorous and pitiable in their ignorance. Experienced firefighters quickly inducted the uninformed, however, as shared action was necessary for everyone's safety and prosperity. As settlement continued, the infrastructure that Euro-Americans imposed on the landscape—the roads and plowed fields that were a part of the newly introduced agricultural economy—eventually played a role in limiting the threat of the fires. Prairie fire, however, was not easy to control, and settlers' attempts to do so were not without consequences. Fighting fire gave Plains people a sense of power over the landscape, power over a threat to their families and livelihoods. But fighting prairie fire, they discovered, was also very hard work.

The work and anxiety began long before the fire's actual arrival. Days and moments preceding a fire were difficult even for

Theodore R. Davis, "The Western prairie farmer running the 'fire-guard.'"
Harper's Weekly (March 28, 1868). Courtesy of the Library of Congress.

seasoned Plains settlers. Uncertainty about the location and path of the fire; potential wind changes; and all the myriad factors that might determine if, when, and how a prairie fire arrived loomed large in settlers' minds. In some ways all they could do was hurry up and wait. Prudent settlers, however, took precautions to try to limit damage and casualties should the worst possible fire scenario develop.

One thing they could do ahead of time was to construct fire-guards. In the absence of natural guards such as rivers or broken topography, both of which were excellent barriers against prairie fires, settlers on the open prairie plowed and burned their own, creating human-made obstacles to stop the fire's progress and to protect lives and belongings. The guards, also called firebreaks, were rows of plowed and/or burned earth. When a fire reached bare ground, with no grass cover to serve as fuel, it would fizzle out. Settlers typically plowed three to ten furrows of ground around anything that needed protecting—buildings, haystacks, fields, and even larger areas such as the perimeters of farms and towns.

A plowed fireguard might stand alone against a prairie fire, but a more common method combined plowing and burning. To create this type of break, a settler plowed several furrows around the desired area, then moved the plow several yards beyond and created another series of furrows parallel to the first. On a calm day the dried grass between the furrows was burned off, creating a larger (and therefore more effective) fireguard.[10] Burning a guard, however, could be dangerous, and many a prairie fire started when a controlled burn took an unexpected leap out of the guard area. "Any mistake might send the fire across miles of precious grassland," noted Nebraskan Minnie Calhoun.[11]

Fireguards stopped the easy fires—those that did not have a strong wind behind them. They were also marginally successful at stopping side fires. As a fire moved across the prairie, often smaller lines, or side fires, broke away and continued to burn behind or in a slightly different direction away from the main line. If a head fire moved fast enough, for example, it might burn over the ground so rapidly that some fuel was actually left behind. Side fires broke away and consumed that "leftover" grass. They had less fuel to work with and consequently were much less intense than the primary fire, which helped the fireguards hold against them.

Fireguards were far less effective, however, at curtailing a head fire—the main line fed by a continuous supply of fuel and driven by a vicious wind. The wind often blew burning grass flakes, cow chips, or tumbleweeds over the guard, which immediately started the fire burning on the other side. As one county historian from Texas stated, a wind-driven head fire only "laughed at the pitiful plowed guard around fields and homes."[12] Nonetheless, a firebreak was the best advance preparation available to limit damage. Some even viewed fireguards as a responsibility rather than a choice. A Kansas judge, for example, threw a suit against a railroad whose train had sparked a fire out of court on the grounds that the farmer whose property was affected "should have put in a day or so plowing fireguards."[13] The message: Living on the Plains required fireguards. Settlers must do the work or live with the consequences. "God pity the settler who had neglected to have good fire guards," Mary Lou Zimmerman of Kansas noted. "He was in luck if the fire kept away even with . . . guards."[14]

The procrastinating Plainsmen who did neglect their duty often found themselves running for the plow with a fire on the horizon. In March 1916 Beatrice Moyer of Haskell County, Kansas, noticed a cloud in the distance. She went to her husband, Forest, who was plowing in the fields, and asked him about the oncoming prairie fire, but he thought the cloud was only a dust storm. He kept plowing his field. Later a neighbor telephoned word of the oncoming blaze, and Forest, finally realizing the danger, hurried to plow fireguards around his buildings. It was almost too late, however, and several outbuildings, including the cow shed, caught fire. "I am glad we have a place to live," Beatrice later wrote to her parents in Indiana. "We have just gone through a terrific prairie fire."[15] It is unknown whether or not Mrs. Moyer gave in to what must have been an overwhelming temptation to utter four little words to her husband—"I told you so."

J. O. Rochat, who settled near Council Grove, Kansas, in the 1870s, learned that firebreaks were necessary to protect his home not only from wild prairie fires but also from a controlled burn gone wrong. "Well at last I have got things ready to write you a little more tonight, but it will be short, for I am very tired," Rochat wrote to his brother. "I have been fighting prairie fire this afternoon and that will tire a wooden man." That April afternoon Rochat had decided to burn off a portion of the field he was preparing to plow. The fire got out of control and headed for his house,

> and it had but a short distance to go. Well if you never saw any one plow with mules on the jump you could have seen it if you had been here. . . . I ran and hitch[ed] the traces and hit the mules with the lines and yelled at them and away they went, throwing dirt five or six feet. I plowed three or four furrows that way and stopped the fire going in that direction, but it was spreading at other places, and I tell you it took work to get it checked.

The frantic event seemed to cause Rochat some stress. "You think hoeing onions and digging potatoes hard work," he concluded, "but if you ever fight prairie fire, you will say the other is fun compared with it."[16] At least an April day in Kansas allowed for emergency plowing—something that was not always true on the Northern Plains. In early spring, 1898, some South Dakota residents frantically tried to save their buildings but could not use the plow to do it. "Even though it was the seventh of April," stated local lore, "the ground was frozen so hard that it was impossible to plow a fire break."[17]

Such anxieties could not be avoided when a prairie fire was nearby. The situation, dependent on the wind and dozens of other factors, was just too volatile for comfort. Getting fireguards ready well in advance of the fire, however, could somewhat lessen the strain. Lovenna Barnes remembered that when her father acquired land in Oklahoma, the first piece of land he plowed was a good firebreak.[18] In Dakota Marie Torbenson recalled that her father, Thore Syverson, moved to the homestead early to prepare it for the rest of the family. In addition to such chores as breaking the fields, digging a well, cutting hay, and hauling wood, Syverson plowed a fireguard around his homestead. Before he could finish his preparations and move his family there, a prairie fire swept over the country. The fireguards, however, held the fire back and saved the buildings.[19]

Many individual settlers carried out a yearly fireguard plan, which varied slightly depending on the condition of the grass in any particular year. New fireguards were plowed and old ones maintained. In 1886 the Norton family of western Kansas started fireguard plowing in July. The work went on for three days, and the family decided to make use of a wagon track, which, because it was bare of grass, functioned as an excellent guard. "July 21 [1886]: I plowed a fire guard partly around the North side of our preemption," one of the Norton brothers wrote in the family diary. "It is only about six furrows wide. We intend to burn the grass between it and the wagon track when the grass dies." More than three months later they did just that—following through with their fire protection plan. "Nov. 3 [1886]: Curt and I burned the grass between the road and the fireguard we plowed along the N. side . . . last summer." The work was completed the next day. "[Nov] 4 [1886]: We burned another stretch of fireguard this evening after dark."[20]

Young children often helped burn fireguards on quiet evenings near the start of fire season. "Father would take us with him and we took wet sacks and kept it from getting away," a Nebraska woman remembered. "We thought that was lots of fun."[21] Many families made the chore an annual custom, sometimes even allowing children to put the torch to the grass. Some years, however, were more exciting than others. When Harriet Walter was eight, for example, she went out with her father, as usual, to burn off the pasture. All went as planned Saturday evening. "As there was no wind, we all assisted in the 'burning off,'" she recalled. "Sunday afternoon the wind veered to the north and a cowchip which had smoldered unnoticed was blown into some trash along the hedge row and the mischief was done." Harriet happened to witness the fire's rebirth and "my childish mind was filled with horror as I ran to my father to tell him the awful news. He sent me to a neighbor a quarter of a mile away for help and I ran, gasping for breath when I arrived."[22]

The larger the area that had to be guarded, the more organization and manpower (not childpower) it took to achieve any measure of fire security. On the XIT in Texas, noted one history of the ranch, "cowboys were regularly detailed to plow fireguards. It was mean, back-breaking work." One hand estimated that he plowed 150 miles of guards in a single summer.[23] John Armstrong, manager of the southern division of the XIT, was perpetually concerned about getting the unpleasant work done. "Have got nine men now," he remarked in 1906, and "we can soon finish up the weaning and get to burning guards which I am anxious to get at [as] we have had three fires now."[24]

Large guards were especially needed along railroad tracks, as trains were a primary cause of prairie fires. The *Colorado Clipper* in 1882 called for stockmen to prepare a large guard surrounding the tracks.[25] Charlie Lummis, who had never seen fireguards before arriving in Kansas, was impressed by one railroad's efforts to protect the prairie from fire. "They have a big plough attached by long side-arms to a flat car," Lummis observed, "and an engine drags this along, turning several tremendous furrows 8 or 10 feet from the track."[26] In the 1890s the North Dakota Stockgrowers Association held the Northern Pacific Railroad Company responsible for providing fireguards along its route. J. E. Phelan, superintendent of the railroad, wrote to John S. Greene, secretary-treasurer of the Stockgrowers Association:

Regarding fire breaks along the main line west of Mandan, we have tried to burn the right of way between the fire break and the track, and so far have been unable to do so on account of the condition of the grass not being dry enough to burn. . . . Further west, in Montana, where they had less moisture than here, we have succeeded in burning the right of way so that we have been free from fires. You can be assured that everything will be done by the company looking to the security of its interests and the interests of residents along the line.[27]

The stock growers did not take the railroad's word for it, however, and insisted on meeting to discuss the issue. In 1891 Northern Pacific signed a contract with W. E. Martin for plowing fireguards between Mandan, North Dakota, and Glendive, Montana. The importance of fireguards to the stock growers' livelihood is reflected in the contract, which imposed very specific conditions on Martin's work. The fireguards had to be at least six furrows and on both sides of the tracks. "Said furrows to be plowed not less than three hundred feet from the center of the main track," the contract continued. "It is also expressly agreed that the fire breaks are to be made continuous. That is, where there is vegetation existing that cannot be plowed to advantage, a strip not less than six feet wide must be broken and have the vegetation destroyed by pick and shovel or similar tools." Representatives of the Stockgrowers Association had final approval over the work, and the Northern Pacific would not pay Martin until its inspection was complete.[28]

Like the organization of stockmen, town governments and newspaper editors called for fireguard plans to protect rural areas and towns alike. The Dodge City *Globe-Republican* argued in 1893:

> One thing of much importance to the farmers of this part of Kansas is safe fireguards. Every township should organize and proceed upon some methodical plan. If the time wasted by some townships in working imaginary roads were devoted to preparing against these devastating fires, it would be a blessing to the county. Every township in the county should get to work in this matter before it is everlastingly too late.[29]

The editor clearly believed that the suppression of prairie fire was a vital part of settlement. Guard against fires first, he argued, and worry about roads later. Yet another Kansas editor used an 1896 fire to demonstrate the effectiveness of fireguards, noting that one township that had good guards in place was protected from damage. "If the fire guards had been made [elsewhere] . . . and well burned out much of the damage might have been saved," the editor noted. "No one who has ridden along the line of the fire and seen the beneficial effect of these fire guards can doubt their value."[30]

An early resident of Junction City, Kansas, perhaps not entirely familiar with plowed fireguards, proposed a more creative solution to the fire threat. The prairie fire danger was real, he argued, and history should teach people to safeguard the town's future. To do this he proposed that streets around the city be plowed and then seeded with clover, a "tame grass" that would remain green longer than the prairie grasses. Green grass would not burn as easily, and the cattle would eat the clover close to the ground so that there would be little grass left to burn. The townspeople and farmers alike should adopt this practice, the citizen argued: "Thus I think they will be secure against fire." Although his suggestion was not widely adopted by towns seeking protection against prairie fires, the concerned Junction City resident did see a need for debate on the subject. "If any man has a better suggestion than mine," he concluded, "let us have it."[31]

A better suggestion, adopted by many Plains towns, was to plow around the perimeter of a town just as farmers plowed around their buildings. The citizens of Anthony, Kansas, took the fireguard advisories to heart and organized a company to establish and maintain guards. Notices in the local newspaper called for volunteers to congregate at 5:00 P.M. for the work because the wind was typically light at that time of day.[32] A traveler in Nebraska noted that the townspeople of Brewster, in 1918, plowed a fireguard around the entire town and backfired from the guards as a prairie fire approached.[33] A backfire, if successfully controlled, extended the width of the plowed fireguards by creating yet another section of fuel-deficient ground. If firefighters allowed the backfire to burn long enough, the head fire would eventually meet it. When that happened, and the fuel was gone, both fires would burn out.

Burning fireguards could be dangerous; plowing them took a lot of work; and once completed, the guards were only marginally reliable. Still, many Plains settlers credited their "good luck" in avoiding prairie fires to the guards. They were a practical first step that settlers took to conquer prairie fire. "We were never burned out but we sometimes lost some hay. We had good fire guards," Charley Becklam explained.[34]

Even settlers with good guards remained watchful, however. Those acquainted with the Plains could almost feel when conditions were right for a blaze. If the rain stopped, making the high prairie grasses "as dry as a political speech after election," if the wind blew unusually hard, kicking up dust clouds and sending tumbleweeds "chas[ing] one another across the prairie like fat people running," this was the time to be watchful.[35] On such days Orland Esval's father sent him out on horseback to ride to the highest point near their North Dakota farm, "scouting for possible fires on the windward side." In spite of the seriousness of the situation, young Esval daydreamed of galloping home to heroically sound the alarm and rouse a firefighting expedition.[36] In Kansas a mother noted the direction of the wind and gauged the likelihood of fire. "The last act at night," she noted, "after seeing that the children were all asleep, and all quiet among the livestock . . . was to sweep the entire horizon for signs of flame."[37]

If the fire came as the household slept, often it was an eerie red glow, lighting up the night and spilling into bedroom windows, that alerted sleepers to possible danger. Jenny Hill, in Nebraska, purposefully left the blinds on her windows up so that the light from an oncoming fire would be bright enough to wake her.[38] Others relied on nervous neighbors for warning. "We had a widow lady south of us that was our fire alarm," J. H. Pieper of Albion, Nebraska, remembered. "She would come in the night and holler, 'Hyland get up, Prarrie fire acoming.' Papa would get up and look around and if they saw it was going the other way he would tell her 'you better go home and go to bed.' She never missed seeing a fire."[39]

Depending on how close and how intense the fire was, the light could be quite bright. The *Emporia News* reported in 1867 that a fire 8 miles away was bright enough to light up the streets of town.[40] Young Robert Crawford, writing to his cousins about his fire adventure, bragged that a prairie fire in "deep grass" produced enough light to read by when it was a half mile away, and one Plains adventurer claimed that an intense fire lit up the night so that a person could pick up a pin anywhere on the prairie.[41] During the day the effect from the light was less dramatic, but at times there was a "weird, coppery light . . . seen when the sun shines through smoke."[42]

Smoke was the most significant sign of an approaching fire in daylight. "During the dangerous season we were ever on guard, watching for the slightest sign of smoke," Merton Field remembered. "Every low hanging cloud was a potential enemy and was regarded with suspicion until proved innocent." At first the smoke might seem almost harmless, just a wisp off to the west, but the tiniest bit on the horizon could set off a flood of emotions within terrified settlers. "A brisk wind was blowing," one Dakota woman wrote after viewing such a wisp, "and all the tales of prairie fires which we had heard came crowding into our minds."[43]

Smoke could appear several days before the fire reached the observer, if it did at all. Everything depended on the fuel supply and, most importantly, on the wind. Longtime residents, especially calm ones, took the uncertainty in stride. Arthur Towne, in Dakota Territory, sometimes spotted smoke on the horizon but usually did not pay it much attention because he felt protected by his firebreaks.[44] Longtime Kansan Elam Bartholomew watched an oncoming prairie fire with practiced ease. "April 5 [1890]," Bartholomew recorded in his diary. "Worked in the A.M. at planting potatoes, and a big prairie fire coming in from the southwest[.] Shortly after noon the time until 4 o'clock was spent with a large number of the neighbors in fighting the fire. We than got it extinguished."[45]

Jumpier settlers could not focus on anything as practical as potato planting. If the wind was unfavorable and the smoke increased, tentative preparations began. Trips to town were postponed and children kept home from school.[46] Even the unconcerned Towne family started making plans at a certain point. "One morning early mother called us, saying there was considerable smoke and other signs of a prairie fire off to the southeast. There was a strong wind coming from that direction. We got up and while eating breakfast father and grandfather speculated regarding the fire."[47]

Training in firefighting started early. Teachers organized prairie fire drills at schools to give children the opportunity to practice their firefighting skills. At a school in South Dakota the boys pumped water to wet pieces of carpet and then dragged the carpet along a pretend fire line while the girls followed behind with wet brooms, putting out any pretend stray sparks.[48] Among adults, newcomers made costly mistakes that seemed ridiculously naive to experienced settlers, prompting advice to those just arriving from the East. When a local man near Albion, Nebraska, noticed newcomer Frank Blough hauling a load of lumber onto his land, the neighbor visited Blough and advised him, just in case of prairie fire, to burn off his building site before he unloaded.[49] Another Nebraska immigrant no doubt wished that someone had told him not to stack his hay so close to his buildings. The location was a convenient place for his feed, but when the hay caught fire it nearly burned his buildings as well as the prairie for 5 miles around. The speed at which the fires traveled was a wonder to many new settlers. "The fires started way up in the sand hills and was coming against the wind," one observer noted. Then "that morning right after we were up the wind changed and it was down there sooner than it takes to tell it."[50]

During a fire experienced settlers mobilized themselves, then checked on neighbors, particularly newcomers. "When a fire was on the rampage it was everybody's business," a South Dakota writer explained, so when the W. G. Santee family observed a smoke cloud out near newcomer Al Yoder's farm, they organized a "small but efficient fire fighting unit" consisting of a wagon loaded with water barrels, mops, drinking water, a plow, and gunnysacks. The Santees drove to the Yoder place and found the farmer "with his arms hooked over the clothes line . . . observing the fire, headed straight for his house. It was disaster staring him in the face but he knew not what to do. When asked about his plans he said that he was going to put his wife and the seven kids in the house and climb on a hay stack himself."[51]

Yoder's helplessness was not unusual. Newcomers were known to waste precious time and energy moving all their supplies onto plowed ground instead of fighting fire, or huddling inside their houses and simply hoping for the best.[52] Such inaction sometimes threatened the safety of nearby farms. After noticing a smoke cloud on the horizon, Merton Field and his brother rode over "to see how our neighbor, a Mr. May, was fixed for firebreaks. He had come [to North Dakota] only that previous spring and we doubted if he knew the dangers from fires. As we surmised, he had done almost nothing in the way of protection." The Field brothers worried that May's failure would allow the fire to get too close to their own range. "It was truly time for action," Field surmised. "My brother and I worked frantically for we knew our danger unless we could get the firebreak [in place.] Mr. May, not sensing the danger, rather held back."[53]

It was easier to cope with the anxiety that accompanied fire watchfulness and preparation with good neighbors like the Merton brothers nearby. Settlers who encountered fire alone and on the open prairie were far more vulnerable, and the experience could be terrifying. Surrounded by fuel, with no place of safety or even a wind block nearby, travelers in such a situation struggled to keep their rising panic in check. Isaac Hammond, traveling alone in eastern Kansas in 1868, at first felt that a distant prairie fire was "quite insignificant to me. . . . nevertheless, the thought of those broad prairies, with such a tall growth of grass, being on fire and fanned by a high wind . . . would occasionally flash through my mind." By the next morning the situation had escalated and Hammond "began to think that it might be possible that I should experience the much-dreaded prairie fires, which I had often heard described by scouts and ranchmen as being the dread of the plains. . . . The thought of being chased by the prairie fires appeared worse to my mind than being chased by wolves in Russia." After trying and failing to reach a place of safety, Hammond set a backfire, hoping to jump his horse over the flames before they became too high. The horse, however, assaulted by smoke and heat, refused to cooperate. Hammond rode on and fortunately found a buffalo trail, clear of grass. He lit another backfire, and when the flames hit the trail the fire went out. Hammond and his horse moved onto burned ground and endured the heat until the prairie fire moved on.[54]

"Woe to the traveler who may be unprepared for, or may lack nerve to meet the emergency," C. A. White wrote in 1871. Another observer argued that all travelers who "would dare cross the prairies when the grass was heavy and dry and the winds were strong" needed specific, detailed instruction in firefighting.[55]

Training and courage were no doubt useful, but, as Hammond's experience demonstrated, matches were the real key to survival. "If [a traveler] has a box of matches and ordinary coolness of judgment he is in no personal danger," White remarked, "for he has only to stop and set another fire, extinguish that part of it upon the windward side before it has increased beyond his control, and pass into the space that has been burnt free from grass by his own fire." White's description of backfiring makes it sound simple, and indeed the creation of a burned safe area, or a "charmed circle," as White phrased it, saved many Plains travelers. Even children who traveled across the open prairie to school were sometimes given matches to carry with them as well as instructions about how to create a backfire if necessary.[56]

Often, however, things did not go as planned. Too many people risked travel without matches, accidentally left them behind, or lost them to the same wind that was driving the prairie fire toward them. Ignoring warnings that he should stay until a fire had passed, a Kansas doctor on a house call decided to start for home, 80 miles away, in the hope that the fire would be checked by plowed fireguards. When he left, a ranch hand gave him a large handful of matches and told him to strike several at a time to set his backfire. The doctor insisted that he had too many matches but when pressed took them anyway. Later, with the fire approaching, the doctor lit one match at a time instead of following the hand's directions, and each was instantly snuffed out by the wind. Finally he did what he had been told and was able to burn a strip clean, lie down on the ground, and wait for the fire to pass.[57]

Lying prostrate on burned ground waiting for a fire to come and go took great courage, but the natural inclination to run was rarely a good idea. If a fire was not intense—if there was no wind or little fuel—a horse or sometimes a person could simply step or jump over the flames onto burned ground. When a large fire was pushed by wind, however, it could move fast enough to catch a running human and even a horse. An 1887 fire in Texas traveled over 16 miles in just two hours, and a 1910 Nebraska fire went 6 miles in forty minutes. Observers clocked a modern prairie fire in Colorado moving at an incredible 30 miles per hour.[58] If close to home, a threatened person might find shelter there, but it was best to run fast. A half mile away from home, an Iowa man saw a fire coming that he later determined had started 1.5 miles from his farm. He started for home and arrived just seconds ahead of the fire, which had gained 1 mile on him during the time it took him to run the half mile.[59] In Oklahoma a woman who had gone to a neighbor's place for milk had to make a mad dash to a plowed fireguard to save herself from a sudden fire while her two daughters watched from the yard. She made it, and so did the bucket of milk.[60]

On the open prairie travelers focused on saving themselves. Fire-fighting was unplanned and improvised, undertaken only when the fire could not be otherwise evaded. When a prairie fire threatened a home or a town, however, protecting property and life was the goal. Possessions both practical and sentimental—cattle, crops, fences, chickens, furniture, dishes, quilts, diaries, books, photographs—were all part of the lives lived on the Plains, and very little could be moved on short notice. Early settlers faced many hardships as they tried to create lives for themselves in the foreign and often harsh Plains landscape. Fighting fire to protect property and family was one way the settlers could assert power over their lives and the land itself.

Defending homes was most effective when people worked together. A Nebraska family was not at home one day in 1904 when a fire swept across its farm, destroying the barn and all its contents. The work of the neighbors, who gathered in the family's absence, saved the house from destruction.[61] A Kansas woman, home alone during a 1916 burn, attempted to start a backfire to save her property but failed in the task. About to give up and run, she was in the barn gathering the horses when a car pulled up and a group of anonymous men hopped out and began fighting the fire. In the confusion the woman never learned who they were, although she later wrote to her parents, "they sure did work as though it were their own home."[62]

Ideally, fighting prairie fire was not a solitary endeavor but a community one. It united friends, strangers, and even enemies against an immediate danger that all faced together. The fires were everybody's business and everybody's responsibility. They were unpredictable, so totally dependent on the wind that nobody felt safe until the fight was won. The firefight was born out of a need for self-preservation, but the task also encouraged neighborliness and community action, binding people together in the midst of crisis. In this way, Plains people's reaction to prairie fire became part of both their individual and community identities. They were a people who knew how to survive in this environment and demonstrated their knowledge by fighting fire. The action bound them to the land and to each other.

A fire brigade, wagon and buggies full of supplies, rushes to fight the "Big Prairie Fire" near Stuart in north-central Nebraska in November of 1912. When a large fire raged, volunteers (and in this case, even canines!) were needed to combat the threat. Photographer unknown.

Townspeople and farmers alike worked to protect homes. Frank Ball remembered fires when people ran from town to defend farms. Many of them carried brooms and mops that local grocers donated to use as firefighting tools.[63] Nebraskan John Springer, grateful for the entire community's efforts, placed a notice in the local paper: "I wish to thank all my friends and neighbors and even my enemies for the assistance rendered in putting out the fire at my farm last Thursday."[64] Eppie Barrier owed her very existence to a prairie fire. Her parents met while fighting fire near Lubbock, Texas.[65]

The occasional news of an entire town's destruction inspired others to fight "with almost superhuman efforts" to save their own settlements.[66] In November 1873 the citizens of Yankton, Dakota Territory, heard "dismal rumors on the street" that the neighboring town, Vermillion, was "having a warm time of it." The telegraph went down and, without news, everyone feared the worst. The next morning the prairie fire, which had illuminated the sky all night long, rapidly moved toward Yankton. "The whole town rallied under the direction of the town Marshal, with teams and plow, and fire guards were broken," the local newspaper later reported. A train stood by in case evacuation became necessary, but the citizens intended to put up a fight until that time. The Vermillion River helped protect Yankton and with "the greatest exertion the flames were not permitted to get a foothold east of that rubicon, although in several instances the flames leaped the barrier and made a beginning." Yankton remained unscathed, and in fact even Vermillion escaped serious damage.[67]

Rarely was there a shortage of volunteer firefighters, but, as one Texan phrased it, "there couldn't be too many helpers at a fire fight, for this was hard work."[68] Near Dodge City, Kansas, 500 firefighters successfully defended the city in 1916. In 1858, near Hyatt, Kansas Territory, citizens fought fire for thirty-six hours before the danger passed.[69] In Ness City, Kansas, the city council, in the dry fall of 1893, instructed the marshal to hire an assistant and burn fireguards around the town, authorizing him to seek contributions of money and labor from the citizens to pay for the job.[70] When faced with the threat of prairie fire, the people of the Plains knew what to do. "Fight fire when necessary," the *Texas Live Stock Journal* instructed its readers; "fight together and fight it out."[71]

With the fireguards in place, a check made on any newcomer neighbors, and all eyes on the smoky horizon, the only thing left for communities to do was to wait and see where the fire might go. Nervousness and inexperience led some to exaggerate the urgency of the situation. Gladys Shattuck, while teaching school in Nebraska, became concerned one morning when ashes and smoke filled the air around her schoolhouse. "I dismissed school early thinking the prairie fire was near," she remembered. "I mounted my horse, riding it hard all the way home, so that I might die with the family, but found out when I arrived there that the prairie fire was twenty miles away."[72] Luna Warner, in Kansas, captured the uncertainty and changeful nature of the prairie fire watch in her diary. "There was a prairie fire beyond the bluff all day," Warner wrote one November 1 in the 1870s. "In the evening it came over in sight. We sat up quite late keeping watch of it, but thought it would go out, it was so still." Her family went to bed, but Warner kept guard. Sure enough, a breeze picked up and the fire came closer. The family woke, dressed, and once again went out into the cold to watch the fire. Once again it seemed to die down, and the family went back to bed. Warner, however, was too nervous. "I kept watch and before long the fire was raging again as hard as ever—one continual line from east to west. . . . We got up and dressed the second time just as five men and some boys came up with bags to put out the fire." The family fought until 3:00 A.M., then went to bed for the last time that night, feet aching with cold. The next morning, November 2, Warner woke and, ironically, built a fire to warm up.[73]

As Warner's case showed, at some point—always depending on circumstance and always subjective—the tentative watching and waiting phase shifted to serious, immediate preparation. Warnings went out both to inform those unaware of the fire's approach (especially in cases when there was little advance notice) and to serve as a call for volunteers. Within communities, church bells pealed and train whistles blew to alert the population.[74] In South Dakota, church members adjourned a business meeting early to rush home and fight fire. They had been holding special meetings to pray for rain, apparently to no avail.[75]

Individual warnings to neighbors were part of the ritual of firefighting. In the spring of 1889, Abe Squires went to the post office to mail some letters and was in the process of completing one when "a fellow ran in to the post office & says Squires there is a big prairie fire raging up your way[.] I sealed the letter and started for home as fast as the mules would go."[76] Children served as messengers, circulating news while the adults stayed home and began other preparations. In later years technology helped get the word out faster as warnings went out over rural and city telephone lines. Telephones also provided more detailed information about the path of the fire and where volunteers were needed. "Several came out from town Saturday to fight fire west of Claude Ellison's," the *Akron Weekly Pioneer Press* reported from Colorado in 1916. "Adney Drum drove from town to Ellison's in just 23 minutes and Ade Layton in 20 minutes. They must have moved some."[77]

One of the first decisions made once it was clear the prairie fire was approaching was how to protect the children. Children at school were often kept there, since the schoolyard, worn of grass from years of recess play, served as a convenient firebreak.[78] One Kansas teacher told only her oldest pupil of an approaching prairie fire, so as not to panic the younger children. Teachers sometimes had difficulty convincing students, who were worried about their families and frightened for themselves, to stay inside the building, even if it was the safest place. "Sim and Io were at school," one mother wrote of her sons' experience, "and Sim [who was twelve] was going to come home fire or no fire but the teacher would not allow it."[79] In Kansas frightened children ran out of their school but almost immediately came back in, "crawling through windows and door to escape the heat and smoke."[80]

While teachers took charge at school, parents had to decide, sometimes very quickly, how to keep their children safe at home during the emergency. As the house on any farm was the building most vigorously defended, it was the best choice in a situation with few good ones. When Mrs. Austin Taylor of Cloud County, Kansas, discovered a fire burning toward her home in March 1879, she made a critical decision. "It certainly took nerve to leave a little babe in the house and go to the north side of it and back fire and fight the fire fiend, but she did it all the same and saved [her] home," a local reporter noted with grudging admiration and, perhaps, a hint of disapproval. "Mr. T[aylor] was away from home," the writer offered in way of explanation.[81] Clara Hileman's mother put her in the house with simple instructions: "'Pa and I are going out to fight the fire,'" she said. "'You will be perfectly safe if you stay right in the house. Don't leave the house and you will be all right.' It took an awful lot of faith for me to stay in the house when I saw the fire coming," Hileman continued. "It went right past . . . not more than three or four hundred feet from the house."[82]

Houses made from prairie sod offered one of the safest places during a prairie fire, although, as the fire passed over, the dugouts held the heat like "bake ovens and it was difficult to breathe." Nevertheless, they were remarkable structures. "I tell you sod is the stuff in this country for houses and barns," Mrs. Clifford Jencks wrote to her family after a large prairie fire. "The fire passes over them and never harms them."[83]

Some Plains parents opted to take their children to water, plowed ground, or other safe places. A South Dakota mother took her children to the middle of a plowed field, wrapped them in wet blankets, and waited for the fire to pass. More extreme options were to go above- or belowground. One woman held her child with one arm and climbed a windmill with the other, waiting there while the fire passed below. Another used the same technique in the other direction, lowering herself and her child into a well.[84] Older children were often put in charge of taking the young to a field or a garden—

anywhere the fire might not find fuel.[85] Other children were kept ready to run—just in case. Mrs. C. W. Fleek of Nebraska hitched up the team, placed her children in the wagon, and drove it to the north side of her house (the protected side, as prairie fires usually came from the southwest) to wait out the fire. A Dakota woman remembered the neighborhood girls waiting, dressed in cloaks and hoods, ready to leave instantly if necessary.[86]

Stock also needed protection. If moving cattle or sheep out on the prairie when a fire approached, the herder hurried to find a safe spot, such as previously burned ground or a body of water. In the absence of anything better, cattle might be driven into green grass that was less likely than dried grass to burn.[87] Edwin Ramey, in Texas, noted that when facing a prairie fire, cowboys would put the stock into the lakes—Panhandle style. "You know what I mean by the lakes[?]" Ramey asked his interviewer. He meant any area devoid of grass—whether it held water, whenever it fell, or was just an old buffalo wallow.[88] Farmers with fewer animals could keep them safe by putting them inside the house, which was protected first.[89] We "caught the chickens and put them in the house all but four which we could not catch," Mrs. Jencks wrote to her family after a spring 1910 fire in South Dakota. Two of the four elusive chickens died in the fire, and the other two were so badly scorched that the family soon finished the job. The rest of the flock, however, waited out the emergency in comfort, along with the Jenckses' supply of corn, which was also placed inside for safekeeping.[90]

Once children and stock were safeguarded, settlers turned their attention to treasured household goods. Some did not bother with such items, preferring instead to put all their energy into fighting fire. Others, however, could not bear to have both their house and their possessions go up in flames and so worked to separate the two. In South Dakota Hattie Erikson dragged her trunk to the middle of a plowed field and set her children on top. She then made several trips back to the house, carrying out bedding, clothes, dishes, a lamp and kerosene, food, matches, tools, and even "my small pile of wood from the hills that I had to be careful with." Some items she reluctantly had to abandon. "I had to leave the stove and 3 big new grain sacks of flour that Tom had gone to . . . Minnesota for not long before. It was to be our year's supply. . . . No one knows how hard it was to leave that flour there to burn, but I could not manage to move it." The fire came and went, burning close but not touching the house. Hattie must have decided that moving almost everything but the kitchen sink was too much work, or else she never felt quite as vulnerable again. "I have seen many prairie fires since," she concluded, "and fought them too—but I have never emptied the house because of them again."[91] Of course moving goods was risky. In North Platte citizens moved furniture and other possessions to plowed ground, only to watch the fire bypass the house and instead catch the items removed. Panic caused people to do strange things. One man "heroically dragged his cook stove out of the kitchen into the yard, and returning, he gathered up the breakfast dishes and threw them out the window."[92] People more in control of their senses buried important items underground or stored them in another safe place, such as in tin cans or a strongbox. A Nebraska teacher instructed her students to dig a pit and bury their schoolbooks before the fire got too close, and another Nebraskan buried her heirloom silver in the garden.[93]

As settlers prepared to fight fire they eyed the progress of the smoke and flames carefully, but other senses also charted the fire's path. The sound of a prairie fire, most often described as a crackle or a roar, could be loud enough to wake a person from sleep. Robert Crawford heard the sound a half mile away, and one Texas cowboy claimed that the roar, which sounded "like the beating of a heavy surf on a rock-bound coast," was "audible for miles."[94] After a person heard the "appalling roar" once, it was not easily forgotten. In Nebraska Harriet Pierce heard a prairie fire coming before she could see it and warned her husband in time to get a fireguard plowed.[95] Of course, as with all aspects of prairie fire, listeners' reaction to the sound was subjective and highly dependent on circumstance. Whereas a Kansas boy, covered by a blanket and crouched in the bed of a wagon, was so frightened by the roar that he sat up, threw off his blanket, and was overwhelmed by the flames, Albert Myer, on the right side of the wind and safe in his tent in Texas, listened to the fire's pleasant crackle as he drifted off to sleep. "Its hum comes to be a kind of lullaby," Myer remembered.[96] Artist H. B. Mollhausen gave a particularly romantic description of the hum and the emotions that it inspired, even before the appearance of the fire itself:

A peculiar disquieting sort of sound accompanies these prairie burnings. It is not thundering, or rushing, or roaring, but something like the distant hollow trembling of the ground when thousands of buffaloes are tearing and trampling over it with their heavy hoofs. It sounded threateningly to us in camp and it was with a thrilling kind of admiration we contemplated this awe-inspiring spectacle.[97]

Smell was yet another early warning sign. Even the slightest whiff of smoke merited an investigation, as no one wanted to ignore the chance that a prairie fire might be just over the next rise. Burning grass gave off a distinct odor that was not unpleasant if the fire caused no angst among the population. Of course the smell elicited the opposite reaction when danger loomed: "The atmosphere in Manhattan [Kansas] was almost suffocating last night, with the smoke and odor of burning grass," the *Republican Journal* reported. After dark the source of the odor revealed itself as the fire appeared on the bluffs southwest of the town.[98] Just as odor was a warning sign for fire, the absence of it was also telling. In North Dakota a panic started by a fog that looked remarkably like smoke eased when an experienced Plainsman pointed out that there was no smell of smoke in the air.[99]

Fog did not bring high temperatures with it either, but real prairie fires brought intense heat. As the fire got closer, Arthur Towne remembered, people preparing to meet it felt the advance heat "borne to us by the wind," which sucked the moisture out of everything it touched, further preparing the environs to burn.[100] Ed Grantham, in Nebraska, noted that the fires were so hot that the grass would "sink 30 yards ahead of the flames."[101] Another settler described the heat as a blast furnace that "made me gasp for breath" and "seemed as though a shovelful of sand was thrown into my mouth."[102] As it passed over, the fire's heat did strange and terrible things. Hogs, cattle, and even human beings were literally roasted by intense fires that drew energy from a plentiful fuel source. In Harvey County, Kansas, in 1879 two men trying to save their mules and wagon were caught by a fast-moving prairie fire. Their clothing was incinerated and flesh burned off their bodies. The local newspaper did not spare the graphic details: "The doctor reports that the fleshy fat under the same was actually cooked brown for half an inch deep."[103] Heat from prairie fires reportedly cracked window glass, evaporated ponds, made the earth hot to the touch, and melted heirloom silver buried underground for safekeeping. Catherine Yahna, in Grand Forks, North Dakota, was baking bread one day in 1895 when a prairie fire swept over her homestead. The bread dough, abandoned in the kitchen when Yahna went to fight the fire, rose to incredible heights from the heat.[104]

A final curiosity in the minutes before a fire was the behavior of wild animals. A variety of creatures such as antelope, wolves, bison, and turkeys fled for their lives before an oncoming prairie fire. "It was always a bad day for jackrabbits and all non-burrowing animals," Roscoe Logue remarked.[105] Fires were known to cause buffalo stampedes and to set prairie chickens ablaze. The birds would fly up into the flame, one Nebraskan recalled, and come down so fast it looked like they had been shot.[106] Fast-running jackrabbits were even a hazard because the animals frequently caught fire and, in a panic, took off running. As they ran they became living, traveling fire torches, setting new blazes wherever they went.[107] Perhaps the strangest migration before a prairie fire, however, was that of snakes. One homesteader remembered a fire in which snakes slithered "in droves" across his yard. "Never saw such a sight before nor since," he said. Likewise, Evelyn Grandy, who taught school in Nebraska, remembered that her students always looked forward to the controlled spring burns near the school building. Many snakes and other animals traveled through the schoolyard to escape the fires, only to meet another untimely fate. "Nineteen snakes were killed by the boys and girls one spring not including those that the boys put in their pockets alive," Grandy noted. "They were just harmless garter snakes."[108]

The children, animals, and possessions stowed away, attention in the moments just before the fire arrived turned to planning how to fight the fire face-to-face should it become necessary. Once placed inside the house with her siblings and told to stay there, Daisy Wright watched from the windows as her mother filled a barrel with water and gathered gunnysacks, placing them on the rim of the barrel in case they were needed to fight fire. She then threw buckets of water against the side of the house and, as best she could, onto the roof. "She kept carrying water until the fire came," Wright noted.[109] The unprepared, uninformed, or unfortunate settlers had

Not every fire was "the big one." Small fires, not pushed by a significant wind, could be extinguished by residents wielding gunny sacks. Note the tongue-in-cheek comment written at the bottom of this postcard: "Observe the raging? fire!" Photographer unknown.

to get ready with what they had. A. S. Kimball, in a perilous position near Larned, Kansas, "planned how to fight with two buckets of water and a long-handled dipper."[110]

Prudent Plains settlers kept gunnysacks, old blankets, and carpet pieces around as firefighting equipment. In the absence of old scraps, Mrs. W. H. Gill sacrificed her Brussels carpet that she had brought to Kansas from Iowa, cutting it into pieces and soaking them in water to use as a firefighting tool. Even a person's good Sunday coat might be sacrificed in a pinch.[111] When asked how he fought prairie fires, Everett Evans, longtime Oklahoma resident, answered simply: "Well, we took sacks and whooped them out."[112] Dry cloth worked for whooping, but wet was more effective, although water was usually scarce if it was available at all. "We were so careful lest a drop of the precious fluid should be spilled or wasted," Emily Combes noted. She and her fellow firefighters even stood on the gunnysacks while they doused themselves with water to ensure that every drop served some purpose, either to protect the firefighters or to aid in putting out the fire. Beating was warm work because it required people to stand very close to the flames, but ultimately it was one of the most effective fighting methods, especially for side and short-grass fires.[113]

Another method of extinguishing fires on the short-grass prairie was to smother the flames using a green cowhide. Workers killed a cow, spread the carcass on the ground (slimy side down), and tied a rope to the front legs and another to the back. Then two riders attached the ropes to their saddle horns and, on horseback, dragged the cow along the fire line, smothering the flames as they rode. One rider placed his horse on the burned ground where the fire had already passed, while the other unlucky cowboy (and horse), to stabilize the dragging carcass, rode in front of the fire, the heat and flames licking at the horse's hooves. If it got too hot to stand, the riders switched places. Meanwhile, other men followed the drag, moving along the fire line on foot with wet blankets or sacks to beat out any leftover hot spots. [114] Once a carcass dried out it was discarded, and, if necessary, firefighters slaughtered another animal to take its place. One North Dakota rancher remembered that he used six cows to help put out a particularly large prairie fire. According to some settlers, the beef-drag technique was learned from the Indians, but there were variations. [115] A higher-tech version of the drag used chains tied to twenty feet of small pipe instead of cows and rope. The chains and pipe were expensive but could be used more than once, whereas cows killed for a drag represented a permanent loss for the rancher—although not as great a loss as the damage from a prairie fire.[116]

Using technology, or invention, to fight fire was an attractive option. An 1870s settler in Cloud County, Kansas, for example, invented a wheelbarrow to help firefighters with their task. The wheel was 12 to 15 inches wide and 3 or 4 feet in diameter and was attached to a platform that rested on the handles of the barrow. The inventor set a keg on top of the platform with a spigot positioned to run a steady stream of water over the wheel, a feature the local newspaper judged "may or may not be an advantage." The ultimate goal was to smother the fire with the wheel. "To use [the invention]," the *Kansas Farmer* explained, "the man simply trundled it over the margin of the fire, going on the run. If there is a stiff wind blowing, two of these barrows could be worked to advantage." The *Farmer* did not explain how firefighters could avoid setting themselves or their clothes on fire as they wheeled directly along the fire line, but the editor did give detailed instructions for construction. "They are easily made," he wrote. "Any farmer of ordinary skill can make them, and we urge upon those living where they are exposed to these terrible visitations [of prairie fire], to manufacture, *at once,* one or two of these implements, and keep them on hand."[117]

Farther north a lawyer from Mandan, North Dakota, invented a "Prairie Burner" to help settlers guard against fires. Many settlers were reluctant to burn fireguards around their property for fear that a wind might come up unexpectedly and cause their "controlled" burn to get away from them, possibly setting the entire county on fire. Ezekial Rice designed his Prairie Burner to burn guards safely, containing the fire under the machine so that it could not jump from the intended burn area. The Prairie Burner was 8 feet long and 4 feet high and could be operated by two men (although Rice recommended three) and one team of horses. Burners ran along the bottom length of the machine, and a fan blew against the fire line to help contain the burn, simulating a "high wind upon the prairie" except that the breeze worked for containment instead of pushing the fire forward, as it would in an uncontrolled blaze. An opening at the back of the Prairie Burner allowed smoke to escape, and a series of optional cast-iron trailers ($5 extra per trailer) ensured further fire containment. Finally, Rice attached gunnysacks by rope to either side of the machine and trailers. He weighted the sacks down with a shovelful of dirt each, and as the horses pulled the machine forward the sacks dragged behind, digging "into all holes and crevices and keep[ing] the fire from spreading and in the rear put[ing] out any that might linger." Green cattle hides might be used instead of gunnysacks. Rice acquired a patent and offered to sell his invention to settlers for about $100 (trailers not included).[118]

The Prairie Burner caused quite a stir among residents of North Dakota in 1889–1890. A Gladstone man wrote to Rice:

> I have read . . . a good deal about your firebreak burner, and as we in this vicinity have just had a most bitter experience of the might, power, and devastation of a prairie fire I write you for particulars in regard to the cost of one of your machines, what it will do, and how it is managed, in fact a full description so that we can understandingly negotiate for one of them.[119]

Another prospective buyer in Towner, North Dakota, wrote for his entire community. "We are already having prairie fires. The grass is very heavy this year," he noted in his August inquiry. By October, after no word from Rice, the buyer was more desperate:

There has been some very disastrous fires this fall and people are very anxious to see the machine work. . . . Every one wants to know what they will cost. I told them that I thought about $150.00. They seemed to think that a big price . . . but if [the machine will] do the work there will be no trouble to find a market for a great many of them—this thing of prairie fires is gathering to be a very serious matter.[120]

Clearly the threat of destruction by fire caused significant worry among Plains settlers, and any hope for aid in fire control and suppression was worth investigation. Maybe, the residents of North Dakota seemed to think, technology was the answer.

Other settlers put their faith not in science but in Providence. Stories of panic-stricken prayers for rain and salvation from fire abound in oral histories. Judge W. D. Crump remembered of a prairie fire in Lubbock County, Texas:

When I saw the smoke, I hurried over to Mr. Beal's house. It was looking pretty bad and when I got there I told [Beal] that he had better start praying for rain. That is just what I am [doing] he said. We could not tell what was overhead with all the sand and smoke . . . but all [at once] it began to rain, it simply poured down and in a few minutes the fire was all out.[121]

A rain that extinguished a prairie fire was rare, but it did happen, whether as a result of earnest prayers or simply of good fortune. On April 7, 1878, the picture near the Norton family farm in Kansas was bleak. A prairie fire burned nearby, and the Bishop farm and wheat fields were threatened. Concerned about their neighbors and their own farm, the Norton men went to see about the fire. "It crossed at Bishop's road," one of them recorded in the family diary. "Bishop came home drunk from the fort, or rather Mrs. Bishop went and brought him home." That night, however, rain fell and put out the fire, solving everyone's problems (except, perhaps, Mr. Bishop's).[122]

No matter the techniques for fighting fire—fireguard, backfire, gunnysack, fire machine, or urgent prayer—settlers considered the task to be primarily the responsibility of men. Despite the emphasis on community participation, society's assigned gender roles nevertheless created a division of labor in the midst of a prairie firefight. Most often men went out to fight the fire first, and women followed only in extreme circumstances. Plains people even gendered the language of firefighting: "Our citizens all turned out and fought the fire manfully," the *Emporia News* reported in 1859.[123] Likewise, the romanticized memory of fighting fire, told in published reminiscences years later, often took a decidedly gendered point of view. Edith Kohl, who praised her and her sister's experience as "lively women homesteaders," succumbed to this tendency. "Men went to work," she reported, "fighting fresh outbursts of flames and putting out fire on the ruins. Women hovered about us in sympathy, some with tears streaming down their sunburned cheeks under the straw hats and bonnets."[124] Archibald R. Adamson, who wrote about the 1893 fire near North Platte, Nebraska, was even more blatant about assigning specific emotions and actions to both genders. "Women and children fled in terror," Adamson wrote, describing the approach of the deadly flames, "while men scorched by heat, and well nigh blinded by smoke did what they could to save life and property."[125]

Eliminating Kohl's and Adamson's romanticism and sweeping generalizations, there is some historical truth to their statements. Society indeed expected more of one gender during a prairie fire than it did of the other. Men fighting fire was normal and expected. Women fighting fire was abnormal but was considered heroic if it became necessary. Stories of pioneer women who, despite being alone when a prairie fire threatened, fought it off until the men arrived to take control are common and were even a point of pride. The *Garden City Herald*, in 1899, reported that two Kansas girls had fought a fire by themselves, stopping the blaze within 1 foot of the barn and feed sacks. One girl's clothes caught fire, and she had to roll on the ground to suffocate the flames. "That is the stuff of which western Kansas girls are made," the reporter bragged.[126] Another Kansas writer noted that his town appeared doomed to destruction from a large prairie fire moving in from the southwest. "But the fire brigade came out and saved us," he continued. "The ladies were heroic turning out with wet sacks in their hands and fighting side by side with the men."[127] Men were only doing their duty, but women who fought fire were heroes.

The primary responsibilities of women in a prairie fire, barring any extreme circumstance that might force them to go to the main fire line, were to protect the children and provide food for the firefighters. Louise Day, who grew up in Texas, remembered her mother wrapping her and her siblings in wet blankets, placing them in a buggy, and then going after a nearby flare-up fire with blankets and a broom. Meanwhile, the men were out on the main fire line doing the same, only without the added responsibility of protecting three children.[128] Women viewed food preparation as part of the overall community response to the emergency. "When there would be prairie fires," Mrs. C. C. West of El Dorado, Texas, explained, "they would gather at our place for food and we never disappointed them." Likewise, Martha Smith, in Oklahoma, baked biscuits and made coffee for the firefighters despite the condition of the interior of her house, which was covered in burned grass. Smith worked to wash her kitchen so that she could cook something more substantial as the men rotated in from the fire line.[129]

Men often used women's clothing as an excuse to keep their wives, daughters, and sisters away from a firefight. Daisy Wright's father, for example, was afraid for his wife to get too close to the fire for fear her dress would catch. "Even so," Wright explained, "Mother helped as much as she could, her skirts pinned up in the fashion women of those days did when scrubbing floors or doing other work."[130] Indeed, the situation could be quite dangerous. In the aftermath of a firefight a Nebraska woman discovered that her skirt had literally been burned off her body. "I had caught fire repeatedly," she realized, "but I would grab up my skirt and rub out the sparks until it was nothing but tatters and I just hadn't thought of my clothes in the excitement."[131] Not all women escaped so easily. The flames of a controlled burn in Oklahoma, fueled by a gust of wind, suddenly moved underneath the skirts of a woman who was supervising the burn. She realized what had happened and in terror, began to run. Her husband pulled her to the ground, but the damage was done. Doctors came from Stillwater and wrapped her in blankets soaked in linseed oil, but the woman died later that night.[132]

Women were just as concerned about the threat of prairie fire as their husbands, sons, and brothers. They understood the potential for economic devastation and the threat to human and animal life that came with a prairie fire, and women worked very hard during a fire emergency to prevent such disastrous results. Yet Plains people still regularly defined firefighting and prairie fire prevention as a masculine activity. Take, for example, the letters of Javan Bardley Irvine, a lieutenant stationed first in Kansas and then in Dakota Territory in the 1860s and 1870s. Irvine corresponded for years with his wife in Minnesota, and later, as his son got older, also sent separate letters to him. In both sets of letters Irvine told of army life and gave poetic descriptions of the Kansas and Dakota prairies. Prairie fire, however, appeared only in Irvine's letters to his son. The lieutenant clearly viewed the fires as a masculine topic. In April 1874, when Irvine was stationed at Fort Sully in Dakota Territory, soldiers observed a prairie fire burning near the post. Irvine explained that the general had expressed an interest in catching a wolf, and they thought the fire might be just the way to do it because wild animals were known to run in front of a grass fire. The fire, therefore, became an aid for hunting. Irvine was impressed by the burn. "The fire was running in streaks," he wrote, "shooting out its tongues and licking up the long grass far in advance of the main body, rolling forward its firey billows like the ocean breakers, now advancing rapidly through the long grass, and again lulling and apparently receding as the grass became shorter." Then followed Irvine's thrilling description of a hunt in which dogs chased a rabbit through the fire and Irvine urged his horse to jump the fire line. No wolves appeared, although the fire moved very rapidly and for a time the fort was threatened. "The fire had no regard for Genl Stanley, or his assertion that 'it would not cross that ridge,' but it came right over and crossed the prairie about two miles back of the river . . . advancing rapidly over the short grass—where the Genl asserted 'it would not run!'"[133]

Based on the length of his letter and on the obvious excitement with which he described the afternoon's events, Irvine enjoyed his experience with the prairie fire. He wanted his son to read of every detail, every emotion associated with the event. His wife, however, received no such description. In fact, no mention of prairie fire appears in the hundreds of letters that Irvine sent her over the many years of his military career, during which he likely witnessed many such fires. Only when Irvine's son was old enough to appreciate the danger and adventure did the father include the tale—one he intended for male eyes only. The soldiers' attempt to use fire as a tool for hunting, yet another "masculine" activity, is further evidence of the fire's gendered status. Prairie fire, Irvine said through his verbose words to his son and his silence toward his wife, was something that men fought; men controlled; and men, if they wished, used for their sport.

Firefighting and suppression, therefore, involved many people, much effort, and a variety of strategies and techniques. Plains people, most of whom believed that eliminating the fires was best for all concerned, were largely but not entirely successful in their goal. Over time the number and scope of the fires did decrease. In part this was inadvertent, due to the continually developing infrastructure on the Plains. The first infrastructure intrusion was the railroad: Locomotives threw sparks and started fires instead of stopping them. But, in the long term, railroads facilitated town and road building and permanent agricultural settlement. Surveyors divided the grassland into neat townships (6 miles square), and then partitioned each township again into 1-mile square sections (640 acres), as dictated by the Congressional Land Ordinance of 1785. Thus, the new arrivals imposed a checkerboard onto the land, dividing it for orderly settlement and conversion to agriculture.[134] Fires did not respect survey boundaries, but some elements of the new infrastructure that accompanied settlement, such as roads and plowed fields, acted as firebreaks.

Roads naturally followed township and section lines, and settlers eagerly put the plow to the soil. Still, the addition of infrastructure was gradual and not inclusive. It was well into the twentieth century before even 30 percent of the Plains felt the plow. Kansas's Hamilton County maintained an open range until 1931.[135] Plowed ground and fuel-free roads thus assisted with the active suppression agenda, but the imposition of infrastructure onto the vast Plains landscape was so gradual that it was well into the twentieth century before the threat from prairie fires truly diminished. As late as 1947 over a quarter of a million acres burned in a South Dakota fire. Even on the modern, long-settled Plains, prairie fires still occasionally threaten despite the degree of settlement and the new technology used to combat them.[136]

Prairie fires, therefore, continued to be a significant threat even after the process of settlement was well under way. The vigilance that early settlers maintained against the fires, however, proved difficult to sustain. Some grew complacent in their watchfulness, perhaps thinking the fight was won. Newspaper editors continually warned against inaction and contentment, sensing that disaster was imminent if settlers relaxed. In 1891 the *Norman* (Oklahoma Territory) *Transcript* reported on a rash of prairie fires in April. "Prairie fires in the territory have done an immense lot of damage during the past two weeks time," the writer stated, "and the danger period has not yet passed."[137] Although the Oklahoma writer referred specifically to the fires that month, the same statement might be used to describe the broader situation, starting in the 1890s and beyond. Euro-American settlement was by then three decades old on some parts of the Plains, but the prairie fire "danger period" certainly had not passed, no matter how much settlers might wish to believe the contrary.

In some ways the fires had actually gotten worse. Fire suppression and the elimination of controlled burns had worked too well. "Western Kansas papers are calling attention to the fact that the unprecedented growth of prairie grass will add greatly to the danger of the usual prairie fires this fall, making it necessary that all possible precautions for guarding against the ravages be taken without delay," the Dodge City *Globe-Republican* cautioned in 1896.

Indeed, after a few years of active fire suppression, the resulting unprecedented growth of grass, shrubs, and trees began to gain notice. Arthur Harbottle, in Nebraska, made the connection. He remembered one prairie fire that had swept near his parents' farm after a ten-year hiatus from burning. "The blue stem was as high as the door," he noted. The fire "was a big one. And a hot one."[138] Likewise, Dick Rice, in Oklahoma, remarked on the changes to his father's land in just a decade without fire.[139]

It is no surprise, then, considering the increase in the amount of vegetation on the Plains, that when the fires came back, they came with a vengeance. Some settlers, like Harbottle, understood the connection between fire suppression and an inevitable return of fire at an increased intensity. Others, however, were slower to make the association. John L. Finley reported to the Kansas State Board of Agriculture in 1894:

It seems that for a number of years after the pioneers and cowboys got possession of this country, and civilization began to come in, prairie fires were to some extent stopped. Grass and vegetation began to grow to a considerable extent; and in 1884, when I came to Ford county [Kansas], there had been two or three years of more than usual moisture. . . . The result showed in the vegetation, although in the spring of 1884 the country was swept by a very destructive fire.

Finley became convinced that prairie fires caused prolonged patchy vegetation in western Kansas and argued that total fire suppression was needed for the grass and planted crops to succeed. Failing to recognize that a heavy grass cover caused by fire suppression was particularly vulnerable to a high-intensity burn and refusing to believe that occasional burns were inevitable, Finley seemed mystified at the inability of Kansans to keep their well-cultivated grass cover forever. In western Kansas during the late 1880s and early 1890s, Finley continued,

the plains became a solid mass of buffalo grass, and large patches of blue stem came in and made a luxuriant growth. . . . As a consequence, crops became more certain and heavier, buffalo grass, in some places, was cut for hay. . . . But in the spring of 1892, from some unknown cause, fires became more frequent and of larger extent. Flames from the heavy crops of matted grass seemed impossible to control, and a large area of the county was burned over.[140]

Finley, like many others on the Plains, refused to acknowledge that human beings did not have complete control over prairie fire. Settlers had partial control, and this gave them delusions of grandeur. As Frederick Law Olmsted had noted, fighting a prairie fire as part of a community effort, and winning, was incredibly satisfying.[141] A feeling of power accompanied the act. For farmers in a new and volatile environment such as the Great Plains—where they routinely lost crops to hail, drought, and other hardships, sinking further into debt as a result—feeling power over any threat to their property must have been a heady experience. No reasonable Plains resident claimed to have power over other natural phenomena, such as tornadoes and blizzards, but the ability to curtail prairie fire gave them false confidence that the threat from fires, at least, could be totally eliminated. Such was the goal, despite the lingering suspicion, still held by some, that fire might actually be good for the prairie grass.

After several decades of vigilant fire suppression, then, in the early twentieth century came reports of "the worst" fires in many years. "The worst prairie fire in 17 years swept over the country south of Dickinson, North Dakota, recently, destroying livestock and burning many farm buildings," a Colorado newspaper reported in 1906.[142] Such statements were not uncommon as second-generation settlers, who perhaps thought that the prairie fire threat was behind them, were forced to combat the blazes just as their parents had done years earlier. "The worst" fires were likely a combined result of settlers' relaxation in fire prevention, a thick mat of grass cover that was the result of suppression, and a not-yet complete infrastructure. In November 1895 the Dodge City, Kansas, *Globe-Republican* reported on a significant prairie fire near the city that destroyed the property of several rural citizens, including that of Nic Mayrath, who lost considerable feed, fencing, trees, and pasture grass. "Mr. Mayrath's land had not been burned off for eighteen years, and the heavy grass made sweeping flames," the reporter concluded.[143]

Across the region, years of firefighting and suppression had had their effect. Sedentary, permanent settlement of the Great Plains made Euro-Americans, as they pushed out onto the wide prairie expanse, initially more vulnerable to prairie fires than the more mobile Indian peoples had been. Over time, however, particularly by the last half of the twentieth century, the ever-expanding infrastructure that accompanied permanent settlement helped to curb the destructive effects of the fires. The land changed through the application of the plow and the road and also through the reduction of fire. The "improvements" that came with settlement, the fragmentation of the land, and the reduction of intentional burns, combined with the vigilance that settlers displayed toward fire prevention and protection, allowed the campaign against prairie fires to succeed. Whether success was a good thing, however, hinged on perspective. Now a people who knew how to fight fire, Plains residents would have to contend with both the benefits and the consequences of its absence.

Chapter Six

"A Horrible World of Cinders and Blackness"

The prairie lay black, smoking, and covered with bodies. Scattered between one-quarter and one-half mile from the schoolhouse, all seven victims were charred and naked, their clothes now ash around them. Not all were dead. Frank Davis, director of the rural school in southwest North Dakota, and William Pike, father of one of the victims, were the first to reach the scene. "Words cannot describe its horror," Davis stated after viewing the carnage. "Here a hand moved, there a head, and again another was past movement."[1]

Davis and Pike were not the only witnesses to the horrific aftermath of the fire that swept the prairie near Belfield in November 1914. When the men arrived, five uninjured students sat huddled in two fire-safe locations. Three stood on plowed ground, and two others, having run through the flames to safety, rested on the bare land where thick prairie grass had grown a mere few minutes before.

It took a week for the full story to emerge. About 1:00 P.M. that Friday the teacher, Gladys Hollister, began gathering her students, ranging in age from seven to thirteen, to resume their studies after the noon break. It was then that she spotted the fire coming from the southwest directly toward her school. Hollister, a twenty-one-year-old Iowa native, had but a few moments to make a critical decision—one that many Plains teachers faced during the first years of settlement. Should she keep the children in the school and pray that the worn ground around the building would act as a fireguard, or should she seek safety for herself and her students outside the vulnerable wooden structure? Believing the school to be doomed,

Hollister ordered the children to run for plowed ground north of the building. Some obeyed, but in their panic, and possibly confused by thick smoke, five of the boys veered toward the south into the path of the fire. Seeing their mistake, Hollister and an older student, Ruth Olson, stepsister to one of the errant boys, rushed after them. The heat and smoke were too intense, however, and all five boys as well as the girl and teacher were overcome. The children who ran in the proper direction escaped all but minor injuries. The schoolhouse was also unharmed.[2]

Two of the boys and Ruth Olson died immediately. Three boys and Gladys Hollister, not so lucky, were alive when Davis and Pike arrived. Pike found his son and listened as the burned boy told of how he was "so hot." Davis encountered the teacher not far from the school, over 95 percent of her body burned. Covering her with his shirt and wiping dirt and ashes from her mouth, Davis heard Hollister ask to see her sister before she died. Davis left Pike to care for his own son and carried the woman to the school for other rescuers to watch over before gathering the remaining two boys in his car and driving 16 miles to town and a doctor. The boys died later that evening as Hollister, conscious and in agony for several hours, blamed herself for her decision to lead the children out of the school. She died sometime after midnight.[3]

Hollister's body was sent to her parents in Iowa, but the town of Belfield held a group funeral at the opera house for the six children. The service was conducted in two languages, English and German, and 700 mourners were in attendance. Seventy rigs made up the funeral procession, and children from the city school served as pallbearers. Townspeople eulogized Hollister and Olson, in particular, for their brave attempt to save the boys in the face of overwhelming danger. "Words fail us in our effort to express the dark gloom which fell over the city, or the horror stricken faces of our citizens," one editor remarked.[4] "Horrors of this calamity will forever remain in the minds of all."[5]

Although a prairie fire might sweep over a town, a farm, or a school in mere minutes, the consequences of the blaze, both human and financial, lasted much longer. When the fires caused human suffering, all benefits of burning were erased from victims' minds, and the suppression agenda was justified. The people who worked to create a life on the Plains only to see that life literally turned to ashes around them were hard-pressed to find hope in the minutes and hours following the fire, although hope did lurk even there. If fighting prairie fire was a way to assert power over the land, then the postfire situation, particularly when the firefight had not gone well, was one in which settlers felt an acute loss of power. After the fire passed by, it seemed as if all the people could do was to get up, take stock, and start again. Facing the aftermath of a destructive prairie fire was, in the eyes of those who endured it, another way for Plains people to earn their place in the region. The postfire scene was also, undoubtedly, stark evidence that the Plains environment was still a very active participant in the ongoing "conversation" with the human beings who proposed to live there.

Most postfire scenes did not create such a horrific image as the prairie fire at the Belfield school, but they nevertheless left a long-lasting impression on observers. Already emotionally drained and physically exhausted by their encounter with the fire, witnesses had little positive to say about the "blackened waste" that a fire left in its wake.[6] To these observers, fire was the destroyer that drastically altered the appearance of the prairie, and it often happened all too abruptly. "Twenty miles of country . . . without a bush or a tree or a sign of human inhabitation, but every foot of it covered with this beautiful Bluestem," a Nebraska man mused. After a prairie fire "the picture was vastly or ghastly different, a black desolation."[7] Other witnesses agreed, describing the charred landscape as "frightful black," "a perfect blackness," and "black as death."[8] Many people already believed they had entered an "empty" land—a treeless, uninhabited place—so a fire's destruction of the thing in the landscape they valued most, the grass, was disheartening. Moses H. Sydenham, a freighter and settler in the Platte River Valley, described the burned prairie as "a perfect picture of despair with hope left out."[9] "I had expected to find things looking bad," the visiting Abbie Bright wrote of her first postfire view, "but my imagination was short, far short of the fact."[10]

The transformed landscape was disorienting, adding to the despair. It was not uncommon for firefighters or spectators to get lost on the dark prairie on the way home. Merton Field remembered one dangerously blind night ride, "every moment of which I expected [my horse] to step into a hole and throw me. . . . We finally reached our destination without mishap, but I shall never forget that six mile ride over the blackened prairie."[11] The experience was not much better for walkers. C. A. Murray spent one evening enjoying the beauty of a prairie fire from a distance but found when the fun was over that he "had much difficulty" finding his way back to camp. "The night relapsed into its natural darkness," he remembered. "The prairie at my feet was black, burnt, and trackless, and I could see neither stream nor outline of hill by which to direct my steps."[12] A newspaper writer concluded that "after the fire was over it was almost impossible to find one's way over the black prairie."[13]

The enveloping darkness was worse for those caught in the emotional exertions of fighting fire. A perfectly executed backfire resulted in instantaneous and "absolute darkness" when the two fires met. The effect was startling for eyes accustomed to the bright light of the fire.[14] Not all fires went out so suddenly, but Kansan Adela Orpen noted that when they did the contrast between the frantic communal activity of firefighting and the lonely aftermath was frightening. She wrote:

> The darkness that follows the going out of a prairie fire is something portentous. From being the center of a lurid glare you are suddenly plunged into the bottom of a bucket of pitch. Nothing reflects any light, and there is nothing to steer by. You don't know where you are nor where the house is; everything is black. . . . If you call to your nearest pal on the back firing line the chances are that he or she has moved away, and may be half a mile distant. You may feel as if you were the last survivor in a horrible world of cinders and blackness.[15]

Besides being dark and depressing, the scorched landscape was inconvenient and uncomfortable. Ash was everywhere, sometimes forming drifts like snow against fences and houses. Blown in the eyes, one traveler complained, the ashes "hurt like blazes."[16] Another overlander, at dinnertime, was not appreciative of the prairie fire remnants that blew into his "victules."[17] Horses stumbled over the uneven burned ground, stepping on bones of animals that had died in the fire. Merton Field noted that his horses' hooves were bleeding after traveling across sharp, stubbled postfire ground: "It was pitiable to see them mincing along on feet so sore they were agonized by the torture."[18]

Adding to the discomfort was the lingering heat. One Plains-man told of several men who rushed out of their house the instant a head fire passed, eager to beat out flying sparks that might have leaped over the fireguards. They just as quickly rushed back in, however, as the air was still too hot to endure.[19] After two Nebraska men ran their team and wagon through an oncoming fire, someone noticed that the jug of drinking water, which was sitting in the back of the wagon, was too hot to touch.[20]

The ground held the heat best. One Dakota mother and her youngest child darted through a fire and tumbled exhausted and "strangled by the dense smoke" onto the charred ground. Both mother and child died when their clothes were ignited, not by the fire itself but by the heat the fire had left behind.[21] The ground heat dissipated slowly. Emily Combes provided a rough timetable for one 1871 fire in Rice County, Kansas, noting that she and her neigh-bors fought fire from Monday evening to about 2:30 early Tues-day morning. When Combes set out to drive across the prairie on Wednesday, more than twenty-four hours after the fire was out, "the ground was hot in some places and the prairies still smoking here and there."[22] While a captive of the Sioux, Fanny Kelly took part in an intense fight to save the Indian camp from fire. That afternoon, she remembered, everyone involved took a rest, not only to regain strength but to allow the ground time to cool so that people and horses could travel.[23] The danger persisted much longer on occa-sion. A Nebraska woman noted that three weeks after a blaze that had almost destroyed her home, one of her children burned his foot when he stepped in a partially burned-out fence-post hole. There was still fire lodged in the remaining wood belowground.[24]

That heat did terrible things to animals, both wild and domestic, and the postfire prairie was often strewn with dead or grotesquely injured beasts. In Dakota, near the Pembina River Post in November 1804, the hunter and explorer Alexander Henry found the

Plains burned in every direction and blind buffalo seen every moment wandering about. The poor beasts have all the hair singed off; even the skin in many places is shriveled up and terribly burned. . . . It was really pitiful to see them staggering about, sometimes running afoul of a large stone, at other times tumbling down hill and falling into creeks not yet frozen. In one spot we found a whole herd lying dead. The fire having passed only yesterday these animals were still good and fresh, and many of them exceedingly fat.[25]

While Henry enjoyed his impromptu barbecue, another prairie fire interrupted Richard Dodge as he skinned a deer. Dodge found a safe spot to wait out the fire, and when he returned to his kill he found the deer "literally cooked," although "not very artistically, as the outside was burned to a cinder, the inside being raw."[26]

Many wild animals, including antelope, skunk, badger, snake, fox, and coyote, were victims of prairie fires.[27] People were shocked at the sheer number of animals killed. "For a day after," a traveler wrote, "the air was black and stifling, and our course was strewn with the bones of animals that had fallen prey to the fire."[28] Prairie chickens, nesting comfortably in the tall grass, would fly up, startled by the disruption, then be overcome by the heat and smoke and drop dead onto the burned ground. "Birds of all kinds were burned to death in countless numbers," one settler remembered, and their carcasses remained scattered on the prairie after the fire was over.[29]

Large numbers of domestic animals also died in prairie fires, contributing to the gruesome postfire scenes. An 1887 fire in Nebraska trapped, burned, and killed forty-seven horses in one small pasture. "This was the worst sight I ever beheld, with the exception of [a] battel field after the battle was over," remembered B. G. Mathews.[30] Part of the postfire experience for many Plains residents was to put injured animals out of their misery. Edwin Walters, a teacher in Kansas, remembered one day in 1872 when 12 men with rifles and axes relieved the suffering of an estimated 800 animals. "Many of the poor creatures kept on their feet after their horns and hoofs had dropped off," he recalled. The carcasses were then moved onto the open prairie and left for the coyotes.[31] Another man remembered, as a child, riding in a wagon across the burned prairie and along the way seeing farmers in their yards and pastures shooting their hairless, blind horses and cattle.[32] The dead animals fouled the very air. Martha Smith smelled burned hair on the wind after an Oklahoma blaze, and Mary Bickett, in Nebraska, noted that days after a fire "the prairie stunk with so many rotting carcasses."[33]

Metaphorically, however, prairie fires were not entirely a stench in the nostrils. Out of scenes of doom and despair came hope. For one thing, as a Nebraskan pointed out, the fires killed a lot of rattle-snakes.[34] Residents also gathered the thousands of newly exposed animal bones and sold them for fertilizer, gaining a little income in a time of need. In 1884 the *Boston Transcript* reported that a "cargo of skeletons" from Texas had recently arrived in Philadelphia, some of them blackened by prairie fire. Hazel Shaw, who moved to the Oklahoma panhandle just after the great prairie fire of 1913, found the thousands of bones depressing reminders of the disaster, but she acknowledged that gathering and selling them was a way to recoup a small portion of the economic loss caused by the fire. Ranchers "would haul these bones to the nearest railroad station" to sell, she noted. "Of course they didn't get much out of them, but they didn't have anything else to sell that year."[35]

By laying bare the prairie, a fire offered other small, but sometimes useful and amusing, benefits. It made the gathering of prairie-chicken eggs easier. One Nebraska woman made a habit of going to the burned area and taking her pick of as many eggs as her basket would hold. Another, discussing the gathering of prairie-chicken eggs in general, noted that the nests were so well hidden in the grass that she frequently stepped on them. "After a prairie fire," however, "is a good time to go egging, the nests being in plain sight, and the eggs already roasted."[36] Mr. F. C. Simon, an early Kansan, benefited from a land-clearing prairie fire in a different way. Two months before the fire Simon lost his pocketbook on the prairie, but the morning after, with the land clear of grass, he found it again. The wallet contained ninety-six dollars, and only one bill was damaged.[37] Simon likely was one of the few Plainsmen to actually make money rather than lose it as a result of a prairie fire.

A far more important advantage of the melancholy postfire landscape was its protection of residents from further fires. Farmers who saved their property from a prairie fire could rest relatively easy until the grass came in again. One Plains woman wrote to her parents in Indiana of her experience. "Don't worry about us," she reassured them, "for there is no grass to make another prairie fire."[38] Comte Philippe de Trobriand, commanding officer at Fort Stevenson in Dakota Territory, recalled one desperate fight to save the fort from a prairie fire in November 1868. With much effort the soldiers managed to stop the fire about 200 meters from the buildings. "There it went out," de Trobriand wrote with relief,

and what had been our danger became our protection. In fact
the fort henceforth was completely surrounded on three sides
by a wide zone of ashes and burnt-over ground. The fourth
side being formed by the Missouri and its sand banks, the fire
might for the future go wherever it would in the prairie. From
whatever direction the wind might blow it could not approach
us any longer and must perforce die at the edge of this black
sea of charred earth. . . . Our isolation becomes henceforth our
security.[39]

Plains settlers quickly recognized the paradox of the prairie
fire—an enemy that threatened to destroy a farmer's livelihood in
one minute might in the next become his salvation. The paradox
continued with the renewal of the grass. What was a "wasteland"
became an expanse of "velvet green," the green actually enhanced by
the so-called destroying element.[40] Observers viewed the phenome-
non as a sign of hope. As early as 1798, David Thompson, exploring
on the Red River of the north, noted that "if these grasses had not
this wonderful productive power on which fire has no effects, these
Great Plains would, many centuries ago, have been without Man,
Bird or Beast."[41] Even that "productive power" maintained the paradox, as the reemergence of the grass could be at the same time sudden and subtle. George Dawson, who observed many prairie fires
while surveying the Canada–United States international boundary
line in 1873, noticed this irony. He saw "a large area burned about
a month ago & now looking beautifully green from a distance but
black & bare when traveled over."[42]

As important as the renewal of the prairie grass was (and is),
human suffering in the aftermath of a prairie fire masked all benefits. Even minor injuries were painful, although most people acknowledged that things might have been much worse. Almost every person who vigorously fought fire walked away with singed
eyebrows and hair, a natural consequence of the gunnysack method
of firefighting, which required fighters to get close to the flames.
Some settlers (as well as their horses) got blisters and fairly severe
burns on exposed parts of their bodies—extremely painful but not
fatal in most circumstances.[43] Some minor injuries had the potential
to be much worse but for a combination of luck and presence of
mind. When his clothing caught fire, a Kansas man fought back his

panic and jumped onto a piece of burned ground, rolling in the ash until the flames were gone. A Nebraska woman had a "harrowing" experience when, upon noticing a bright light outside her window, she "went to the door and stepped out, [and] like a flash a great sheet of flame swept over her head. She slammed the door shut and raised trembling hands to her hair to find it literally burned off her head. Only a short, straggly mop remained."[44] One Plainsman, trapped and burned over by a 1925 fire in Nebraska, miraculously survived the event relatively unscathed. "I learned a lot that day," he mused fifty years later.[45]

Clarence Cline also lived to tell the tale of his encounter with a prairie fire, but his experience was far more severe. The catastrophe happened in March 1910 near Tryon, Nebraska. Cline, who served as treasurer at the courthouse, was at work when he was told that a prairie fire was heading toward his home south of town. Worried about his wife, children, and farm, Cline did not pause to gather information or to think of the safest course of action but simply set off on foot—a colossal mistake. He ran through dust and smoke and was halfway home when he saw the flames, felt the approaching heat, and heard the crackle of the fire. Understanding his mistake and realizing that he could not run faster than the fire, Cline lay down on a narrow cow trail and dug a small hole in the dirt to shelter his face. As it approached a prostrate and terrified Cline, the fire hit a section of tall grass, which only magnified its intensity. The heat was unbearable, and as it passed over the man it left him, according to one disturbing account, "like a barbecued beef." Despite his injuries Cline rose to his feet, his clothes still burning, and ran for home—beating out the flames as he ran, "a living torch." When he arrived at his farm, Cline threw himself into the cattle tank, his clothing entirely gone by then except for his boots.

After the fire passed, Cline's wife, Signa, brought her children home to see the damage done to the house and outbuildings. The family had fled the area at the approach of the flames and had never been in danger. Mrs. Cline believed her husband to be safe at his office and was therefore shocked to see his horribly scorched body in the stock tank. With her brother's help, Signa Cline carried her husband into the house and sent for the doctor, but she must have felt the situation to be without hope; perhaps she even prayed for her husband's pain to end quickly. The doctor arrived and cut Cline's boots off his feet, using oil to separate the leather from the man's cooked flesh, which was literally falling off his bones. For treatment the doctor soaked Cline's entire body in linseed oil and left instructions that he was not to be moved and could have neither clothes nor blankets touching him. Most prairie fire victims burned so severely died within a few hours. Distant newspapers, such as the Oklahoma City Oklahoman, picked up the story and prematurely reported Cline's death, making a logical assumption that he could not possibly survive such a severe trauma. Cline indeed lingered close to death for several weeks but eventually recovered, and after many months he returned to his job as county treasurer, carrying physical (and likely mental) scars of the tragedy on his entire body.[46]

There are countless other such stories, many almost as tragic as Clarence Cline's. Occasionally children were severely injured, like young Zora Hull, burned in the Lawton fire of 1904. People, like animals, were sometimes blinded by prairie fires. They lost limbs, hands, and feet, their appendages "charred nearly to the bone."[47] To survive such horrific injuries, victims such as Clarence Cline and Charles Bergren, who dragged his burning body into a creek to extinguish the flames, had to fight hard. Bergren, noted one newspaper, saved himself "by an almost superhuman effort," and "as he is not burned internally, and has a good constitution, strong hopes are entertained of his recovery."[48]

Today medical professionals place burns in three different categories—first, second, or third degree. First-degree burns are minor and affect only the top layer of skin. These superficial burns, although painful, do not have long-lasting effects. Second-degree burns involve deeper layers of skin, which may blister and seep fluid. Swelling of the skin is also common, and the burns may leave scars. The most serious burns are third degree, in which all layers of skin and underlying tissue, sometimes including bone, are involved. Third-degree burns may look charred and may or may not be painful (at least at first), depending on the extent of nerve damage. The more serious the burn, however, the greater the risk of infection owing to the exposure of tissue. Infection was undoubtedly an even greater threat to prairie fire victims because of the unsterile conditions (a sod or a frame house) in which the victims were placed during recovery. Also, the victims of third-degree burns, such as Clarence Cline, can suffer from severe dehydration—especially if the burns cover a large percentage of the body. Severe-burn victims have trouble breathing, and the body, without the protection of the skin, often cannot satisfactorily regulate its own temperature.[49]

Those who did recover from severe injury experienced disfigurement or other lingering reminders of the tragedy. Neddie Clark's scarred appearance made a lasting impression on young Rachel Ball. Clark, who had been severely burned while visiting in Kansas, eventually recovered well enough to move back home to Nebraska, where he frequented a store owned by Ball's father. "His body was so terribly burned that he was deformed," Ball recalled, "making it difficult for him to walk." Kansan Oscar Lilly, severely burned on his upper body by an 1893 prairie fire, lived despite the odds against it but finished the remainder of his life with no ears or nose. Meanwhile, in Colorado, a young girl's "troubles have been many," reported a local newspaper, "since she was burned in a prairie fire at her home near Walden three years ago."[50]

Yet another consequence of prairie fire injury was the inability of the victim to work during or after recovery, which caused even more economic hardship to fire-impacted families. Ed Grantham's neighbor, he remembered, allowed a controlled fire to get away from him and burned himself very badly. Not only did the neighbor lose a horse, 300 bushels of wheat, and all his corn, but he was not able to work for months. Mrs. Ross, in Nebraska, noted of her husband, "The Mr. got his hands burned in a prairie fire and then he couldn't help anymore with the milking."[51]

Most of those burned to the point of disfigurement never recovered. Burn victims got into trouble in a variety of ways. Many were simply caught unawares by the fire, and others risked too much to protect their property. Some of those burned were firefighters who became trapped when a sudden wind shift sent the blaze in an unexpected direction, or who got too close and set their clothes afire or inhaled flames. Some victims were burned while trying to help other people escape.

Daniel and William Anderson, brothers from Manhattan, Kansas, came so suddenly upon the fire that killed them that they had too little time to assess and deal with the situation. Traveling by wagon near town, the brothers saw the fire coming but were unable to navigate their frightened horses through the smoke to safety. The men fell from the wagon, and their clothes caught fire. Later the doctor said one of the brothers was "literally cooked. . . . His finger and toe nails are burned out, his eyes consumed, and his entire body a crisp." Remarkably, however, before his cries attracted the attention of neighbors, he had risen to his feet and walked "several rods," either in an attempt to get help or in a state of agonized confusion. Both brothers died several hours after the fire.[52]

Men, who were always in the vanguard of a firefight, sometimes risked too much to protect the property they had worked so hard to obtain for themselves and their families. John Koch of Broken Bow, Nebraska, lost his life while trying to protect his haystacks, which represented his cattle feed for the coming winter and therefore his livelihood.[53] Often, though, it was not men who lost their lives but women and children. These casualties were directly related to assigned gender roles. Men were the primary firefighters; although women often fought fire, some waited until things got desperate before joining the fight. This might have been because women were needed to watch children during the fire, because of a gendered labor division in which firefighting was a specifically male role, or because husbands instructed their wives to stay away from the fire. This hierarchical, gender-based system for fighting prairie fire had its consequences. Men and older boys rushed to the scene when fire was first discovered, leaving the women and children on the farm. Thus, if the fire took an unexpected turn and bore down on the home while the men were elsewhere, the job of protecting property fell to the women and children. Such a situation developed in Cottonwood Falls, Kansas, in 1876. "The city was on fire at various places," a regional paper reported, "but the bravery of the women (the men being at the front of the fire) saved the town."[54]

Not every scenario turned out as well. Nineteen-year-old Mrs. Daniel Borversox, in March 1879, was newly married and had recently immigrated to Republic County, Kansas, from Illinois. The prairie fire that killed her started slowly on a Thursday morning in a light wind but increased in intensity and shifted direction, along with the wind, that afternoon. Many men of the county were already out fighting fire, one newspaper account related, and were trapped by its unexpected movement. They were not able to return to their houses to combat the blaze, and "the women were compelled to do the best they could." While her husband and other male neighbors found safety in a dugout, Borversox, who was home with her mother-in-law, saw that the fire threatened the stable where several valuable horses were lodged. She tried to free the animals but was overcome by smoke and heat. Her body was found in the remains of the building next to the burning horse carcasses.[55]

In South Dakota, two brothers, Michael and John Donley, went out to fight a fire in October 1880, instructing their seventy-nine-year-old mother, Mary, to stay inside the house until the danger passed. While they were gone, however, the fire threatened the Donley home, and Mary went out alone to fight it, catching her clothes on fire in the process. The house, ironically, was saved by a last-second wind change, but Mary died two days later.[56]

The deaths of settlers who put themselves in danger to help neighbors were particularly tragic. Robert Montgomery and his son were burning a fireguard when a sudden wind change turned the fire toward them. Two plowed fields were nearby, and the boy and his dog ran toward one while the father moved to the other. Passing by this scene on a mule, neighbor Isaac Pfaff rode to Montgomery and told him to get on the mule. As Montgomery did so, he saw his son engulfed by the flames—a sight that caused him to lose "all presence of mind." In his panic and grief, he threw his arms around his rescuer, interfering with Pfaff's ability to control the mule, and caused both men to tumble to the ground and be severely burned. Both Montgomery and his would-be good Samaritan died after several hours of agony.[57]

Death by burning was not the only danger people encountered when fighting prairie fire. Heart attacks brought on by the sheer effort were not uncommon. Neighbors of Walter Heath in Nebraska noted Heath's quick efforts to put out a fire before it could do much damage but became concerned when the farmer did not come home after the fire was out. They found him sitting on the ground against a wagon wheel, apparently the victim of a fatal heart attack. The *Akron Weekly Pioneer Press*, in 1911, reported that a local store had shipped a coffin northeast of town "intended for a man who died from over exertion in fighting a prairie fire." The man in need of the coffin, the journalist continued, was "a new comer and came to eastern Colorado for his health."[58]

A far more common, if considerably less dramatic, way in which prairie fire affected the lives of Great Plains residents was through property loss. In fact, the threat of property destruction was the primary thrust behind the settlers' avid drive to suppress. In part this was because loss of hay, livestock, a barn, or even a house seemed to most Plains residents a plausible threat—something that might easily happen to them—whereas loss of life or severe injury by prairie fire was less conceivable. In the abstract, settlers knew that what happened to Clarence Cline might happen to them, but, perhaps because it was too horrible to contemplate, most seemed not to believe it would. Property loss, however, was all too likely.

No one on the Plains, from the poorest farmer to the largest ranching operation, was immune from fire. Large ranches occasionally lost staggering numbers of livestock. "There is a report here that the Hall brothers and Sam Doss have lost about eight hundred head of fat cattle which they were driving to Kansas City," the *Colorado Weekly Chieftain* recorded in 1877. "The report is to the effect that they were overtaken by a prairie fire in Kansas and the cattle all suffocated by the fire and smoke."[59] A later fire in the Texas Panhandle caught two bands of sheep, totaling thousands of animals, and reportedly burned every one to death.[60] The memory of a big livestock loss could last a while, even if the loss was not your own but your neighbor's. Some forty years after the event, Ed Wright of North Platte, Nebraska, identified "the big fire" as the one that "got 96 head for Jes Long."[61]

The greatest concern for large ranches was not livestock but grass. Some individual Plainsmen were cavalier about such a loss. "Charlie and I went to a prairie fire Mr. Norland has set," a Kansas farmer wrote in his family diary. "It burned nothing but grass."[62] Newspaper writers who sputtered and raged when homes or barns or livestock were destroyed often dismissed the loss of the range as an afterthought. "A prairie fire was accidentally started in our vicinity Wednesday," the *Akron Weekly Pioneer Press* remarked, "but no damage was done except the burning of the grass."[63] The *Texas Live Stock Journal*, however, made different comments regarding the range: "Look out for prairie fires and be on hand to put them out before much damage is done. We cannot spare the wealth of the grass."[64] To ranchers, who depended on the energy in the grass to nourish their livestock, the loss of the range was just as significant as a crop loss to a farmer or a business loss to a merchant.[65] To a ranchman, range lost was, effectively, property lost. "When a ranchman lost his grass the backbone of his industry was broken," Roscoe

Logue argued in *Under Texas and Border Skies*. "It meant a transfer to other ranges, resulting in the loss of flesh and the deterioration of his cattle."[66] Even if a suitable transfer location could be found, the good grazing areas became crowded quickly. "There are still some ranges untouched," a Dakota newspaper reported, "but they are liable to be pretty well crowded this winter by cattle from the burned ranges." Not every herd got new grazing. One man remembered seeing starved Texas cattle in Kansas during the mid-1870s. After a late-fall fire, "all their grazing had been burned off. If there is any grass on the ground at all them Texas cattle can get it," he noted. But when the ground was "as bare as a peeled onion" they could die by the hundreds or thousands.[67]

The managers and foremen of the very large, often corporately owned ranches in the Texas Panhandle worried constantly about unplanned prairie fire and the resulting lack of grazing range. In their 1894 monthly reports, foremen of the various divisions of the XIT ranch frequently mentioned fire and the condition of the grass. "Grass [is] very bad," the Spring Lake Division foreman wrote on November 29. "Prairie Fire came in on west line about twenty miles wide on night of 25th and has been burning since—just now have it out. We have considerable grass yet, but will have to move some cattle."[68] A month later, things were under control. "Have moved [the cattle] off the burnt country and have them shaped good on grass sufficient to carry them."[69] The search for grazing caused much anxiety, however. Another division foreman noted at year's end that "I leave everything [in] a[s] good shape as I can. The fire has caused some things to be a little out of shape thoe."[70]

The anxiety over grazing did not stop with the foremen. John Armstrong, manager of the southern division of the XIT in the 1910s, used a significant amount of pencil and paper over the years in trying to explain to his superiors the extent of the burned area and his plans for dealing with the situation. "We burned out yesterday, everything is burned," he wrote in November 1906. "We will haf to move all the dry cows now and the suckling twos that are at Tiera Blanco. . . . I am going back to Coral Lake in the morning and will get all cattle off the burn just as soon as possible. . . . I am out of men again and it is going to make it bad moving the cattle off the burn." At the end of his letter Armstrong added, "We had some cattle burned up I know but am in hopes we haven't lost many."[71]

Judging by the content of his letter, which until the very end focused primarily on range loss and the resulting movement of the herds, prairie fire's threat to the range was even more significant, in Armstrong's opinion, than the hazard it posed to the cattle.

Extensive property loss to cattlemen and farmers prompted sympathy and assistance from relief organizations. "The work of relief has begun and every possible effort is being put forth to find homes for the homeless," a reporter from the *Oklahoman* wrote after the terrible March fires of 1904. "More than a thousand people are homeless and penniless and many are in need of medical assistance," a Colorado editor reported.[72] Just as neighbors gathered to fight an oncoming prairie fire together, they also congregated after the fire passed. Because very few settlers carried insurance that covered destruction by prairie fire, victims had to rely on help from friends and family. "After the fire," a Nebraska man remembered, "several of the neighbors offered to share their homes with us" and helped build a new and better dugout than the one lost.[73] One young man who was planning a spring wedding was not home when the fire approached and lost everything. "The neighbors went together and gave him grain and machinery and took up a collection in town among the people and got enough to buy him another team," one person recalled. "Several men let him have a cow to milk so he got on his feet again. [The fire victim and his fiancée] got married as planned and were lovely neighbors." Neighbors in the Texas Panhandle were also generous, noted Eppie Barrier. "They were all right there to help. . . . [They would] go home and bring [victims] a feather mattress . . . they'd just take everything, food, clothing, and everything."[74]

Spontaneous donations were common, and thousands of generous acts doubtless went undocumented. Some victims, however, inspired newspaper editors to make public pleas for assistance, pulling at the heartstrings for donations. "S. M. Anderson," noted the editor of the *Emporia* (Kansas) *News* in 1864, "was burned out of house and home on Thursday last by prairie fire. . . . Mr. Anderson is a poor man, and his loss will be heavy. We hope our citizens will contribute liberally for his relief. Mr. Anderson, it will be remembered, was severely wounded [in the Civil War] at Prairie Grove, [Arkansas,] from which he has not yet entirely recovered."[75]

Other private relief efforts were more organized yet. After a disastrous prairie fire in Kansas, citizens of Stockton, themselves in the midst of the economically difficult 1890s, circulated a subscription paper "for the relief of the sufferers." "Everybody was ready to help to the extent of his ability and by noon of the following day [after the fire], it had reached the sum of $357.40, of which $265 is cash and balance merchandise." The donations were sent to the county commissioner with an attached condolence letter. "It is the wish of the donors," a Stockton representative wrote, "that you in your official capacity use these contributions impartially where in your judgment you think best."[76] After an 1873 fire in Saline County, Nebraska, citizens of Brownville formed an official committee to organize relief donations for the "Saline Sufferers." The committee gathered $176.40 in cash, plus clothing and provisions valued at $200. They made arrangements to send the donations, along with a large box of "bed clothing" assembled by a woman from Leavenworth, Kansas, who was a sister of one of the victims.[77]

The majority of relief efforts were private or community-based endeavors. Still, some victims appealed to the state for help or satisfaction in their plight. Mrs. Anton Matoush wrote to Governor Willis J. Bailey of Kansas in 1904, describing a series of calamities that had affected her and her husband, including a prairie fire that had destroyed much of their property. Her husband, she wrote, was "all broken down over it and am sorry to say he is almost crazy over that big loss."[78] More than a decade later, A. M. Hopper, a farmer from Scott City, Kansas, wrote to Governor Arthur Capper to beg for help for his neighbors and justice for those who had set the prairie on fire. "Herewith I am send[ing] you a partial account of damage done to some of my neighbors by careless, if not criminal, citizen[s] of our state," he wrote. "Thes people are all producers. . . . the greatest asset to our state and national growth that we possess. . . . Surely justice demands that the state or nation, or both, reinstate its builders to their former statis of efficiency, and take charge of the culprit causing destruction of homes." Hopper suggested that the careless or criminal party who caused prairie fires be put to work until he earned enough money to reimburse the state for rebuilding costs. The governor's reply, via his secretary, was telling:

> There is no law that can reimburse the loss either by the state or nation. These fires were caused by persons deliberately setting them. Those persons s[h]ould be prosecuted. . . . The Governor,

like you, feels sorry for the stricken people but as I stated there
is no way they can be given state or national relief. The only way
the state money can be expended is through an appropriation
by the legislature. No funds are set aside by the legislature to
pay losses sustained by prairie fires.[79]

The lesson, Governor Capper's representative seemed to say,
was that prairie fires, like the one that devastated Hopper's friends
and neighbors, were human-caused disasters that could be tamed
if Plains people only tried hard enough. Prairie fires had no legiti-
mate place on the "civilized" Plains. When fire was adequately suppressed, injury and loss such as those experienced by the people of
Scott City would no longer occur.

Until they were controlled, however, injury, both physical and
economic, would accompany the blazes that swept the landscape.
Communities would continue to face the fire's aftermath just as they
faced the fire itself. The people would continue to be a people who
fought and then recovered from prairie fire. Both the fight and the
recovery were hardships but represented much more to those who
experienced them. The suppression agenda continued, but in the
meantime, prairie fire and the people's reaction to it, the hardship
they endured as a result of the fire, earned them the right to be part
of the place in which they lived. Just as the fire identified the Great
Plains, so did Plains people's response to it help identify them.

Although the postfire experience could be bleak, there was a
reward that accompanied the blaze. After the fire had passed, the
people sat back and waited for the inevitable greening of the land
that followed the blackness. The greening, like the beauty of the fire
itself, was, ironically, a benefit of the very force that suppression enthusiasts so longed to eliminate. Prairie fires were dangerous. Prairie fires destroyed. Prairie fires threatened. Prairie fires could not
be allowed to remain on the Plains. But prairie fires were beautiful.
Drawn in by the beauty, the people could not keep their eyes off it.

Chapter Seven

"Awfully Grand"

The prairie was burning to the east—the light on the horizon told the exploring party that—but it was so far away that they were not much concerned. At supper that night, however, discussion turned to the prominent smell of burned grass and the "very much augmented" glow around them, muted somewhat by a hill near camp but nevertheless stronger than before. About 8:00 the party became concerned enough to climb the hill to check on the progress of the fire. One anonymous observer later wrote:

> A spectacle presented itself to us the most grand that can well be conceived. The night was very dark, but as far as the eye could reach, all across the horizon, about four miles in front of us, was a broad, bright lurid glare of fire, with a thick canopy of smoke hanging over it, whose fantastic wreaths, as they cured in the breeze, were tinged with the red reflection of the flames.

Alarmed and chagrined, for the party was inadequately prepared to fight fire, the men set to work to safeguard themselves, the animals, and the camp as best they could. "We had not time to look at the picturesque," the observer remembered, but nevertheless he could not resist going to the top of another nearby hill, even though the danger had not passed. "I ran up for an instant . . . and shall never forget the scene," he wrote. Three parallel lines of fire stretched across the darkness, one just below the hill and two others "licking up any little spots of grass" that had managed to escape the first. "Although still half a mile off, the fire seemed close to me, and

the heat and smoke almost intolerable, while the dazzling bright-
ness of the flames made it painful to look at them."

Returning to camp, the errant observer found the other men
cutting the mules loose, allowing some of the animals to run instinc-
tively to the river and guiding others to a patch of burned ground
that the party had just backfired. They waited there and watched as
the fire, upon hitting their blackened safe area, turned itself to seek
out unburned grass in another direction. "All danger was over," the
observer noted, "but the sight of the three lines of fire stretching up
the rising grounds behind the camp, just like the advance of a vast
army, was magnificent. . . . The whole scene lasted altogether about
two hours, and nothing could be conceived more awfully grand."[1]

The beauty of the prairie on fire was a guilty pleasure. As for
the anonymous observer, it could draw a person away from his responsibilities in a time of crisis. It meant admiring or, even worse,
secretly longing to see a force that had the potential to cause great
harm to oneself or to others. It was an unholy emotion in the midst
of war—what was supposed to be a postscript to a larger story
that, for many observers, became the story itself. It was virtually
impossible to resist, fleeting but, ironically, embedded in collective
memory more than other more tangible aspects of prairie fire. The
guilty pleasure made prairie fires an exhilarating experience and
made fire suppression, regardless of its supposed benefits, a dreary,
melancholy one.

Prairie fires were more than just a threat to the prevailing Euro-
American economy and land-use strategy. They did more than just
endanger the newly imposed "civilization" in the region, and their
suppression meant more than just a forever altered Plains environment. Prairie fires inspired emotion. They stimulated nearly every
conceivable reaction within those who experienced them—shock,
awe, terror, curiosity—and later familiarity, wonder, and pride.
Through the communal act of fighting fire, but also, paradoxically,
through the shared beauty of the fires and the guilty pleasure, Plains
people adopted prairie fire as part of their identity. Thus, prairie
fires took on added significance, even in the midst of suppression.

The anonymous observer was not the only visitor to experience
prairie fire in contradictory ways. It was fairly common, in fact,
for witnesses, both terrified and awed by what was before them,
to oddly juxtapose their emotions when later asked to describe or

write about their experience. This, in fact, was the essence of the guilty pleasure. Large, wind-driven prairie fires, certainly, were absolutely terrifying. They also were astoundingly beautiful. Observers were sometimes powerless to tear their eyes away, even in the face of possible danger. Paul Wilhelm, duke of Wuerttemberg, while traveling on the Missouri River in the 1820s, noted that "it was truly horrifying but at the same time a magnificent sight as we drifted along in the middle of the river and watched the banks of [the] giant Missouri as it appeared for miles a sea of flames. At night the spectacle defied description."[2] An explorer on the Northern Plains called a burning fire "a gorgeous yet a dismal sight," while a traveler on the Santa Fe Trail in one breath described the fire as a serpent's tongue that might very well burn up his camp and in the next called the spectacle "grand and beautiful."[3] Even an 1893 prairie fire in Rooks County Kansas, which destroyed thousands of dollars' worth of property and killed a local farmer, was called by a newspaper reporter "truly awful in its grandeur."[4] Henry Hind, quite simply, called it "awful splendour."[5]

Despite the danger posed to human life and property, despite the fear that the fires triggered in those that encountered them, and despite the changes in fire use over centuries of Plains settlement, the impressions of beauty remained constant, spanning both time and place regardless of the viewer's nationality, gender, or age. The Sauk chief Black Hawk, after his tour of the United States in the mid–nineteenth century, was asked what he thought of the great cities and works of art that he had seen. He remarked that "'they were very fine, but that they were not half so grand as a prairie on fire.'"[6] Prince Maximilian of Wied, a German naturalist and explorer who traveled the Great Plains in the 1830s, noted that during "a great prairie fire . . . fiery smoke filled the air; it was a splendid sight! A whirlwind had formed a remarkable towering column of smoke, which rose, in a most singular manner, in graceful undulations, to the zenith."[7] Twelve-year-old Robert Crawford put it more succinctly: "It looks like fireworks," he wrote to his Eastern cousins. "Wouldn't you like to see a great long line of fire two or three miles long[?]"[8] A more cerebral James Price, meanwhile, called the fire "a sight, the impression of which cannot be erased while life lasts."[9]

It is no wonder, with descriptions in such widely read publications as *Harper's Weekly* and James Fenimore Cooper's *The Prai-*

rie, that Easterners came to the Plains with a secret desire to see a prairie fire.[10] Some visitors simply could not wait for the inevitable and put a match to the grass themselves. A group of young men in Prince Maximilian's traveling party set a fire after dark "to give us the pleasure of seeing how the fire spread." The wind did not cooperate, however, and the pyro-enthusiasts were disappointed with the results.[11] On a March day in 1839 Francis Chardon, a bored fur trader at Fort Clark, first allocated chores for the other men and then, perhaps with even less forethought than Maximilian's party gave to the matter, found something more stimulating to occupy his own time. "I set the men to clean around the fort," Chardon wrote in his diary. "Having nothing else to do, I set fire to the prairies."[12] Such a flippant action might enliven a dreary Dakota day, but it was not without risk. "I and my two guides reproached ourselves for having set fire to the prairie every night for . . . the enjoyment of a fine spectacle," Count Francesco Arese, yet another 1830s Plains explorer, reported. Both Arese and his Sioux guides knew the potential consequences. "It might have attracted the attention and the curiosity of our enemies' war party," Arese admitted, "but that didn't happen."[13] Settlement brought more potential for destruction of property and human life, which curtailed such unnecessary burnings, and as settlement continued, social pressures and stigmas further discouraged would-be fire starters.

Many of those who gave in to temptation would never admit their weakness but might instead claim that a fire had been started by accident or an unknown cause. James Pratt, a supply trader from Wyoming, conveniently placed the blame for a purposeful fire on a commanding officer. One April morning in 1871 Pratt, who was settled at Fort Randall for a time to trade with the military, decided to take a look at the country with a party of four soldiers and a black servant. The day was mild but windy. It hadn't rained in a while, and the group passed through some old grass—very tall and dry, perfect for burning. The wind was strong but was not blowing in the direction the men were traveling, so Captain Miner, the leader of the group, decided to burn the prairie—just to see what a prairie fire looked like. The blaze started easily, but as it did the direction of the wind shifted, and soon the soldiers and Pratt were running for their lives. The fire threatened the wagon and team, and the men scrambled to find safety. In the end the group "escaped all but a good scare," and, Pratt reported almost as an afterthought, they even "began to enjoy the sight when we felt safe."[14]

Feeling safe was usually a prerequisite for prairie fire enjoyment. A letter to the editor published in an 1862 Kansas newspaper argued that if farmers would create guards and otherwise prepare for fire, then when the fires came they could relax and "look on with much pleasure" as the flames passed around them.[15] The *New York Press*, reporting in 1890 on a series of fires, remarked, "It is hardly possible for the people in this part of the country to understand, even by the imagination, how a great western prairie fire looks. . . . When, as in this instance, no tradgedy is . . . included, our minds may dwell with interest and a degree of pleasure upon the descriptions given by those who speak from personal observation."[16] Like James Pratt, the Eastern writer gave himself and his readers permission to admire a fire only when it posed no danger to persons or property. Still, observers had to take advantage of opportunities for viewing. In the middle of the night on October 14, 1870, Philip Bright woke his sister Abbie, a Pennsylvanian who was visiting Kansas, from a sound sleep. "He said I should wrap up well and come out and see the fire," she wrote, "that it was not likely I would ever see the like again. The scene was grand beyond description. . . . To the west there was fire beyond fire. . . . I can't give a description of the wild, fearful—yet fascinating sight."[17] Abbie Bright was the luckiest of observers. Nothing was more breathtaking than a large prairie fire at night, and her enjoyment was unspoiled by fear because the wind, if it was a factor, did not cause the fire to threaten the Bright family.

Observers' first (and safest) view was often from a great distance. From a moving train in 1876 Mabel Hubbard wrote—because she could not yet phone—her relative Alexander Graham Bell about the sight. It was "unlike any other fire," she observed, "a graceful sinuous line . . . coming from [a] great distance on the horizon."[18] J. William Lloyd described his twilight view of a fire from his seat on the Kansas Pacific Railroad. "Miles away I could see it, trailing like a red serpent up and down the rolls in the yellow plain." Throughout that entire night's journey, looking out his window onto the dark Kansas prairie, Lloyd was "never out of sight of some fire."[19]

The view was little less dramatic on the ground but substantially more disconcerting, as the potential for danger loomed. "The other day a long line of dark red smoke skirted the western horizon,

showing that the grass upon the plains is already turning to fire,"
a newspaper editor observed. Indeed, on many autumn days the
pervasive red glow, the "sea of crimson," would not let settlers forget the peril that burned around them.[20] As the official naturalist of
the joint British and American Boundary Commission charged with
surveying the prairie section of the international boundary, George
Dawson witnessed several fires on Canadian prairies in 1873. "After dark," he wrote in September, "the glow of a distant prairie fire
reflected in the sky far to [the] S[outh]." At that point the nonthreat-
ening fire "glowed," and Dawson recorded the event in his journal
as an interesting and agreeable occurrence. A month later, however,
his tone changed. "After dark the Prairie fire to the S[outh] began to
look very threatening. Bright reflection in the sky & lurid glare along
the horizon. . . . Sat up reading & watching the fire. After a time the
reflection disappeared but smoke began to fill the air & the moon
now risen, looked blood red through it."[21] The "glow" of September
had changed to a "lurid glare" in October. As Dawson contemplated
a fiery challenge, he sat up watching the enemy, not out of curiosity
or appreciation but with thoughts of red blood in mind. Eighteen-
year-old Emily Combes, a newcomer to Rice County, Kansas, had
similar feelings. She, too, noticed a light on the horizon but became
fearful when the wind carried the source of that glow toward her.
"All day smoke had been drifting across the prairie," she divulged
to her fiancé in West Virginia, "and as the night came on we could
see . . . flashes of light here and there—a burst of flame then the dull,
sulky looking red glow like the eyes of an angry animal."[22]

As a raging prairie fire bore down on a farm or a town, sometimes moving faster than a horse could run (or, by the early twentieth century, faster than an auto could drive), thoughts of aesthetics
were few.[23] Still, some observers recognized the remarkable quality
of the sight in spite of their terror. Merton Field, on his father's farm
in Dakota, recalled a single moment amid hours of grueling battle
against a prairie fire: "Pausing in our work to turn around we saw
the upper strata of the smoke column borne like a celestial canopy
in our direction, its under surface seething in deep red as the smoke
billowed and rolled. . . . We stood awed at the spectacle. . . . But this
was no time for gazing. Our task was yet unfinished."[24]

As with Field's "deep red" smoke column, color was a significant element of prairie fire aesthetics. Jim Metzger described the

contrast of colors within a slow-moving fire in Nebraska. The advancing flames, he noted, "looked like a red fringe to a large, black rug that was being unrolled" over the muted green and brown tones of the grass.[25] H. B. Mollhausen, the German artist who accompanied the Whipple expedition across the Southern Plains, noted the interplay between fire, smoke, and grass and the resulting changes in the color of the flames and reflecting clouds.[26] Paul Kane, an artist who would incorporate his view into his 1849 painting, *Prairie on Fire*, observed the contrast between light and dark on the burning Canadian prairies. "The scene was terrific in the extreme," Kane wrote. "The night being intensely dark gave increased effect to the brilliancy of the flames."[27]

As a child in Nebraska, Minnie Calhoun was astonished not by the color of the burning fire but by the absence of color when the fire was suddenly extinguished. Calhoun witnessed a well-placed backfire directly encounter a headfire. "It was an awesome sight to behold the two fires come together and light the sky in one great blast of fire," she remembered years later. "In the next few minutes there was absolute darkness. Not even the spark of a burning weed could be seen from our house and yard. We had all been watching . . . in awe at the spectacle. . . . We watched a while longer, but the fire was dead."[28]

Transfixed by speed, light, color, or just overall grandeur, prairie fire observers were occasionally almost paralyzed by the lure of the flames—not only from fear but from sheer astonishment at the sight. An 1860 correspondent for the *London Times* concluded his romantic view of fire on the "Grand Prairie" by noting the siren call of the flames. "Hour after hour you will stand, fascinated with the terrible beauties of the scene," he wrote, "as the mass of red, sultry ruins grows and grows each minute, till your eyes are pained and heated with its angry glare and you almost dread the grand, fierce sheet of fire, which has swept all trace of vegetation from the surface of the prairie."[29] This was what witnesses meant by "awful splendor." Although the London newspaper writer was in no actual danger from the flames, his point is nevertheless a good one. Prairie fire did have the power to mesmerize, and the results were potentially deadly. A fire that threatened newly settled Americus, Kansas, in 1862 was so beautiful that a group of six boys, who likely had never seen a prairie fire before, decided to wander out of town to take a closer look. They got a little too curious, however, and lingered too long. Before the boys knew it they were running for a nearby creek while the fire gained on them from behind, nipping their heels before all six finally made it to the safety of the water.[30] A child near Abilene, Kansas, was not so fortunate. In March 1910 a six-year-old girl was playing in her yard when a prairie fire, driven by a high wind, suddenly approached. The little girl "stood fascinated by the unusual spectacle" and did not respond to her mother's warning calls. The mother attempted to pull her daughter to safety but did not reach her before the fire ignited the girl's clothing. She was severely burned and died soon after.[31]

Even if no lives were lost, a fire, at minimum, left behind a much-changed prairie. The land was blackened, an effect that many found unsettling and melancholy, especially after expending so much energy and emotion fighting the fire that had caused the "wasteland." Thomas Christy, on his trip across Nebraska, noted how "discouraging" the burned-over ground looked,[32] and Alan Cheales, on a hunting trip in the Cherokee Strip, walked for many miles before he found anything that was not burned. "Nothing to be seen but burnt prairie ashes blowing in one's eyes," Cheales complained.[33]

More hopeful and beautiful sights, however, also emerged out of the blackened prairie. Merton Field saw the areas of "dense black" land as a refreshing change from the "drabness" of the dead, dried grass that covered the remainder of his view.[34] In the spring the burned-over land promised new growth. "Mother Earth, in our neighborhood, has donned a garment of mourning," the editor of a Junction City, Kansas, newspaper observed after a prairie fire. "Blackness covers the face of the earth as far as the eye can reach. But in a few weeks it will be replaced by the lovely garb of vegetation peculiar alone to our beautiful prairies."[35]

The editor's comment is revealing. Prairie fires and the landscape they helped create were part of an emerging identity among Euro-American Plains residents. Fire, although destructive and frightening, created something unique, or peculiar—"our beautiful prairies"—a place that Easterners could not understand and that inspired awe, even as settlers did their best to change it.

Expectations for and reactions to prairie fire depended on perspective and changed over time, depending on what vision or purpose the observer might have in mind for the Great Plains. Easterners who stayed home and read about prairie fires in *Scribner's* had a much different viewpoint than did travelers who went West and saw them in person; earlier Plains settlers had a different point of view than those who came later. The awe was constant, but it manifested itself in a variety of ways.

To newcomers and visitors, and even to Easterners who had only read about but had never seen a prairie fire, the conflagration was an exciting, exotic sight associated with an alien country. An 1884 traveler's guide for the Union and Central Pacific Railroads directed the attention of the modern rail voyager to the fires. "During the first night's ride westward from Omaha," the authors noted, "the traveler, as he gazes out of his car window (which he can easily do while reclining in his berth) will often find his curious attention rewarded by a sight of one of the most awful, yet grandest scenes of prairie life." The sight surely would be a highlight of the trip. "The prairies," the helpful authors continued, "which in the day-time to some, seemed dry, dull, uninteresting, occasionally give place at night, to the lurid play of the fire-fiend, and the heavens and horizon seem like a furnace. . . . We have never seen anything of prairie life or scenery possessing such majestic brilliance as the night glows, and rapid advances of a prairie fire."[36] Although not quite like the World's Largest Ball of Twine, which tempts modern travelers in Kansas to stop along I-135 to see the once-in-a-lifetime sight, prairie fires in the nineteenth century added a touch of the exotic to a landscape that few people, especially those who did not live there, understood.

In her book *Plain Pictures: Images of the American Prairie*, Joni Kinsey noted the tendency of outsiders and newcomers to view the prairies as a land devoid of form and identity, so meaningless in its "original condition" that it could "be defined only by what it may become," not by what it was.[37] Prairie fires, though, were an exception. They were already part of the Plains, and they helped make the Plains special. Grasshopper plagues, it could be argued, also identified the Plains. Few people, however, ever commented on the loveliness of a horde of munching 'hoppers. It was aesthetics that set fires apart from other Plains phenomena.

That magnificence provided a fine backdrop for adventure, danger, and even intrigue. While Frank Root, in his boyhood, admired illustrations of hunters running from a fierce prairie fire, other publications also emphasized that the fires were part of the wild, untamed West—a danger, to be sure, but also a fine adventure in the making.[38] James Fenimore Cooper, author of the first Western adventure novels, included a prairie fire scene in his 1827 book, *The Prairie.* Over breakfast one morning a young couple naively admired the glorious sunrise, which appeared more crimson than usual. Cooper's hero, an old man wise in the ways of the prairie, eyed the "changing, and certainly beautiful tints" of the supposed sunrise and declared that, in fact, the Indians had "'circumvented us with a vengeance. The prairie is on fire!'" The impetuous but uneducated young man wanted to try to outrun the fire, but the old man stopped him from attempting this foolish action and instead, through his knowledge of the fires and the ways of the Sioux, found another way to save the party.[39] Some years after the story's publication George Pope Morris penned a dramatic poem, "The Prairie Fire," based in part on Cooper's "thrilling story of the West." "The sun seem'd rising through the haze," Morris wrote, "But with an aspect dread and dire!/The very air appeared a blaze!—/Oh God! the prairie was on fire!"[40]

Adventure stories flourished as travelers crossed the Plains in record numbers in the 1840s and as Euro-American settlement commenced in the next two decades. In one such drama, published in 1849 in *The United States Democratic Review*, an unknown author told the fictional story of Captain Dan Henrie, an adventurer in west Texas who had one very bad day. Henrie was the sole survivor when hostile Indians attacked his exploring party. Chased on horseback by the warriors, he made the radical decision to ride his horse intentionally through a prairie fire (conveniently burning nearby) as a way to escape certain death at the hands of the Natives. The ride was a dramatic one, as is evidenced by the number of exclamation marks used by the author to highlight the experience: "The fire has struck him with a roaring surge! His hair flames crisply, and the flesh of his body seems to be burning! . . . On! On! Scorching through the stifling blaze! . . . He is safe!" The threat from the Indians and the fire left behind, the unfortunate hero's troubles were not finished, for soon he realized that "more than a hundred" wolves pursued him. "'My God!' he moaned aloud—'wasn't it bad enough for me to pass that hell of flames back yonder? and have I only escaped that to meet a fate a thousand times more hideous?'"[41] Here the largely mythical threats of Indians and wolves were accompanied by another dangerous and thrilling source of adventure—the prairie fire.[42]

Of course, with adventure came danger and tragedy. As settlement continued and reports of prairie fires destroying property and human life began to circulate, accounts of the fires in periodicals and books began to emphasize the dark side of prairie fire adventure. To Eastern audiences, death by prairie fire, particularly the tragic demise of an entire family or several schoolchildren, was part of the calamitous lore of the West. *Harper's*, in 1873, reported on a "terrible prairie fire" in Nebraska that destroyed much property and caught ten school children "in the flames, three of whom perished, three were mortally injured, and four terribly maimed. Mrs. Morley, mother of three of them, endeavoring to rescue them, was also fatally wounded."[43] In an 1879 account of Kansas farming, *Scribner's Monthly* argued that next to the death of a child, "the great besetting fear of the settlers . . . is the coming of the autumn prairie fire, which so frequently menaces their stacks and cribs, their helpless stock, their stables and cabins, and even their lives." Even in this context, however, aesthetics were still a fascination. "Were it not for its known danger and power of havoc," the writer continued, "this tempest and scourge of fire would be a spectacle of commanding force and beauty."[44] The wonder of the fires only added to their mystique, and the tragedy that could accompany them increased, rather than muted, the romance from the perspective of "absent observers" like the readers of *Scribner's*.[45]

The population's increasing awareness of prairie fires and their effects even affected American language. In the mid–nineteenth century, just as Euro-American settlement began to creep onto the Plains, analogies involving prairie fires also began to creep into literature. Suddenly many occurrences—gossip, scandal, the temperance movement, and even love—spread "like a prairie fire." "Until I loved him!" one *Harper's Weekly* romance gushed. "It seems so impossible to realize now that there ever was a time when I did not love him, or to remember what life was like before my love for him came over it like a prairie fire."[46] The most common use of analogies, however, involved politics and war. Because the settlement of the Plains coincided with a particularly volatile time in U.S. history—on the eve of and just after the Civil War—it is perhaps not a coincidence that prairie fire analogies were employed to describe the burning passions of war fever. In 1858, after Kansas had bled and a still larger crisis loomed, *Harper's Weekly* compared war with the prescribed, controlled burning of the prairie grass. "War, in any case, is a dismal misfortune to befall a country," the writer began. However, "it must sometimes be, to avoid a direr calamity. . . . It is the burning of the prairies to limit burning." At the height of the conflict, *Harper's* again used the prairie fire analogy: "The rebellion is to be overcome, as a prairie fire is, by attacking it and trampling it out resolutely to the last spark. You do not make terms with it. You do not negotiate. You fight it wherever it appears, and as long as it burns."[47]

Prairie fires were also useful for political descriptions. "Like the half subdued fire upon a western prairie, which is rekindled into a marching conflagration by the first breath of an opposing wind, so it would seem the Kansas excitements, renewed by the pro-slavery party, are again to sweep over the land with redoubled fury," a correspondent for the *Daily Missouri Democrat* in St. Louis wrote about the territorial drama in Kansas.[48] A presidential campaign song for Abraham Lincoln likened his Western supporters to a prairie fire in the candidate's native Illinois: "Ho! gallant Pennsylvanians, with your Western breth'ren join,/And shout for our hardy Pioneer!/For the prairies are on fire . . ./Their leader's brave and dauntless, and his name all hearts inspire,/'Tis Lincoln, the Pride of the West!"[49] In September 1860 the future vice president, Hannibal Hamlin, congratulated Lincoln on the Republican Party's successes in Maine. "We have carried all our Congressmen and swept the State like a prairie on fire," Hamlin wrote enthusiastically. "We think that will do, and we wait with confidence of the response of the West."[50] During the war, abolitionist Lewis C. Lockwood wrote to officials in the Lincoln administration to argue that the Union's reports of black troops in the southern theater of the war would "inspire Confidence in the slaves." The news "would spread like prairie fire," he thought, "and act as a magnetic incentive to stampedes."[51] Prairie fire symbolized passion, speed, excitement, determination, and great change. It was a force that was difficult to control, difficult to stop.

Despite its still volatile and dangerous nature, however, prairie fire was also becoming familiar. "The plains people are accustomed to prairie fires, indeed, expect them, and hence use precautionary measures," the Chicago *Inter Ocean* reported in 1893.[52] One settler remembered that his family, while watching a nearby prairie fire, decided to go check on the recently arrived Nichols family, who might not know much about fighting the blaze. When they arrived the Nicholses were "right glad to see us coming. They were standing in a frightened group in front of the house. . . . The people were absolutely helpless. They were talking of putting some barrels of water in the wagon and trying to go out and quench the fire with it. Think of it! They had not seen it yet or even they would have known better than that." With obvious pride the seasoned Plains family took charge of the firefighting operation. Recounting the experience, the settler was scornful of the newcomers' ignorance: "West of us and north of us rolled walls of flame and great masses of smoke. That is a prairie fire. Wouldn't they have stood a fine chance of stopping it with a few barrels of water?"[53]

Time and experience brought knowledge and understanding to the first settlers. They learned what conditions caused large-scale threatening fires. They learned how to gauge a fire's danger and how to fight it if necessary. They experienced firsthand fire's beauty and learned something of its benefits. Even schoolchildren were taught how to fight fires—and sometimes they were released from their studies just to watch them burn.[54] As knowledge and experience deepened, prairie fire became embedded in Plains identity.

The process of identification and familiarity was gradual. Consider two separate fire accounts, one from a letter dated 1855 and another from 1887. Albert Myer, who later became known as the father of the U.S. Army Signal Corps and the U.S. Weather Service, in the mid-1850s was in the military and stationed in Texas. In a letter to his future brother-in-law Myer reported on a clash with Comanche near Fort Clark. At camp that night, nervous that the Indians might be planning an attack, officers gave the order to fire the prairie as a way to smoke out any warriors who might be hiding in the grass cover. The fire lit, Myer went to bed in his tent. "All that night the fire rages and I awaking see it shining through the walls of canvas, and look out to enjoy its beauty," he reported. The pleasant crackle, "the flame and its reflection, the broad wavering light, and the solemn grandeur of the scene, at night, are enchanting and I wish that some of you could be with me a moment to enjoy it and then, far away where I know you are safe."[55] The second letter, dated April 15, 1887, was from a mother in Nebraska to her adult son in Massachusetts. "By the way," she noted, "there is at this moment a splendid prairie fire blazing just west of us. Some of your Wor[c]ester [Massachusetts] people never saw *such* a sight with all their privileges."[56]

The authors of these letters wrote about similar sights but from strikingly different perspectives. Both focused on the beauty of the sight, and both were awed by it. As a visitor to the Plains, however, Myer treated the prairie fire as alien—beautiful and romantic because it was exotic and unfamiliar. He wanted to share it with his friends and family but at the same time was relieved that they were not in any danger from the fire or other unfamiliar phenomena in Texas. The Nebraska mother's account, written thirty-two years later, when settlement of that state and the rest of the Plains was well under way, is much more matter-of-fact. She wrote of the fire almost as if it were an afterthought—a relatively common occurrence—but clearly one she cherished. Whereas the fire that Myer witnessed was something that should be shared with the outside world, the Nebraska mother's fire was something to keep for herself. She bragged about her good fortune in seeing something so magnificent and also reflected an air of superiority. The fire—*her* fire—was something that only she and other Plains people possessed. Easterners were left to their envy.

The beauty of the prairie fires thus became a significant piece of Plains identity. The fires, however, were also a hardship that settlers faced together—a collective, often traumatic experience that contributed to identity. A newspaper told of a Kansas farmer named R. D. Dukes, who, within a fairly short time, experienced the flooding of his crops, cholera in his hogs, a collapsed shed that killed two cows, and the death of his wife—caused by an exploding lamp that also severely injured Dukes himself. Just after the farmer recovered, his mother died. While he attended the funeral a prairie fire came along and burned his house and all his belongings.[57] An extreme case, to be sure, but the point is clear: Prairie fires were one of many hardships that all Plains people faced, either in fact or as an ever-present prospect. Even the shared prospect contributed to regional identity.

Fictional stories of adventure and humor provide further evidence of prairie fire's role as a distinctive feature of the Great Plains.

One told the tale of the daughter of the famed Indian Geronimo, who saved a sleeping Texan from not only a raging prairie fire but also from the cattle stampede that it started. The two fell in love in the midst of the chaos and planned to be married.[58] Another story involved "Plain Pete," a poor, homely, unintelligent boy who saved an elderly woman from a prairie fire. "'I always knowed my boy was no common dirt,'" Pete's fictional father stated. After his heroism, Pete started getting lots of dates.[59]

Other stories were classic tall tales: "Several prairie fires occurring during the recent warm spell down in Kansas are attributed to fire flies setting fire to the dry grass," a Colorado newspaper joked.[60] A Texan wrote that a criminal, fleeing punishment, "ran [his horse] so fast that his feet got so hot that it set the grass afire."[61] Finally, an "avalanche of thistles" (tumbleweeds large enough to crush horses, cattle, and even farm houses), which supposedly pounded the Central Plains in 1909, became an even greater problem when the population tried to burn off the weeds. The tumbleweeds, which even under normal circumstances made excellent windblown firebrands, in such gigantic proportions set off a monster of a prairie fire.[62] The tall tales, designed to amuse, are also reminders that prairie fires set the Plains, and therefore Plains people, apart from other regions.

Fire's symbolic role on the Great Plains is complex and conflicting. Because fires were so beautiful; because they were a hardship to be overcome that, once past, bound Plains people together; and because they became an integral part of regional identity, prairie fires were, in a way, difficult to surrender. They were simply fascinating. "The Seventh Congressional fight is attracting a great deal of attention in the short grass country, but not as much as the prairie fires," the Kansas *Liberal News* quipped in 1905.[63] As problematic as prairie fires could be, they made for interesting stories and were exciting to watch and remember.

Historian Elliott West, in *The Way to the West*, described two contradictory outlooks that Plains settlers had toward their new surroundings. The first was that the Plains were an empty landscape, open to manipulation and devoid of a past. The second, often overshadowed by the first, was the feeling that the new land was something to be savored and enjoyed, a place that would cleanse the visitor with its "wildness." West noted the settlers' ability to hold both outlooks in their minds without detecting the contradiction.[64]

Plains residents demonstrated this inconsistency in their reactions toward prairie fire. Their first response reflected the desire to "fill" an "empty" landscape. Fire suppression was necessary both to correct this aesthetic flaw and to protect the settlers' sedentary lifestyle. The second reaction complicated the first and conflicted with the tree-obsessed aesthetic ideal that the Euro-Americans pursued. The absence of prairie fires might make the Plains safer for settlement, but it also made the region a more melancholy, less interesting place. With the suppression of prairie fire, the guilty pleasure was gone.

For practical reasons, however, combined with an insatiable desire to "remake" the Plains, fire suppression was the overriding concern. Still, prairie fire did not lose its symbolic value. Beyond the actual consequences of fire suppression, and however successful or futile the settlers' efforts, the *action* of suppression itself took on symbolic weight. As a conscious attempt to manipulate the Great Plains landscape—a way to struggle against nature and, sometimes, to win—fire suppression became a measure of gaining mastery over the land by defeating an elemental natural force. Eliminating prairie fires meant the triumph of conquest, the successful transition from one era of Plains settlement to another.

No Great Plains town trying to attract settlers wanted bad press about prairie fires. In 1873 the *Fargo Express*, taking a jab at its rival, remarked, "Prairie fires are already prevailing near Bismarck, so dry it has become. We should smile to see the tall luxuriant green grass in the Red river valley [near Fargo] on fire." The *Bismarck Tribune* responded in kind: "Somebody has been 'stuffing' the *Express* man, or he is culpably wrong. . . . No prairie fires have occurred near Bismarck this season, and we will wager our best beaver that we can show him taller, more luxuriant green grass . . . within a few minutes walk of Bismarck than ever grew near Fargo."[65] The absence of prairie fires, to these editors, implied a flourishing civilization, a place that could lure new settlers in and then usher them into prosperity. A Kansas booster, writing for the *Walnut Valley Times*, waxed poetic about the coming of civilization following the Civil War:

> Three years ago you might travel for weary miles and not be gladdened by the sight or sound of humanity. . . . At that time, settlements . . . followed the water-courses and clung to the belts of timber, and the wide, wide prairies were left to

the unrestrained raves of the prairie fires. But at this date one can scarce get beyond hearing of the shrill locomotive whistle. . . . Farms are being opened upon every quarter-section; comfortable houses are on all hands visible; the school house is quite as frequent as in New England; and all the graces of civilization and high enlightenment are visible.[66]

Despite the inconvenient fact that sparks flying from one of the great symbols of conquest, the locomotive, were a primary instigator of prairie fires—an observation that the Kansas booster chose to ignore—the point is clear. To this writer, just as to the editors of North Dakota, prairie fires were part of the unconquered Plains. They had no role in the newly civilized region, and their very absence, like the coming of the locomotive, was a source of pride, a sign that human will and action had triumphed over nature.

As settlers increasingly interpreted the reduction of uncontrolled prairie fires as a sign of conquest, they began to forge a new outlook toward the fires themselves. "The wedding dress has been purchased, the prairie fires are all out, the Indian have departed, the buffaloes have gone to parts unknown, so what shall I write about?" Emily Combes quipped in 1871.[67] It might not have happened that early, but as successive generations of settlers gradually realized their dreams of a "new" prairie, complete with houses, crops, and trees, they began to look back on the "old" one with greater affection. Once a degree of safety was in place, Plains people allowed themselves to enjoy the fires and the memory of them. Nostalgia took hold, and the beauty of the prairie fires, which at one time had seemed otherworldly, was now seen as a unique aspect of the region's past. "The prairie fire of today is a miniature affair," Roscoe Logue wrote in 1935 with some regret. "Like other events of the long ago it is preserved only in the memory of man; the country being plowed into fields and a highway surrounding each section, there is nothing bigger than a horse pasture to catch fire."[68]

As they continued their quest to suppress prairie fires—now part of settler identity—those living on the prairies found safe, alternative ways to immortalize the fires while preserving their way of life. Images of the fires were transferred into expressive cultural mediums such as poetry and art, and confinement within a book or a picture frame allowed prairie fire to take on an even greater appeal, preserving something that had been lost with the old prairie. Joni Kinsey noted that early artists, such as George Catlin (*Prairie Meadows Burning*, 1832) and Paul Kane (*Prairie on Fire*, 1849), emphasized the breathtakingly powerful image that the burning grass created on the prairie.

The artists, with their emphasis on historical nature and emotion in landscape, reflected the Romantic movement of the late eighteenth and early nineteenth centuries. Romanticism emphasized beauty combined with power. Such emotions revolved around the concept of the Sublime, which, philosopher Edmund Burke argued, was beauty that originated from something powerful and terrible. Such splendor produced in witnesses "the strongest emotion which the mind is capable of feeling." The Sublime, others argued, was the imagination's conception of something that is "immense, nebulous, beyond exact description."[69] Prairie fire observers, also speaking the language of Romanticism, became frustrated with the inadequacy of their words and their inability to satisfactorily communicate the "awful splendour" before them.[70] Artists confined prairie fire to canvas, thereby rendering it harmless, but nevertheless attempted to convey and preserve the beauty of the fires—the power, the magnificence, and the terror.

By the late nineteenth century, however, in the midst of settlement and suppression, art reflected nostalgia more than power and grandeur. In 1888 Meyer Straus's *Herd of Buffalo Fleeing from a Prairie Fire* combined two vanishing forces on the prairie—fire and bison—into one dramatic painting. An anonymous artist, in *Prairie Fires of the Great West* (1872), portrayed a fire threatening a passenger train as it traveled across the Plains. Although the title maintains that the fire is the main subject, it is the locomotive that is at the center of the painting, its progress clearly unimpeded by fire. The not-so-subtle message is that although fire once was a considerable force, it now had to join the buffalo and the Indian as part of the nostalgic past.[71] By 1890 the message was even more obvious when a New York journalist made the familiar comparison between the waving grass on the prairies, sometimes overtaken by billowing fire, and waves on the wide expanse of ocean. The ocean, however, is eternal "The far stretching expanse of unbroken prairie, dotted only by the dwellings of man as ships dot the sea, is a thing of yesterday and partly

Meyer Straus (1831–1905) *Herd of Buffalo Fleeing from Prairie Fire.* Oil on canvas, 1888, 18 × 30 inches (45.7 × 76.2 cm). Amon Carter Museum of American Art, Fort Worth, Texas.

of to-day also," the writer observed, "but will be gone after a few more to-morrows. Such prairie fires as we have tried to describe are coeval with the buffalo and wild Indian. The places that know them once will soon know them no more forever."[72]

The journalist's tragic and romantic words were only partially accurate. Certainly Euro-American settlement brought great changes for buffalo, Indians, and prairie fire, but none of the three simply faded from the Plains. The reduction of actual prairie fires and their transfer to unobtrusive cultural mediums, however, to Euro-Americans, was symbolic of the process of "civilization." C. L. Edson's poem "Prairie Fire," for example, published in 1924, had no specific mention of fire in its lines. Instead Edson used prairie fire to symbolize Euro-American settlement of the land: "West, from their wooded islands," the author rhapsodized, "They have spread across the earth;/Till the planet has been belted;/By the men of Nordic birth."[73] By controlling fires, both actual and symbolic, Euro-American settlers fused images of this environmental force with their image of themselves and their rightful possession of the land.

Anonymous, *Prairie Fires of the Great West*. Currier & Ives, c. 1872. Courtesy of the Library of Congress.

The "today" and the "few more to-morrows" that the New York journalist mentioned in 1890 have come and gone. Still, prairie fires remain—changed but present—on the modern Plains. What has not changed is the beauty of the blazes, the mesmerizing, terrible, and ultimately magnificent sight that is unique to the grasslands. A nighttime drive through the Kansas Flint Hills during range-burning season even today inspires emotions—including pride that the tradition survives—very similar to those experienced by former Plains dwellers. "I saw it happen many times," one settler wrote of the burning prairie, "but I never got over the feeling of awe, the catch in my breath and the pounding of my heart. . . . It came at night or it came in the day time. It came in the fall or in the spring, but it always came, and it was always terrible and awe inspiring."[74] Even if in modified form, the guilty pleasure continues on the Great Plains.

Chapter Eight

"Burn, Prairie, Burn"

In mid-September 1947 the grasslands of central South Dakota exploded in flames. The first fire started on a Friday morning, the result of a spark from a combine running on the Fanger farm. Driven by a strong wind, the fire spread northwest until it was 12 miles wide. Hundreds of firefighters, professional and volunteer, gathered from numerous surrounding counties to help in the fight. They made little progress in the first several hours as the fire continued to devour pasture land, thousands of tons of cut hay, fence posts, farm equipment, telephone poles, stock, and three farmhouses. Elmer Faulstich lost a full granary valued at $10,000 to $12,000. Plowed fields sometimes curbed the fire's flow, but at other times the wind was so intense that the fire "merely skirted these fields and went merrily on in its destruction." Friday afternoon the wind shifted direction, then shifted again. People who had believed themselves safe because the fire had passed them by in the morning now faced the brunt of its force. The variable winds frustrated the tired workers, who many times believed the fire to be out only to see it start again a few minutes later, enlivened by the wind in a seemingly random place.

The second major fire, east of the first, started just after noon the same day when a passing motorist threw a cigarette butt from a car onto the dry prairie grass. A trucker saw the fire start but, instead of stopping to quickly put it out, drove into town to report the incident, giving the fire more than enough time to gather energy. The flames moved across the prairie, jumped a road, and proceeded, destroying more grass, hay, and stock as they went. Although not as large as the western fire, the new blaze divided the focus of the firefighters, some of whom had to be diverted to the second front. State police officers and game wardens, using the two-way radios in their cars, directed people to where they were needed and kept communication flowing between the two major fire areas. The combined conflagrations kept firefighters busy for a full twenty-four hours. Even after the main emergency was over citizens kept a vigilant watch for two more days as pop-up blazes continued to plague the region.

Postfire activity was almost as frenzied as the firefight itself. Elmer Quirk, who had been hit by a car while fighting fire, recuperated at the hospital in Pierre. Ray Fife, who had broken his shoulder in a fall from a car's running board, did the same. The rest of the firefighters nursed mild burns while the police directed traffic and kept crowds of gawking visitors who had gathered to see the aftermath of the giant prairie fire from clogging the intersections. Locals fielded telephone calls from Chicago, Los Angeles, and other distant places. The national news, it seemed, had reported erroneously that several South Dakota towns had been "wiped out" by the flames, and friends and family called to learn whether the bad news was true. Politicians, from the secretary of the Yankton Chamber of Commerce to the governor of South Dakota, accompanied by newspaper reporters, flew over the burned area, snapping photographs and framing sound bites for the curious and the concerned.

Meanwhile, the local farmers and press looked toward the future. Now unable to keep large herds of cattle on their land during the upcoming winter, farmers and ranchers in the burned areas scrambled to sell their herds or to find new grazing land and alternative feed for their stock. A county commissioner estimated that he would need 100,000 new fence posts. "What this section needs most right now is a heavy rain of two or three inches that will soak up the grass roots and also relieve the dust situation," a local reporter noted. In the meantime, "caution should be exercised by everyone that no fires break out in this or other counties, as all of central South Dakota is just like a tinder box at the present time."[1]

In many ways the central South Dakota prairie fire of 1947 was like those of the nineteenth century. Its origins were familiar (farm equipment and human carelessness), its consequences were the same (destruction of property and human injury), and the frustrations felt by the firefighters were virtually identical to those experienced by earlier generations. Yet there were differences, too. Report-

A prairie fire sweeps across Gray County, Kansas, in the 1940s. Fires maintain a presence on the Great Plains even in the modern period. Photograph courtesy of the Kansas State Historical Society.

ers and politicians examined the burned area by airplane, firefighters communicated through two-way radios, and Elmer Quirk was hit by a car (not a wagon) as he tried to stop the flames.

Then there were the rubberneckers. As the Plains became well settled, with the land broken into sections by the plow and by roads, large prairie fires on the scale of the South Dakota blaze were increasingly rare. As early as 1893 the *Denver Field and Farm* had declared that prairie fires "are for the most part history."[2] Although his pronouncement was a little premature, the newspaper writer had a point. Many twentieth-century Plains people were less personally acquainted with prairie fire than were their parents or grandparents and thus, strangely, became tourists in their own land, wanting to see the fires they had heard about but not experienced themselves. Reporting on a 1950 fire in Kansas, a newspaper writer noted that "oldtimers" who were "skilled in the art" of fighting prairie fire were relied on for their expertise during the emergency. "Such fires . . . were once common on the Great Plains," the reporter explained to his modern audience.[3]

By the mid–twentieth century the blazes were considered part of the "old" prairie that had been left behind. In 1947, the same year that the large fire terrorized the citizens of central South Dakota, a Kansas newspaper ran a "then and now" article detailing the *former* threat that prairie fires had posed to early settlers.[4] Still, the fires remained an important part of Plains culture. The threat was still present, if largely unrecognized by the population, but more prominently, the legacy of the fires survived in nostalgic collective memory. Now well past the settlement era, modern Plains people thought of prairie fires as a legacy of the past. Their influence remained, however. Ranchers continued to clear their land with controlled burns; wildfires occasionally made an appearance; and fires even played a part, gradually but extensively, through their *absence*. Environmentally and culturally, prairie fires even today remain an enduring link connecting the region's past, present, and future.

As the nineteenth century turned into the twentieth, Plains residents began to memorialize those who fought prairie fires, an early indication that they believed that their struggle to suppress fire had succeeded. As early as 1893 a family in Dorrance, Kansas, erected a stone monument in memory of Willie Baley, a twenty-year-old man who had died fighting a prairie fire that same year. The marker, which as late as 1976 stood out in the pasture where Baley presumably suffered his fatal injuries, read simply, "Willie Baley—Burnt—March 12, 1893." Joe Garrett, who found Baley barely alive, carried the young man to his family's hotel, where Baley died the following morning. Apparently touched by the incident, the Garrett family built a monument to recognize the young man's sacrifice.[5]

Most efforts came later as memories became more distant. The 1930s saw a rush of efforts to commemorate prairie fires that had occurred some fifty or sixty years before. In 1936 citizens of Anderson County, Kansas, placed a marker where four members of the Kellerman family had been killed by a prairie fire in 1862. "The monument is a mute memento of the prairie tragedy that almost exterminated a whole family in the pioneer days," a local writer rhapsodized.[6] Plains newspapers also published scores of "old-timers recall" articles in which settlers, now senior citizens, recalled "the worst prairie fire[s]" in the history of their particular piece of the Plains.[7]

As well as a time to remember the past, the 1930s were a volatile period during which the Plains were immersed in crisis. During that decade the Southern Plains, in particular, suffered through one of the most destructive dry spells in the region's history. Complete with high temperatures, high winds, and of course copious amounts of dust, the Dust Bowl nearly brought agricultural communities, already in the midst of the Great Depression, to their figurative knees.[8] Blowing topsoil inspired government agencies and local farmers alike to try to improve land-use techniques in order to lessen the disaster. As a result, the federal government became more interested in planting trees through its shelterbelt program, to try to limit wind erosion, than in maintaining the prairie through whatever traditional burn techniques lingered in the aftermath of the push for fire suppression.[9] In fact, the newly organized Soil Conservation Service and the older Forest Service were both adamantly opposed to the intentional burning of the prairies in the drought-plagued 1930s, claiming that fire was not good for the land.[10]

A 1936 report, "The Future of the Great Plains," written by a committee of New Dealers appointed by Franklin D. Roosevelt, said more through its neglect of fire than its coverage of the topic. The authors divided their report into three sections describing the past, present, and future of the region. Significantly, they mentioned prairie fire only in "The Great Plains Past" section. Although the Indians did not significantly alter the environment, the report maintained, they did kill buffalo and occasionally burned the prairie grass—only mild disruptions in an otherwise flawless system. In general the Native peoples lived in "rude but productive harmony with Nature," but the coming of the "White Man" changed everything. Now the relationship with the land was unbalanced due to overgrazing, overplowing, and a lack of trees. In "The Great Plains of the Future" (another section of the report), however, these trends could be reversed. Suggestions included planting trees, terracing, creating dams, and using "scientifically selected sites" for planting.

"The sun, the wind, the rain, the snow can be friends of man, not enemies," the report concluded. No mention was made of fire's role in this proposed utopia. Prairie fire, the Great Plains Committee implied, was a part of the past, not the future, of the region. The committee's goal of encouraging responsible land use did not include the responsible use of controlled fire.[11]

Pasture burning even came under fire (so to speak) in the Flint Hills of Kansas, where, more than in most areas of the Plains, residents ignored the suppression agenda due to the land's continuous use for grazing rather than farming. In the mid–twentieth century, however, under pressure from government agencies and agricultural scientists to stop burning, particularly in the dry years, some ranchers in the region complied. The increased pressure to suppress fire was a reaction to the dry 1930s and 1950s. Walter A. Jones of Emporia was a vocal opponent of pasture burning. Born in 1886, Jones believed that the frequent burning of the pastures damaged the grass and destroyed the mulch that protected the soil. Jones said as much the year before his death, in a 1971 interview published in a national magazine, and he was not alone in his opinion. "In the 1930s, '40s, and '50s it was easy to get an argument started in the Flint Hills over the pros and cons of burning. Nearly everyone had an opinion," noted one writer.[12] Even county agricultural extension agents were at odds. The longtime agent for Lyon County, who in later years favored controlled burns, remarked, "'Back in the 1950s if you had put a match to a pasture, I'd have strung you up from the nearest utility pole.'" Another agent in a nearby county, however, "knew that pasture burning was supposed to be bad, but he had some lingering doubts, especially when the ranchers . . . had such excellent grass. So he just kept quiet and let them burn."[13] The situation was so controversial that one local grocery store owner remembered ranchers in the 1950s coming into her store and, with a wink, remarking on the "accidental" fires that mysteriously started in their pastures each spring.[14]

Many Flint Hills ranchers continued burning unabated. The Roglers, near Matfield Green, were one ranching family that kept the tradition alive. "'We've been burning pastures all my life and my father's life,'" Wayne Rogler noted in 1972. "'We've been here 100 years. My grandfather, who settled the land, also burned the pastures like we do. Perhaps that's one of the reasons the bluestem

An aerial view of the Kansas Flint Hills. Photograph courtesy of the Berne Ketchum Collection, Kansas State Historical Society.

grass has remained dominant in these hills.'"[15] Folklorist Jim Hoy called Flint Hills ranchers' tradition of pasture burning a "hundred-year outlaw" because only in Kansas did the practice continue without a pause. "Fire is something that Flint Hills ranchers continued to use," Hoy noted, "from the 1870s through the early 1900s, when other Americans quit burning, through the 1930s, when other Kansans quit burning, and right on up to the present day, when ranchers all over the country are being encouraged to start burning again."[16] Preservation of the Flint Hills, the largest section of unplowed tallgrass prairie in the world, is critical. Only about 4 percent of the tallgrass prairie that existed before Euro-American settlement remains, and 80 percent of that is in Kansas. The Flint Hills precluded the plow because of their rocky soil, but the prairie is still susceptible to woody intruders without the frequent application of fire.[17]

By the 1970s range scientists had begun to change their stance on the consequences of burning. Professors at Kansas State University taught their range management students that fire was "the prairie's best ally," and some ranchers who had been reluctant to burn also changed their views.[18] One man near Council Grove who had ranched in the area since 1928 decided to burn his land in the early 1970s. The rancher looked at his own land and looked at his neighbor's, which had been burned regularly since the early 1940s. The former hosted small hedges, weeds, elm and locust trees, and other invading woody species, and the latter supported healthy, nutritious grasses that helped a grazing cow gain 2 pounds per day.[19] The absence of fire had done its work. Paul Ohlenbusch, a range management specialist at Kansas State University, argued that fire was the "cheapest, most natural way to improve grass quality, increase livestock gains, cut down on weeds, brush and trees and increase wildlife vitality." Planned burns also cut down on overgrazing because a good hot burn requires a certain amount of grass, which forces ranchers to leave enough on the ground in the fall to ensure a successful burn in the spring. "That means you don't overstock—which means healthier grass, more gain on livestock, and less soil erosion."[20]

The result of the new research and recommendations is that across the Great Plains more ranchers and farmers are returning to controlled burns. Today ranchers burn approximately 2 million acres (out of 4.5 million total) in the Flint Hills annually. Even outside the Flint Hills, controlled burns are more common. Near Medicine Lodge, Kansas, in the Gypsum Hills, ranchers returned to burning in the late 1970s in an attempt to reduce the red cedar (*Juniperus virginiana L.*) tree population. By the mid-1980s even the overseer of the Cimarron National Grasslands in the southwestern part of the state, on the short-grass High Plains, began burning.[21]

Although new technology is used for controlled burning, the modern process is not all that different than it was 50, 100, or even 150 years ago. Usually neighbors work together to make more efficient work of the task (fires still do not recognize the authority of fences and land boundaries) and to help with safety concerns. Weather is a primary consideration on burn day. Ranchers look for a warm day following a recent rain, with a light wind blowing in the desired direction. Just as in the nineteenth century, too much wind is dangerous and too little wind causes a slow burn that can damage grass and fence posts.[22] Often ranchers will organize burns to begin near nightfall, when the winds typically taper off their daytime gusts. The result is spectacular nighttime fires that light up the dark for miles around.

If the weather is right, fire crews assemble at the designated time to burn fireguards, separating areas that will not be burned from those that will. Sometimes a road or a plowed field can be used as a fireguard, but more often the crews set backfires to burn up the fuel load in the fireguard area. Modern crews often use a cattle sprayer to moisten the grass, then light it and let it burn until it goes out, using the trailing cattle sprayer or (continuing a method used for decades) humans with wet sacks to ensure that the fire stays in the guard area. Once the fireguards are ready, workers set out the head fire, which travels across the burn area until it meets another fireguard on the opposite side. Many ranchers consider pasture burning the most difficult work they do all year. "Starting a prairie fire is not difficult," Hoy noted, "but building a proper set of fireguards and keeping them from escaping into areas not to be burned, requires great mental and physical effort . . . and luck." Again as in the nineteenth century, a sudden shift in the wind can send the fire in an unexpected direction. Workers have to guard against such accidents as much as possible. Carrying a few matches in a pocket for emergency backfiring, just as the first settlers to the area did, is still the best insurance policy should a person get caught in the path of a head fire on the prairie.[23]

To start the head fire itself, workers throw matches from a pickup truck, or ranchers put a modern twist on the Indian method of dragging a ball of burning grass across the prairie by substituting a bale of hay soaked in kerosene or an old tire pulled by a pickup.[24] Researchers and government personnel on public land use commercially produced torches for starting fires and sometimes other store-bought equipment, such as a "firefighter" consisting of a piece of rubber attached to a wooden stick, to put the fires out.[25] Private ranchers, particularly those with deep roots in the region, have their own techniques and equipment. "Undoubtedly the most striking bit of folk technology to have emerged from the annual burning of the Flint Hills," noted Hoy, "is a fire starter called variously a firestick, a firepipe, or a firesetter." It is a homemade device used regionally by ranchers in the Flint Hills since before World War II, with individual design plans and improvements passed through the generations but never adopted by commercial manufacturers. The firestick is a piece of pipe (of varying length, according to the user) sealed at one end and filled with gasoline. The other end of the pipe is plugged and a hole added to the plug so that a bit of gasoline can drip out of the stick. "To use the firestick," Hoy reported, "one sets fire to a clump of grass with a match, then drops the plugged end . . . into the fire. The gasoline ignites and, as the pipe is dragged along (whether on foot, from the rear of a four-wheeler, or the bed of a pickup), the gasoline dribbles and bounces out, setting grass ablaze in a continuous string of fire." Even filled with gasoline, the firestick will not explode because air cannot enter the pipe. If the stick is tipped upright, the flame will go out by itself, or the worker can put it out with a gloved hand.[26] The firestick, as a tool used in pasture burning and as a folk device, is testimony to the long legacy of intentional fire use in the Flint Hills, a practice started by the Indian peoples, taught to Euro-American settlers, and maintained by ranchers today.

Despite the prominence of controlled burning in Kansas and its growing acceptance across the Great Plains, the effects of fire suppression in the region remain evident. Even as burning has become more accepted, suburbanites build houses in traditional burn areas, making pasture burning "a touchier business," and some landowners simply do not burn regularly.[27] The consequences can be profound. Take, for example, the invasion of the misnamed red cedar trees into Kansas and Oklahoma. "For centuries," a recent report stated, the trees, which are actually junipers, "were confined to rocky bluffs where they [had] escaped fires." After Euro-American settlement and the corresponding suppression of prairie fire, however, the trees began to spread onto the wider prairie. In the past government agencies actually encouraged residents to plant the cedars to function as windbreaks, distributing thousands of saplings to aid in the process. Another factor is birds, which eat the cedar berries and then do a little seed distributing of their own all across the prairies. The result by 2007 was a rapidly expanding cedar population. Southwest of Wichita, for example, are areas that contain 400 cedars per acre. Many consider the cedars an eyesore, but an even more significant consequence is water consumption. A single 15-foot cedar can consume 35 gallons of water each day. The proliferation of cedar trees, caused by plantings in the past two centuries and by the suppression of fire, therefore places stress on the semiarid Plains' water supply, a stress particularly felt during times of drought.[28]

Cutting cedars and using fire to discourage them could help reverse the invasion. Still, even as pasture burning has gained favor among scientists and ranchers, the general public, although aware of the spring fires, remains largely uneducated regarding the true value of fire on the Great Plains and the intricacies of a proper spring burn. Occasionally the burns cause controversy. In 1994 a shift in the wind blew smoke across the Kansas Turnpike, which runs through the heart of the Flint Hills. On the stretch of road between El Dorado and Emporia the smoke reduced visibility, causing a multiple-car accident. One person died, twelve were injured, and traffic backed up for miles. Immediately the public and the press began to question the necessity of the annual burns.[29] Ultimately, the burns continued, but the state posted large signs along the highway warning motorists not to drive into smoke.

Another controversy that clearly illustrates common misunderstandings surrounding the burning practice, even among environmental agencies, emerged first in 2004 and again in 2010. In the spring of 2004 state environmental officials sent a letter to agricultural extension agents in Chase County, Kansas, regarding a three-day period in which smoke from the Flint Hills burns, carried to the northeast by the wind, "helped push ozone levels in Kansas City above approved limits." Art Spratlin, U.S. Environmental Protection Agency (EPA) air-quality director for Kansas City, noted that recently implemented higher standards for air quality meant probable tighter restrictions on emissions. "There's a great deal of concern here at EPA and in the states and within the community that we're going to be over that limit and have to do some things to improve air quality in Kansas City after this coming summer," Spratlin continued. The letter, addressed to Flint Hills agents, "hinted that mandatory restrictions on prairie fires are possible" as part of the plan to improve the air quality of a city some 150 miles away. The EPA requested that local officials "work with ranchers to spread out the prairie fires between February and May" and to limit the area burned by each rancher to 160 acres per day.[30]

This request, demonstrating government officials' ignorance of pasture burning, did not go over well among agricultural extension agents or Flint Hills ranchers, many of whom consider themselves stewards of the grass. "My dad was here, my granddad was here. We've looked after grass for over 60 years," stated one rancher, who also noted that if he limited his burning to 160 acres per day it would take him over three months to finish, an impractical plan. The timing of the burns is critical and must be done within a few weeks' time. If burned too early the grass will not renew itself soon enough to prevent wind and water erosion of the soil. Also, fires started too early will not kill dormant woody intruders. If burned too late the already green grass does not produce a fast fire. "At just the right time," noted one specialist, "the fire burns hot and fast. It kills scrub cedar and other woody invaders. It lets sunlight penetrate to the soil, bringing to life fungi that help plant roots."[31] This happens not in February or June but from mid-April to mid-May. Some Flint Hills ranchers still burn in March, a remnant of an older burn tradition. Recent scientific research, however, places the optimal burn time about a month later.[32]

The EPA's request that ranchers distribute their burning over a longer time, therefore, if fulfilled, would essentially negate the benefits of fire on much of the burn area. A Chase County rancher wondered "why Kansas City doesn't take care of its own problems rather than blame them on ranchers in Chase County." Pasture burning only lasts a few days, a writer for the *El Dorado Times* observed, whereas emissions from cars, construction, industry, and other sources are daily events in urban areas. "The farm and ranch industry will continue to keep its controlled burning of the tall grass prairies confined to a minimum time period," he concluded. "Those fires aren't recent phenomena, and they aren't strictly for the viewing pleasure of those traveling up and down our highways." Prairie fires help renew the grass. "That means good things for cattlemen, for agriculture, for rural communities and the Kansas economy. . . . This process is part of the culture of the rural communities that dot the Flint Hills region."[33]

In 2010 the impact that prairie burning has on air quality again inspired controversy, as burns twice caused Wichita's ozone levels to exceed federal air pollution allowances in 2009 and once again in 2010. As more strict EPA standards take effect in the future, officials are concerned that Wichita might be forced to make costly adjustments to comply with the new regulations. To avoid this situation, EPA officials want to adjust Flint Hills burn practices and establish a smoke management plan. Josh Tapp, chief of air planning and development for the EPA's regional office in Kansas City, assured ranchers that the agency did not seek to ban prairie burns. Instead the goal was to maintain the practice while adopting strategies to diminish the impact of smoke on health and air quality. The Kansas legislature, in 2010, passed a resolution asking Congress and the EPA to exempt the burns from regulation due to the special circumstance and the need to preserve the prairie. At least one Kansas extension agent, however, feared that Congress would be of little help, as most members of Congress are unfamiliar with the burn practice and the rationale behind it. For now, a Smoke Management Plan Committee, which includes representatives from the Nature Conservancy, Kansas State University Extension, Kansas Farm Bureau, Kansas Livestock Association, Kansas Department of Health and Environment, and the EPA, among others, has been organized to identify the problems and has recommended a pilot program that will allow ranchers to burn while minimizing smoke production. The plan encompasses such topics as smoke distribution, burn timing, public outreach and education, and long-term research needs. It includes a voluntary smoke reporting plan to gather information about how burn strategies work, plus some regulatory measures such as the restriction of nonessential burning (yard waste and trash) during pasture burning season.

Although the burns are an ecological and preservation concern, they are also an economic issue. According to the Kansas Livestock Association, about 500,000 yearlings graze on burned Flint Hills pasture each year, which allows them to gain 32 pounds more than if they grazed on unburned pasture. That 32 pounds, noted Kansas State University range management professor Clenton Owensby, "can be the difference between profit and loss" for the rancher.[34]

The legacy of fire on the Plains is a long one, and ranchers are quite skilled at applying the fire that helps maintain their livelihoods and the tallgrass prairie ecosystem. Still, new research is constantly emerging and points toward a future of grassland burning that will merge traditional practices with new ideas. One promising area of research proposes that Great Plains ranchers adopt burning techniques that mimic the burning from the pre–Euro-American settlement era. Today, as before settlement, fire and grazing interact to shape the grasslands. The difference, according to researchers Samuel D. Fuhlendorf and David M. Engle at Oklahoma State University, is that fire and grazing application in the modern era is much more regimented than it was two centuries ago, when the grasslands were a "dynamic patch mosaic of plant communities"

maintained by the interplay between fire and grazing. Bison preferred to graze on new growth in recently burned areas, thereby ne-
glecting the unburned grass. The resulting buildup of fuel increased
the likelihood of fire on a different part of the prairie the next
season, especially a hot fire capable of eliminating woody intruders.[35] The theory that the presettlement tallgrass prairie resembled
a mosaic, the result of fire and grazing interaction, intersects with
Stephen Pyne's argument that the landscape of the eastern Plains,
fragmented with natural fireguards, burned as a result of numerous
human-instigated ignition sites.[36] The areas chosen for ignition by
the Native peoples from year to year; the available fuel load; and
the movement of the fire, depending on grass condition, weather,
and other factors, likely combined to create the mosaic effect. Thus
not all parts of the prairie burned every year, and not all parts were
uniformly grazed every year as the migrating bison were drawn to
recently burned ground over old.

A manufactured randomness, labeled "patch-burn grazing"
and not unlike the randomness of the past, should be implemented
on the Great Plains today, researchers argue. Cattle, given a choice,
will graze 75 percent of the time on recently burned patches and
25 percent on unburned patches—a pattern not that different from
that of bison. In any given year, "by season's end," noted biologist
Randy Rodgers, "the burned area had been pounded and the unburned area partially rested. The next year, a different part of the
pasture is burned and the cattle pound it, giving rest to the patch
that was burned the first year and added rest to the yet-unburned
patch." The process is dependent on allowing cattle to choose where
they graze—on unburned or burned pasture. Patch-burn grazing,
therefore, uses fire to "deliberately create uneven grazing," thereby
making the grasslands more heterogeneous. Within the mosaic of
the grasses, the abundance and type of vegetation shifts, creating
varied habitats for the diverse wildlife on the Plains. The year after
a burn, for example, the prairie produces more forbs than it does
during the initial regrowth. Prairie left unburned for a time will, of
course, create heavy grass and litter. Such a mosaic of vegetation is
critical to prairie animal species, not all of whom prefer the same
type of grass cover. The prairie chicken, for example, requires high
grass for nesting but thinner grass with lots of forbs for brood-rear-
ing. Nighthawks and upland sandpipers, who nest in short grass,

"will find exactly what they need in the most recently-burned, heavily grazed portion of the pasture." Other species, such as Henslow's sparrows, are at home in heavy grass that has gone without burning for two years. A random mosaic of grasslands, created by fire and grazing, is therefore a system that can support cattle while maintaining an ecosystem amenable to other animal life.[37]

More research is needed to determine whether patch-burn grazing would decrease smoke production, thereby preventing Kansas's metropolitan areas from exceeding air-quality allowances. Some ranchers in the Flint Hills and in the Tallgrass Prairie Preserve in northeast Oklahoma already use the technique and hypothesize that they do indeed generate less smoke than if they burned more widely. Thus far, however, researchers have not tested the theory. One concern is that although patch burning means burning only about one-third of the grass each year, it also means that the grass on the unburned sections grows taller and, when it is burned later, might generate more smoke than if it had been burned annually. Other skeptics argue that patch burning might require more firebreaks (thus more work) and more equipment (thus more expense) than traditional burning. Finally, it is uncertain yet whether patch burning would be frequent enough to block woody intruders from the prairie.[38]

Prairie fire, at least in its controlled form, is therefore a subject of lively debate, with a seemingly positive future, at least in limited areas of the settled Plains. The fires have come to symbolize many things, including terror, adventure, conquest, danger, passion, and lust. The fires are tradition, a way to care for the land and a way to perpetuate the efforts of those who have come and burned before. With the prominence of prairie fire in its annual controlled form, in its occasional wild form, and as transformed by cultural media, prairie fires are part of the identity of the Plains.

Still, the taming of the red buffalo has had its consequences, not only for the land but also for the people who live there. The awareness that modern people have of prairie fire, too often, is based in pop culture caricature or misunderstanding. Travelers in the Flint Hills, native and out-of-state, stop their cars at the next town, anxious to report what they think are wild, uncontrolled fires to the authorities.[39] Occasional accidents and rare wildfires, covered extensively by the media, give the public the impression that all fires are bad.[40] At the very least prairie fires are considered part of the past—something that the Indians, pioneers, and maybe Gene Autry contended with, but not something that affects modern Plains life. Only when tragedy strikes, evacuation is needed, or the air gets smoky for a couple of days in the spring do the fires get much attention, and then only as an anomaly or in a negative context.

Even the annual newspaper articles about the burning in the Kansas Flint Hills reflect this attitude. The fires are beautiful, of that there is no doubt. The beauty, in fact, is perhaps their most consistently noted feature; they are described as "riveting" and "compelling," a spectacle at which to marvel.[41] Yet modern writers also describe the fires in other ways that are remarkably similar to descriptions from an earlier era. "Red, eerie, and farther away than they look," remarked a writer for the *Wichita Eagle* in 1997; "flames light up the night. . . . The fires are part of the annual spring preparations by cattle handlers for grazing season in the Flint Hills—but for the unknowing, they look like a scene from the end of the world."[42]

Among modern Plains people, therefore, is a strange conjunction of awareness of and unfamiliarity with prairie fire. The fires, still beautiful and awe-inspiring, continue to stir the fascination they did 200 or more years ago. Yet the beauty and the purpose of the fires, as for the earliest Euro-American explorers in the presettlement era, are once again mysterious, alien, and otherworldly. The way Plains people see prairie fire has come full circle. Mesmerizing yet alien in the presettlement era, the fires became recognizable, if still threatening, during the process of nineteenth-century settlement. Even in the midst of their campaign to rid themselves of the blazes, the people retained a familiarity with the fires, accompanied by pride that the sight belonged to them and to their new home. Most modern Plains peoples, in contrast, even when armed with a vague awareness of prairie fire's legacy, feel no such connection. The fires are of the past and, except for the occasional outbreak and for a select few ranchers each spring, have little to do with the Plains present and future.

Nothing could be further from the truth, of course, as prairie fires, whether present or absent from the Plains, continue to be a significant force. Perhaps this message has started to resonate with some in the region. Take, for example, an event in Kansas called "Flames in the Flint Hills," in which rancher and native Kansan

Jan Jantzen, starting in 2003, turned pasture burning into a tourist attraction. The business venture resonates of the past, when nineteenth-century settler George Munger took his visiting Eastern relatives out in the wagon to see their first prairie fire. Originally at the Jantzen ranch and now at the Flying W ranch, where Josh and Gwen Hoy have continued the practice since Jantzen's retirement, prairie fires are once again a curiosity for native Plains people as well as for those from outside the region. Visitors come and, for a fee and under close supervision, fire the prairie and watch it burn. Included in the package price is an "all-day party" of sorts—snacks, dinner, and a live bluegrass band. Also included, however, is a little education about fire's role on the prairie—not only its past role in creating and maintaining the prairies but also its importance for the present and future of the region. Visitors come from as far away as Louisiana, Pennsylvania, and even Finland, but most customers are people who live on the Great Plains. When he started "Flames in the Flint Hills," many of Jantzen's ranching neighbors could not imagine why tourists would want to pay to do ranch work, but for those who did come—especially those who had roots and homes in the region—the burning was an act that connected them to the land.[43] Prairie fires are still something privileged, something that Easterners can visit and see but cannot truly claim for their own. Prairie fires, ultimately, belong to the Plains.

Pasture burning tourism is, in part, a celebration of a landscape. Such activities are welcome on the Plains, a landscape that, for whatever reason, is not celebrated as often or as universally as others. The people of Cottonwood Falls, Kansas, however, find plenty of reasons to party at their annual Prairie Fire Festival, an event held each spring during burn season. The festival invites people to Chase County, in the heart of the Flint Hills, to have a little fun and perhaps learn something about the tallgrass prairie and fire's role in maintaining the region. If festivalgoers are lucky, they may even get a spectacular view of the controlled burns. Flint Hills ranchers are privileged to continue the burns that keep the region's unplowed prairie healthy, a tradition they believe well worth celebrating.[44]

Art featuring prairie fire also contributes to the celebration. Kansas native John Steuart Curry in 1941 included a prairie fire in his famous John Brown mural at the state capitol in Topeka. Meant to symbolize the Bleeding Kansas struggle of the 1850s and the con-

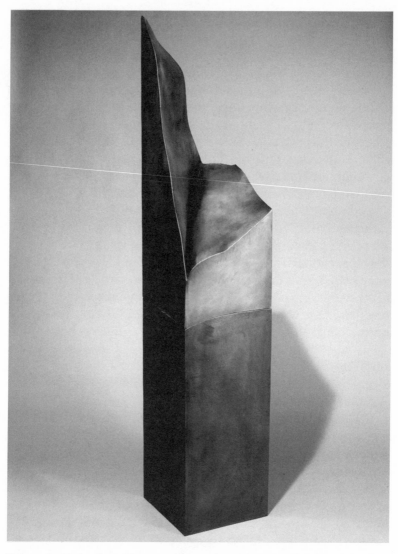

This sculpture makes reference to the Loess Hills of western Missouri and Iowa and the Missouri River. A line near the top of the bronze sculpture acts as a geological baseline denoting limestone strata with the loess soil and hills atop. For thousands of years, prairie fires sustained the abundant and lush tall grass landscape of the hills. This sculpture references spikes of fire as well as the spires of the hills. *Prairie Fire*, 1994 by Thomas Stancliffe (American, b. 1955). Patinated steel and bronze. Gift of the artist. In the permanent collection, Brunnier Art Museums, Iowa State University, Ames, Iowa. Photograph by Bob Elbert, 2011. ©University Museums, 2011. All rights reserved.

troversy over statehood, Curry's use of fire reflects Brown's desire to purify Kansas from the evils of slavery.[45] James Cook's painting *Fire at Night, Kansas* (1982) hangs in the Wichita Art Museum and, according to art historian Joni Kinsey, "demonstrates that fire, even without the implicit danger and drama favored in the last century, provides a compelling visual subject for contemporary artists that is both conceptually intriguing and visually expressive."[46] Saskatchewan native Robert Scott's modern abstraction, *Prairie Fire*, appeared in 1993, and Blackbear Bosin's striking *Prairie Fire* from 1955 provides a modern interpretation of an ancient hunting tradition.[47] The terror that prairie fires inspired is absent from modern art, but the symbolism, power, and beauty remain.

Modern artists such as Cook, Scott, Bosin, and perhaps most notably Larry Schwarm are using their talents and the magnificent prairie fires to draw the public's attention to a region often described as "empty" and "monotonous." Schwarm, professor of photography at Kansas's Emporia State University, photographs the controlled burns in the Flint Hills. He published a book of photographs titled *On Fire* in 2003 and has also displayed his photographs at the National Museum of Art at the Smithsonian in Washington, D.C.[48] The photographs certainly celebrate the beauty of the fires, but more than that, noted Kinsey, Schwarm's work "is informed by the contemporary awareness of fire's role in the survival of the prairies."[49] *On Fire*, in other words, combines the legacy of the fires with their future and helps to ensure that prairie fire remains a part of regional identity. The attraction of the modern fires, in addition to their beauty, comes not from their endangered (and therefore nostalgic) status, as in the nineteenth century, but from their perseverance and their role in preserving the prairies. The fires of the "old" prairie have a definite place in the "new."

"A Prairie Fire Came upon the Place"

On a bitterly cold winter night in 1867 a train out of Chicago overtook a fire burning across the open prairie. It was an unusual night for a prairie fire. The wind blew a gale, which was typical, but snow fell, which was not. Snow lightly covered the ground, but the tall grass towered above it and provided fuel enough for the fire to flourish despite the small amount of moisture present. Although the wind rapidly pushed the fire over the landscape, the train managed to catch up. An occasional gust allowed the burn, for a time, to keep pace with the methodical churn of the train's engine. Locomotive and fire traveled along parallel paths. The "race," noted George Bungay, who witnessed the contest from inside the train, was on.

Bungay was enthralled. "It was a picturesque and grand race between the fire steeds of the prairie and the iron horse," he rhapsodized. "On and on, they sped through the thick and stormy night. One crackling and whispering in the wind . . . [the other] pressing forward with a tread that shook the ground." Eventually the locomotive, unaffected by such variables as wind, gained the advantage and "left the fiery cavalry in the distance, fighting with the wind and the snow, and leaping over the creeks and the ponds in its course." The experience left Bungay pensive. "Whether [the fire] swept away any human habitations in its path, I cannot say," he mused, "but it was a most attractive sight, and so full of suggestion."[1]

Indeed. The encounter between train and prairie fire, the "race"—at least in Bungay's mind—is in many ways symbolic of the larger contest between Euro-American Plains settlers and prairie fire. Bungay's interpretation of events suggested as much. He noted, for example, transformative power in both the train and the fire. The train carried settlers onto the Plains who in turn planted crops and trees and constructed towns, houses, and roads. But in human hands fire too was powerful. Purposeful burning at the hands of the Indians had helped create the vast Plains. The prairies were free of trees and primed for the plow in large part because the Indians had "put out" fire. Under the "civilizing" influence of Euro-American settlement, however, the Great Plains were changing. The power that prairie fires possessed was no longer needed. In fact, that power was dangerous to life, property, and above all the imagined future of the region.

Bungay's train and fire were thus, by the mid–nineteenth century, identifying characteristics of the vast expanse of prairie that dominated the interior of North America. Both train and fire, he argued, were also beautiful. The fire was "a most attractive sight," but the train was a wonder of human ingenuity—"poetry in motion—ringing with the rhythm of progress."[2] New Plains settlers could readily embrace the locomotive and all it symbolized but should approach prairie fires with caution. They *were* lovely. "It is worth traveling ten thousand miles to be an actor in a scene so sublime," a traveler noted after witnessing a prairie fire in 1837.[3] The beauty, however, could not compensate for the threat that the fires represented. The sublime scene that the presettlement traveler admired could, after settlement, be preserved only in art and literary description. The fire outside the train was Bungay's guilty pleasure, to be sure—exciting and beautiful—but "behind it was a charred and blackened wake of cinders" that he could not ignore.[4]

Safeguarding and subduing the Plains meant controlling fire. Bungay's fire was not controlled—at least not when he viewed it—but prairie fire in general was a force that most settlers believed they could manipulate and manage. Usually *started* by humans, the fires would also be *contained* by humans intent on "civilizing" the Plains landscape. It thus seemed appropriate to Bungay that the quintessential symbol of conquest in the American West, the locomotive, quickly outmaneuvered the prairie fire. The two "raced," separate but parallel for a time—long enough for Bungay to admire the fire's beauty—but then the engine inevitably outpaced the flames. Prairie fire was an impressive force, to be sure, but one that would invariably and necessarily be left behind in the wake of advancing settlement.

To a degree, Bungay and the many others who commented on prairie fire's demise had a point. Settlers' suppression efforts, in combination with an ever-expanding infrastructure, did eventually reduce the size, scope, and frequency of prairie fires by the mid–twentieth century. As early as 1856 an author argued that "no insurmountable obstacle exists in the way of settlements upon the Grand Prairie." Railroads would soon extend into the region and carry building materials to the vast, treeless land. If fires, which threatened newly built settlements, were "excluded," there would be "no serious impediment to the future growth" of the region. Fires prevented trees and threatened fences, farms, and human life. They also got in the way of Euro-Americans' vision of the Plains—the remaking of the landscape into an unobtainable ideal. Thus, the author matter-of-factly concluded in 1856, "the burning of the prairies is then stopped."[5]

But it was not that simple. In a larger sense George Bungay was wrong. It was true that the train he rode that winter night outran the prairie fire in a literal sense, and perhaps *partially* in a metaphorical sense. However, settlers' certainty that prairie fire would soon *exclusively* be relegated to history was misguided.

Again, a story seems appropriate: The prairie started burning near Sioux Falls, South Dakota, one November day in 1870. At first the wind carried smoke and ash into the city, but as night fell it died considerably, and the glow from the fire cast a "crimson light" onto the windows of the buildings. Unnerved but presumably protected by the river, people gathered to watch the fire in the distance as the flames "writhed and twisted, like souls in purgatory." The failing breeze provided further assurance that the river, without a strong wind to fling sparks to the other side, would serve as an effective firebreak. Their safety secured, the citizens of Sioux Falls contentedly listened to the crackling of the burning grass as they "gazed with awe upon the grandest of Western sights." Then they heard another, unexpected, sound. It was like . . . thunder? Thundering . . . hooves? At first the townspeople were mystified. What could be causing the strange noise? Then the first cry rang out through the streets: "Buffalo!" Sure enough, the prairie fire, tamed by the diminished wind and contained by the river but still burning through tall grass, had forced a small herd of bison, moving ahead of the flames, to cross the river and pay a visit to town. People screamed in surprise and ran into their houses for protection. Others got out their shotguns to fire at the animals, who were likely even more terrified by the strange experience than the people of Sioux Falls. Soon it was all over. The bison went on their way, and the prairie fire—the root cause of all the excitement—died quietly along the river's edge.[6]

The moral of this silly yet illustrative story? Prairie fires bring unintended consequences. In this case it was bison running through the streets of a South Dakota town. Most of the time the consequences were not so obvious (or hairy) but proved more significant. Prairie fires burned the grass away, it was true, but they also cleared the way for new, more nutritious growth later—new grass that added weight to the cattle that grazed on it and provided a diverse ecosystem for nesting birds and other prairie animals. It was dangerous work to fight prairie fire, that also was true, but the act of firefighting united communities, fostered neighborliness, and assisted in identity formation. It also got people out of bed at night to see one of the prettiest sights on earth.

If prairie fires brought unintended consequences, it follows that the suppression of them did too because the fires are just as influential when absent as when present. Suppressing fire allowed more trees to grow on the wood-starved Plains. Settlers thought this a good thing: Trees would improve the land. But trees, particularly cedar trees, also sucked enormous amounts of water from the already parched prairie ground. Controlling fire meant that houses, farms, and fences were temporarily safe. It also meant that a thick, "woolly" grass cover spread across the land. When a spark inevitably touched this ground cover, the fire burned faster and more intensely than it had before suppression.

The environment in which humans live, as any environmental historian (or farmer, or person who has ever accidentally gotten caught driving in a blizzard) can tell you, is unpredictable and fundamentally uncontrollable. Humans, despite what we'd like to think, cannot control nature. Occasionally we achieve a modicum of control, as Euro-American settlers did with prairie fire, but there are always consequences. Just when things seem in hand, along comes a herd of bison through the middle of town, or a prairie fire that supposedly had been relegated to history. "About 2 P.M., under a

Signs caution drivers on the turnpike in the Flint Hills of Kansas. Photo by author.

fearful wind, blowing at the rate of at least forty miles an hour, from the south, a prairie fire came upon the place," a reporter succinctly noted of Cottonwood Falls, Kansas.[7] The environment, when people least expect it, and in unexpected ways, continually reasserts itself in the ongoing "conversation."

Bungay's train overtaking the prairie fire was, in truth, largely illusion. Prairie fire still has a profound presence on the Great Plains, and in more ways than one. First, its influence is felt even through its absence. The fires have, to a degree, been tamed, or at least restrained, by Euro-American settlement, but the power of fire's absence is clear through the environmental legacy of suppression. Second, as shown by the resurgence of fires in the dry 1890s, and again the "worst" fires of the early twentieth century, and again the massive 1947 fire in South Dakota, and again the Southern Plains fires of 2006, prairie fire is not completely physically gone from the Great Plains either. Ranchers in the Flint Hills of Kansas and elsewhere in the region still purposefully burn, as their parents, their grandparents, their great-grandparents, and the Indian peoples did before them. Moreover, the research of range management specialists and other scientists continues to prove that prairie fire is still *needed* on the Great Plains.

The taming of the red buffalo has had significant consequences for the Plains and for the region's people. Still, the fire remains in its many forms. Residents and visitors are still captivated by the sight of the "red serpent" all around them, even if accompanied by prudent warnings from the state. "Range Burning Area," read large yellow signs posted along the Kansas highways; "Do Not Drive into Dense Smoke." Like the excluded Easterners of the nineteenth century, who could not even imagine what a Western prairie fire looked like, modern Plains residents must usually be content with pictures and controlled versions of the real thing. One hopes that, even within this limited scope, observers will get a glimpse of the grand event that both identified and shaped their home. Perhaps they will get an inkling of what Abbie Bright saw in 1870 on the Kansas prairies and an understanding of what she meant by her journal entry that day. "Saw [a] prairie fire," she wrote; "such a sight."[8]

The suppression of prairie fire, by reducing by magnitudes one of the region's great formative forces and most striking sights, has shaped the history and culture of America's interior grasslands as much as that other culturally driven event, the great "plow up" and the introduction of large-scale monoculture. As such, it deserves our equal attention. The "master of the prairie," through its occasional return, through its imprint on regional identity, and ironically even through the force of its absence, continues its hold on the Great Plains.

Notes

Introduction: "Think of This"

1. *Walnut Valley Times* (El Dorado, Kansas), October 25, 1872.
2. *El Dorado Times* (Kansas), March 9, 2006; *Wichita Eagle* (Kansas), March 9, 2006; *Augusta Daily Gazette* (Kansas), March 9, 2006.
3. Jim Hoy, *Flint Hills Cowboys: Tales of the Tallgrass Prairie* (Lawrence: University Press of Kansas, 2006), 2.
4. *Arkansas Democrat Gazette*, January 8, 2006, March 14, 2006; *Wichita Eagle* (Kansas), March 9, 2006.
5. Walter Prescott Webb, *The Great Plains* (reprint, Lincoln: University of Nebraska Press, 1981). A sampling of Malin's work includes James Malin, *Winter Wheat in the Golden Belt of Kansas: A Study in Adaptation to Subhumid Geographical Environment* (Lawrence: University Press of Kansas, 1944); *The Grassland of North America: Prolegomena to Its History with Addenda and Postscript* (Gloucester, Mass.: Peter Smith, 1967); and *History and Ecology: Studies of the Grassland*, ed. by Robert P. Swierenga (Lincoln: University of Nebraska Press, 1984). Geoff Cunfer's related discussion is *On the Great Plains: Agriculture and Environment* (College Station: Texas A&M University Press, 2005), 6–9. Cunfer also provides a nice summary of Webb's and Malin's scholarly contributions.
6. Donald Worster, *Dust Bowl: The Southern Plains in the 1930s* (New York: Oxford University Press, 1979); Pamela Riney-Kehrberg, *Rooted in Dust: Surviving Drought and Depression in Southwestern Kansas* (Lawrence: University Press of Kansas, 1994).
7. Elliott West, *The Contested Plains: Indians, Goldseekers, and the Rush to Colorado* (Lawrence: University Press of Kansas, 1998); Andrew C. Isenberg, *The Destruction of the Bison: An Environmental History, 1750–1920* (New York: Cambridge University Press, 2000); Dan Flores, "Bison Ecology and Bison Diplomacy: The Southern Plains from 1800 to 1850," *Journal of American History* 78 (2)

(September 1991): 465–485; and James E. Sherow, "Workings of the Geodialectic: High Plains Indians and Their Horses in the Region of the Arkansas River Valley, 1800–1870," *Environmental History Review* 16 (2) (Summer 1992): 61–84.

8. Richard White, "Discovering Nature in North America," *Journal of American History* 79 (3) (December 1992): 874–891.

9. See, for example, Stephen J. Pyne, *World Fire: The Culture of Fire on Earth* (New York: Henry Holt and Company, 1995); Stephen J. Pyne, *Burning Bush: A Fire History of Australia* (New York: Henry Holt and Company, 1991); and Johan Goudsblom, *Fire and Civilization* (London: Penguin, 1992).

10. See this book's bibliography for published articles, essays, and chapters about prairie fire.

11. Wes Jackson, *Becoming Native to This Place* (Lexington: The University Press of Kentucky, 1994), 60.

12. Linda M. Hasselstrom, *No Place Like Home: Notes from a Western Life* (Reno: University of Nevada Press, 2009), 6.

13. Ree Drummond, "'There's a Fire,'" *The Pioneer Woman*, November 9, 2010, http://thepioneerwoman.com/blog/2010/11/theres-a-fire.

14. Louis S. Warren, *Buffalo Bill's America: William Cody and the Wild West Show* (New York: Alfred A. Knopf, 2005), x; "Pawnee Bill's Historical Wild West Official Program," Box 13, Folder 6, Gordon William Lillie (a.k.a. Pawnee Bill) Manuscript Collection, Western History Collections, University of Oklahoma, Norman, Oklahoma.

15. Denver Bardwell, *Prairie Fire: A Gunfire Western Novel* (New York: Doubleday, Doran & Co., 1940), 21; Hank Mitchum, *Red Buffalo*, Stagecoach Station 41 (Toronto: Bantam Books, 1989), 49–50. For other Westerns that feature prairie fire, see Loula Grace Erdman, *The Edge of Time* (New York: Dodd, Mead & Company, 1950); and John Killdeer, *Fire on the Prairie* (New York: Domain, 1995).

16. Don Pendleton, *Mack Bolan: Prairie Fire*, The Executioner 68 (Toronto: Worldwide, 1984).

17. The first volume of the Spanish Bit Series is Don Coldsmith, *Trails of the Spanish Bit* (New York: Bantam Books, 1980), 131–132, 195.

18. Laura Ingalls Wilder, *Little House on the Prairie* (New York: Harper & Row, 1935), 274–285.

19. "Little House on the Prairie—The Pilot" (1974), Lions Gate DVD; the *Little House on the Prairie* board game was issued by Parker Brothers in 1978. I am a proud owner of one of the few complete versions likely still in existence, and the game board hangs on my bathroom wall.

20. Jim Roberts, *Gene Autry and the Prairie Fire* (London: Adprint Limited, ca. 1956).

21. Betty G. Birney, *Tyrannosaurus Tex* (Boston: Houghton Mifflin Company, 1994). See also Marilynn Reynolds, *The Prairie Fire* (New York: Orca Book Publishers, 2001); Kristiana Gregory, *Prairie River: A Grateful Harvest* (New York:

Scholastic Inc., 2003); and Susan E. Goodman, *Cora Frear: A True Story* (New York: Aladdin Paperbacks, 2002).

22. Patricia Werner, *Prairie Fire* (Toronto: Paperjacks, 1988); Catherine Palmer, *Prairie Fire* (Wheaton, Ill.: Tyndale House Publishers, 1998); Terri Branson, *Prairie Fire* (Dragonfly Publishing, 2001); L. J. Maas, *Prairie Fire* (Nederland, Tex.: Yellow Rose Books, 2002).

23. *The Texans*, Universal Western Collection, 1938 Paramount Pictures Inc.; Elliot Arnold and Lou Vittes, "Prairie Fire," *Rawhide*, produced by Bernard L. Kowalski and Bruce Geller; Marty Robbins, *More Gunfighter Ballads and Trail Songs*, Sony Records, 1990 (originally released 1960); Jane Parker Resnick, *The Everything Bartender's Book* (Holbrook, Mass.: Adams Media Corp, 1995), 48; Anthony Dias Blue, *The Complete Book of Mixed Drinks*, rev. ed. (New York: Quill, 2002), 166.

24. Hoy, *Flint Hills Cowboys*, 2.

25. Jim Hoy, *Cowboys and Kansas: Stories from the Tallgrass Prairie* (Norman: University of Oklahoma Press, 1995), 113. Hoy, a Flint Hills native, is an authority on the region's folklore and folk customs. He, much more than I, is acquainted with the vernacular of Flint Hills burns.

26. Early Nebraska Prairie Fire Accounts Collection, MS No. 18, Folder 1, University Archives Special Collections, University of Nebraska–Lincoln. The story is told in "Prairie Fires and the Nebraska Pioneer," collected and ed. by Donald E. Westover (Lincoln, Neb.: The Cooperative Extension Service, University of Nebraska–Lincoln, n.d.), 20–24.

27. Cunfer, *On the Great Plains*, 8.

28. "Fire, Grazing, and the Prairie," Fire Management, Tallgrass Prairie National Preserve website, National Park Service, http://www.npns.gov/archive/tapr/fire.htm.

Chapter One: "Mass of Grass"

1. John T. Irving, Jr., *Indian Sketches Taken During an Expedition to the Pawnee Tribes*, ed. by John McDermott (Norman: University of Oklahoma Press, 1955), 221–223. Irving is quoted by Kenneth F. Higgins, "Interpretation and Compendium of Historical Fire Accounts in the Northern Great Plains," Resource Publication 161 (Washington D.C.: U.S. Department of the Interior, Fish and Wildlife Services, 1986), 17.

2. Geoff Cunfer, *On the Great Plains: Agriculture and Environment* (College Station: Texas A&M University Press, 2005), 40; Candace Savage, *Prairie: A Natural History* (Vancouver: Greystone Books, 2004), 85.

3. Roscoe Logue, *Under Texas and Border Skies* (Amarillo, Tex.: Russell Stationary Co., 1935), 43.

4. Savage, *Prairie*, 8.

5. *Kansas Farmer*, September 23, 1874.

6. Quoted by Savage, *Prairie*, 6.

7. James E. Sherow, *The Grasslands of the United States: An Environmental History* (Santa Barbara, Calif.: ABC-CLIO, 2007), 33.

8. Savage, *Prairie*, 64.

9. Ibid., 64–67.

10. Ibid., 67–70.

11. Sherow, *The Grasslands of the United States*, 4; see also Daniel I. Axelrod, "Rise of the Grassland Biome, Central North America," *Botanical Review* 51 (April–June 1985): 163–201.

12. Logue, *Under Texas and Border Skies*, 43.

13. Stephen J. Pyne, *Awful Splendour: A Fire History of Canada* (Vancouver: University of British Columbia Press, 2007), 32, 35.

14. Sherow, *The Grasslands of the United States*, 9.

15. Ibid., 10.

16. Savage, *Prairie*, 85, 206; Larry Schwarm, *On Fire* (Durham, N.C.: Duke University Press, 2003), n.p.

17. Cary J. Mock, "Rainfall in the Garden of the United States Great Plains, 1870–1889," *Climatic Change* 44 (2000): 174. See also Anthony J. Amato, "A Wet and Dry Landscape," in Anthony J. Amato, Janet Timmerman, and Joseph Anthony Amato, eds., *Draining the Great Oasis: An Environmental History of Murray County, Minnesota* (Marshall, Minn.: Crossings Press, 2001).

18. Stephen J. Pyne, *America's Fires: A Historical Context for Policy and Practice* (Durham, N.C.: Forest History Society, 2010), xvi.

19. Carl O. Sauer, "Grassland Climax, Fire, and Man," *Journal of Range Management* 3 (January 1950): 20; Axelrod, "Rise of the Grassland Biome," 187.

20. Pyne, *Awful Splendour*, 31.

21. Ibid., 32, 37.

22. Axelrod, "Rise of the Grassland Biome," 186.

23. Savage, *Prairie*, 46–47, 50–51; Roger C. Anderson, "The Historic Role of Fire in the North American Grassland," in Scott L. Collins and Linda L. Wallace, eds., *Fire in North American Tallgrass Prairies* (Norman: University of Oklahoma Press, 1990), 8.

24. Savage, *Prairie*, 53–60.

25. See Waldo Wedel, "The Central North American Grassland: Man-Made or Natural," in Angel Palerm et al., *Studies in Human Ecology: A Series of Lectures Given at the Anthropological Society of Washington* (Washington, D.C.: Pan American Union, 1957).

26. Axelrod, "Rise of the Grassland Biome," 186.

27. James S. Clark, Eric C. Grimm, Jason Lynch, and Pietra G. Mueller, "Ef-

fects of Holocene Climate Change on the C4 Grassland/Woodland Boundary in the Northern Plains, USA," *Ecology* 82 (March 2001): 631, 633.

28. Pyne, *Awful Splendour*, 37–38.

29. Kenneth F. Higgins, "Lightning Fires in North Dakota Grasslands and in Pine-Savanna Lands of South Dakota and Montana," *Journal of Range Management* 37 (March 1984): 100–102. For lightning fires, see also W. F. Rannie, "'Awful Splendour': Historical Accounts of Prairie Fire in Southern Manitoba Prior to 1870," *Prairie Forum* 26 (April 1, 2001): 17–45; and J. G. Nelson and R. E. England, "Some Comments on the Causes and Effects of Fire in the Northern Grasslands Area of Canada and the Nearby United States, ca. 1750–1900," *Canadian Geographer* 15 (1971): 295–306.

30. Stephen J. Pyne, *Fire: A Brief History* (Seattle: University of Washington Press, 2001), 5–6.

31. J. S. Rowe, "Lightning Fires in Saskatchewan Grassland," *Canadian Field-Naturalist* 83 (October–December 1969): 318.

32. Pyne, *Awful Splendour*, 33.

33. William M. Denevan, "The Pristine Myth: The Landscape of the Americas in 1492," *Annals of the Association of American Geographers* 82 (September 1992): 372–373.

34. Stephen J. Pyne, *Fire in America: A Cultural History of Wildland and Rural Fire* (Seattle: University of Washington Press, 1982), 81.

35. Henry T. Lewis and M. Kat Anderson, "Introduction," in Omer C. Stewart, *Forgotten Fires: Native Americans and the Transient Wilderness* (Norman: University of Oklahoma Press, 2002), 4–5, 8.

36. Thomas R. Vale, ed., *Fire, Native Peoples, and the Natural Land* (Washington, D.C.: Island Press, 2002), 296. Vale's edited volume on the American West does not include a chapter on the Great Plains, but the editor noted in his remarks that in his opinion, conclusions about the other parts of the West could be applied to the Plains as well. Another environmental historian who questioned the role of Indian fires is Donald Worster in *Dust Bowl: The Southern Plains in the 1930s* (New York: Oxford University Press, 1979), 77.

37. Pyne, *Fire in America*, 81–82; see also Theodore Binnema, *Common & Contested Ground: A Human and Environmental History of the Northwestern Plains* (Norman: University of Oklahoma Press, 2001), 33–34.

38. Higgins, "Interpretation and Compendium," 7. See also Omer Stewart, "Why the Great Plains Are Treeless," *Colorado Quarterly* 2 (Summer 1953): 40–50; and Henry A. Wright and Arthur W. Bailey, *Fire Ecology: United States and Southern Canada* (New York: John Wiley & Sons, 1982), 80–137.

39. Pyne, *Fire: A Brief History*, 59–60.

40. University of Virginia, Geospatial & Statistical Data Center, Historical Census Browser, http://fisher.lib.virginia.edu.

41. Cunfer, *On the Great Plains*, 8.

42. Richard J. Vogl, "Effects of Fire on Grasslands," in T. T. Kozlowski and C. E. Ahlgren, eds., *Fire and Ecosystems* (New York: Academic Press, 1974), 142.

43. Dick Rice, interview by Frank Benede, June 2, 1973, Oklahoma Oral History Collection, Oklahoma State Historical Society, Oklahoma City, Oklahoma.

44. Charles E. Bessey, "Are the Trees Advancing or Retreating upon the Nebraska Plains?" *Science* 10 (November 24, 1899): 769.

45. John M. Briggs, Alan K. Knapp, and Brent L. Brock, "Expansion of Woody Plants in Tallgrass Prairie: A Fifteen-Year Study of Fire and Fire-Grazing Interactions," *American Midland Naturalist* 147 (April 2002): 287.

46. Jana L. Heisler, John M. Briggs, and Alan K. Knapp, "Long-Term Patterns of Shrub Expansion in a C4 Dominated Grassland: Fire Frequency and the Dynamics of Shrub Cover and Abundance," *American Journal of Botany* 90 (2003): 423.

47. Savage, *Prairie*, 85.

48. Walter Prescott Webb, *The Great Plains* (reprint, Lincoln: University of Nebraska Press, 1981), 17–18.

49. *Globe-Republican* (Dodge City, Kansas), July 7, 1893.

50. Pyne, *Awful Splendour*, 40.

51. Brian Allen Drake, "Waving 'A Bough of Challenge': Forestry on the Kansas Grasslands, 1868–1915," *Great Plains Quarterly* 23 (Winter 2003): 21.

52. Daniel S. Licht, *Ecology and Economics of the Great Plains* (Lincoln: University of Nebraska Press, 1997), 4. Licht is quoted by Drake, "Waving 'A Bough of Challenge,'" 21.

53. P. V. Wells, "Scarp Woodlands, Transported Grassland Soils, and Concept of Grassland Climate in the Great Plains Region," *Science* 148 (April 9, 1965): 247–249. Anderson, in "The Historic Role of Fire in the North American Grassland," 17, argued that fire suppression, combined with overgrazing by cattle, caused an expansion of trees and shrubs.

54. Anderson, "The Historic Role of Fire in the North American Grassland," 9.

55. R. L. Hensel, "Recent Studies on the Effect of Burning on Grassland Vegetation," *Ecology* 4 (April 1923): 187.

56. David J. Gibson and Lloyd C. Hulbert, "Effects of Fire, Topography and Year-to-Year Climatic Variation on Species Composition in Tallgrass Prairie," *Vegetatio* 72 (1987): 182.

57. Elliott West, *The Contested Plains: Indians, Goldseekers, and the Rush to Colorado* (Lawrence: University Press of Kansas, 1998), 52; Webb, *The Great Plains*, 32.

58. Webb, *The Great Plains*, 32.

59. William D. Hoyt, Jr., "Rosser's Journal, Northern Pacific Railroad Survey, September 1871," *North Dakota Historical Quarterly* 10 (January 1943): 49–50.

Chapter Two: "Putting Out Fire"

1. Garrick Mallery, "Picture-Writing of the American Indians," *Tenth Annual Report of the Bureau of Ethnology* (Washington D.C.: Government Printing Office, 1889), 304–305; Edith Eudora Kohl, *Land of the Burnt Thigh: A Lively Story of Women Homesteaders on the South Dakota Frontier* (St. Paul: Minnesota Historical Society Press, 1986), 238–239. The story of the fire (originally published in 1938), Kohl wrote, "was told me by a famous interpreter who had heard the tale many times from his grandfather." These two accounts vary slightly. Mallery places the fire in the winter of 1762–1763, based on a winter count, and describes more elaborate destruction. The story Kohl heard places the fire "three seasons after the big flood of 1812." See also J. L. Humfreville, *Twenty Years Among Our Hostile Indians*, 2nd ed. (New York: Hunter and Company, 1903), 160. Humfreville is quoted by Conrad Taylor Moore, "Man and Fire in the Central North American Grassland, 1535–1890: A Documentary Historical Geography" (Ph.D. diss., University of California–Los Angeles, 1972), 45. Moore's dissertation led me to numerous accounts of prairie fire from the presettlement era.

2. Paul Wilhelm, Duke of Wurttemberg, "First Journey to North America in the Years 1822 to 1824," trans. by Wm. G. Bek, *South Dakota Historical Collection* 19 (1938): 426–427.

3. Stephen J. Pyne, *Fire in America: A Cultural History of Wildland and Rural Fire* (Seattle: University of Washington Press, 1982), 85, 79–81.

4. James E. Sherow, *The Grasslands of the United States: An Environmental History* (Santa Barbara, Calif.: ABC-CLIO, 2007), 14; Pyne, *Fire in America*, 36.

5. Henry Y. Hind, *Narrative of the Canadian Red River Exploring Expedition of 1857 and the Assinniboine and Saskatchewan Exploring Expedition of 1858*, vol. 1 (New York: Greenwood Press, 1969), 336–337. Hind is quoted extensively by Kenneth F. Higgins, "Interpretation and Compendium of Historical Fire Accounts in the Northern Great Plains," Resource Publication 161 (Washington D.C.: U.S. Department of the Interior, Fish and Wildlife Service, 1986), 22, 24. Higgins's compendium led me to many accounts of prairie fire.

6. Matthew Boyd, "Identification of Anthropogenic Burning in the Paleoecological Record of the Northern Prairies: A New Approach," *Annals of the Association of American Geographers* 92 (2002): 471–472.

7. Higgins, "Interpretation and Compendium," 7; Pyne, *Fire in America*, 85.

8. Henry T. Lewis, "An Anthropological Critique," in Omer C. Stewart, ed., *Forgotten Fires: Native Americans and the Transient Wilderness* (Norman: University of Oklahoma Press, 2002), 32.

9. Higgins, "Interpretation and Compendium," 1; Pyne, *Fire in America*, 79.

10. Moore, "Man and Fire," 4, 8, 49, 65, 67, 93, 111–112.

11. Weather Records for Kansas, Fort Leavenworth, Meteorological Register, T907 R176, National Archives, Washington D.C.

12. Pyne, *Fire in America*, 76, 78, 81; Lewis, "Anthropological Critique," 28.

13. Pyne, *Fire in America*, 71; Higgins, "Interpretation and Compendium," 7; Lewis, "Anthropological Critique," 33.

14. Pyne, *Fire in America*, 72. See also Gregory Thomas, "Fire and the Fur Trade," *The Beaver* (Autumn 1977): 34–35; and Theodore Binnema, *Common & Contested Ground: A Human and Environmental History of the Northwestern Plains* (Norman: University of Oklahoma Press, 2001), 119.

15. Pyne, *Fire in America*, 75–76. See also William Cronon, *Changes in the Land: Indians, Colonists, and the Ecology of New England* (New York: Hill and Wang, 1983), 30.

16. Quoted by Lewis, "Anthropological Critique," 33.

17. Stewart, *Forgotten Fires*, 68, 114. Other scholars, such as Pyne, though in general agreement with Stewart, are slightly more moderate in their opinions about fire's influence on the drier High Plains. Pyne believed the short-grass Plains to be more influenced by climate alone, with his focus on the dominance of fire extending primarily to the prairies east of the 100th meridian. See Pyne, *Fire in America*, 84.

18. Moore, "Fire and Man," 59.

19. Elliott West, *The Contested Plains: Indians, Goldseekers, and the Rush to Colorado* (Lawrence: University Press of Kansas, 1998), 67.

20. Higgins, "Interpretation and Compendium," 8; Pyne, *Fire in America*, 78–79, 85.

21. Pyne, *Fire in America*, 79.

22. Moore, "Man and Fire," 112.

23. Ibid., 115.

24. Charles Augustus Murray, *Travels in North America During the Years 1834, 1835 & 1836*, vol. 2 (London: R. Bentley, 1839), 126–127. Murray is quoted by Higgins, "Interpretation and Compendium," 19.

25. William D. Hoyt, Jr., "Rosser's Journal, Northern Pacific Railroad Survey, September 1871," *North Dakota Historical Quarterly* 10 (January 1943): 47–51.

26. Richard Irving Dodge, *Our Wild Indians: Thirty-Three Years' Personal Experience Among the Red Men of the Great West* (Hartford: A. D. Worthington and Company, 1882), 432.

27. Mary McDougall Gordon, ed., *Through Indian Country to California: John P. Sherburne's Diary of the Whipple Expedition, 1853–1854* (Stanford, Calif.: Stanford University Press, 1988), 74.

28. See W. H. Keating, *Narrative of an Expedition to the Source of St. Peter's River*, vol. 2 (London: George B. Whittaker, 1825), 36. Keating is quoted by Moore, "Man and Fire," 12.

29. Walter Prescott Webb, *The Great Plains* (reprint, Lincoln: University of Nebraska Press, 1981), 78–80.

30. Louis Hennepin, *A New Discovery of a Vast Country in America* (London, 1698; reprint, Chicago: A. C. McClurg & Co., 1903), 248. Hennepin is quoted by Moore, "Man and Fire," 13.

31. Annie Heloise Abel, ed., *Tabeau's Narrative of Loisel's Expedition to the Upper Missouri* (Norman: University of Oklahoma Press, 1939), 187; Alexander Ross, *The Red River Settlement: Its Rise, Progress, and Present State* (Minneapolis, Minn.: Ross and Haines, 1957), 269. Both Tabeau and Ross are quoted by Moore, "Man and Fire," 14.

32. J. F. McDermott, ed., *Tixier's Travels on the Osage Prairies* (Norman: University of Oklahoma Press, 1940), 236; Moore, "Man and Fire," 70–71.

33. Moore, "Man and Fire," 72–73. Moore quotes D. J. Onate, "True Account of the Expedition Toward the East, 1601," in *Spanish Exploration in the Southwest, 1542–1706* (New York: Barnes and Noble, 1946), 259; and P. G. Lowe, *Five Years a Dragoon ('49 to '54) and Other Adventures on the Plains* (Kansas City, Mo.: The Franklin Hudson Publishing Company, 1906), 139–140.

34. Moore, "Man and Fire," 26.

35. Edwin James, *An Account of an Expedition from Pittsburgh to the Rocky Mountains, Performed in the Years 1819, 1820; under the Command of Major Stephen Long*, vol. 15 (Cleveland, Ohio: Arthur H. Clark Co., 1905), 38–39. James is quoted by Moore, "Man and Fire," 16–17.

36. Moore, "Man and Fire," 51–52.

37. John G. Bourke Diaries, vol. 25, Center for Southwest Research, Zimmerman Library, University of New Mexico, Albuquerque, N.M., 12–13.

38. Moore, "Man and Fire," 52.

39. Eugene Bandel, *Frontier Life in the Army, 1854–1861* (Glendale, Calif.: Arthur H. Clark Co., 1932), 91. Bandel is quoted by Higgins, "Interpretation and Compendium," 22; and by Moore, "Man and Fire," 18–19.

40. Moore, "Man and Fire," 19.

41. Eugene F. Ware, *The Indian War of 1864* (Lincoln: University of Nebraska Press, 1994), 351–357; Minnie Calhoun Splinter, "Calhoun Chronicles," unpublished manuscript, box 1, 184–185, Minnie Calhoun Manuscript Collection no. 37, Nebraska State Historical Society, Lincoln, Neb.

42. Christian Isely letter, October 24, 1864, Wichita State University Special Collections, Isely Family Letters, MS 88-31, Wichita State University, Wichita, Kans. The Isely letter is quoted by Whit Edwards, *"The Prairie Was on Fire": Eyewitness Accounts of the Civil War in the Indian Territory* (Oklahoma City: Oklahoma Historical Society, 2001), 127.

43. Edwards, *"The Prairie Was on Fire,"* 3–5. Captain Robert Young of Company K, 1st Regiment, Choctaw and Chickasaw Cavalry, also noted the confusion, and perhaps elevated panic, caused by prairie fire during another battle. "The prairie was on fire on my right," Young wrote, "and as we advanced to

the attack I could see very distinctly the enemy passing the fire." Young at first believed that the enemy numbered 200 or 300 troops, "but they were 300 yards away and the prairie was burning very rapidly, and I may have taken the motion of the grass for men." Young is quoted by ibid., 4.

44. James C. Bates, *A Texas Cavalry Officer's Civil War: The Diary and Letters of James C. Bates*, ed. by Richard Lowe (Baton Rouge: Louisiana State University Press, 1999), 27–33; George L. Griscom, *Fighting with Ross' Texas Cavalry Brigade: The Diary of George L. Griscom, Adjutant, Ninth Texas Cavalry Regiment*, ed. by Homer L. Kerr (Hillsboro, Tex.: Hill Junior College Press, 1976), 5–6. Both Bates and Griscom are quoted by Edwards, *"The Prairie Was on Fire,"* 4–5.

45. P. R. Trobriand, *Military Life in Dakota*, trans. and ed. by L. M. Kane (St. Paul, Minn.: The Alvord Memorial Commission, 1951), 51–52. Trobriand is quoted by Higgins, "Interpretation and Compendium," 29. See also Edwin Thompson Denig, *Five Indian Tribes of the Upper Missouri*, ed. by J. E. Ewers (Norman: University of Oklahoma Press, 1961), 107–108. Denig argued that the Indians did not hunt with fire at all, stating, "Firing the prairie is not a custom resorted to by the Indians to facilitate hunting, as it generally supposed. Nothing they desire less and their laws to prevent it are severe. . . . It effectually destroys their hunting by driving away all game and renders the country unfit for pasturage during the winter, especially if burnt late fall. These fires mostly originate in the carelessness of hunters, travelers, or from the petty malice of individuals. Occasionally it is done by passing war parties." Many witnesses of Native use of fire in the hunt, however, dispute Denig's claims.

46. Tom McHugh and Victoria Hobson, *The Time of the Buffalo* (Lincoln: University of Nebraska Press, 1972), 71.

47. Fanny Bandelier, *The Journey of Alvar Nuñez Cabeza de Vaca* (Chicago: The Rio Grande Press, 1964), 92–93. Cabeza de Vaca is quoted by Moore, "Man and Fire," 98. Other writers who cite the fire-surround method include P. F. X. Charlevoix, *Journal of a Voyage to North America*, vol. 1 (Chicago: The Caxton Club, 1923), 188–189; N. Perrot, "Memoir on the Manners, Customs, and Religion of the Savages of North America," in *The Indian Tribes of the Upper Mississippi Valley and Region of the Great Lakes*, vol. 1 (Cleveland, Ohio: Arthur H. Clark Co., 1911), 121–126; and J. Carver, *Travels Through the Interior Part of North America in the Years 1766, 1767, 1768* (Minneapolis, Minn.: Ross and Haines, 1956), 287–288. See also Moore, "Man and Fire," 20–21.

48. Moore, "Man and Fire," 20–21. See also McHugh, *The Time of the Buffalo*, 69.

49. Elliot Coues, *New Light on the Early History of the Greater Northwest: The Manuscript Journals of Alexander Henry*, vol. 2 (New York: Francis P. Harper, 1897), 519. Henry is quoted by Moore, "Man and Fire," 22.

50. Moore, "Man and Fire," 55–56. Moore is quoting Prinz von Maximilian

Wied, *Travels in the Interior of North America*, vol. 23 (Cleveland, Ohio: Arthur H. Clark Co., 1906), 115.

51. Moore, "Man and Fire," 22.

52. Reuben G. Thwaites, ed., *Original Journals of the Lewis and Clark Expedition, 1804–1806*, vol. 1 (New York: Arno Press, 1969), 269. See also A. B. Gray, *Survey of a Route on the 32nd Parallel for the Texas Western Railroad, 1854* (Los Angeles, Calif.: Westernlore Press, 1963), 18; H. B. Mollhausen, *Diary of a Journey from the Mississippi to the Pacific . . .* , vol. 1 (London: Longmans, Brown, Green, Longmans & Roberts, 1858), 107. Clark, Gray, and Mollhausen are quoted by Moore, "Man and Fire," 24, 75, 98.

53. Hind, *Narrative of the Canadian Red River Exploring Expedition*, 336–337. Hind is quoted by Higgins, "Interpretation and Compendium," 23–24; and Moore, "Man and Fire," 28.

54. Binnema, *Common & Contested Ground*, 39.

55. Ibid., 87–89; Pekka Hämäläinen, "The Rise and Fall of Plains Indian Horse Cultures," *Journal of American History* 90 (December 2003): 834.

56. Hämäläinen, "The Rise and Fall of Plains Indian Horse Cultures," 837, 847.

57. Higgins, "Interpretation and Compendium," 8.

58. Hämäläinen, "The Rise and Fall of Plains Indian Horse Cultures," 841.

59. Andrew C. Isenberg, *The Destruction of the Bison* (Cambridge: Cambridge University Press, 2000), 33, 39, 70–72 (see chapters 2 and 3 for an explanation of the shift to nomadism); Elliott West, *The Way to the West: Essays on the Central Plains* (Albuquerque: University of New Mexico Press, 1995), 53, 74, 78–79, 82; and West, *The Contested Plains*, 89. See also James E. Sherow, "Workings of the Geodialectic: High Plains Indians and Their Horses in the Region of the Arkansas River Valley, 1800–1870," *Environmental History Review* 16 (Summer 1992): 61–84.

60. Hämäläinen, "The Rise and Fall of Plains Indian Horse Cultures," 845, 847–848.

61. Moore, "Man and Fire," 67–68.

62. Hämäläinen, "The Rise and Fall of Plains Indian Horse Cultures," 848.

63. Bourke Diaries, vol. 25, 12–13.

64. Moore, "Man and Fire," 28.

65. Ibid., 27, 54.

66. Ibid., 76, 99.

67. Jim Hoy, "To Start a Fire," *Kansas School Naturalist* 39 (March 1993): 7–10.

68. H. A. Boller, *Among the Indians: Four Years on the Upper Missouri, 1858–1862* (Lincoln: University of Nebraska Press, 1972), 307–308.

69. Fanny Kelly, *Narrative of My Captivity Among the Sioux Indians*, ed. by Clark and Mary Lee Spence (New York: Konecky & Konecky, 1990), 153–154.

70. Ware, *The Indian War of 1864*, 373.

Chapter Three: "Master of the Prairie"

1. Mary McDougall Gordon, ed., *Through Indian Country to California: John P. Sherburne's Diary of the Whipple Expedition, 1853–1854* (Stanford, Calif.: Stanford University Press, 1988), 63.

2. Ibid.

3. Ibid., 11, 61 (footnote).

4. Grant Foreman, ed., *A Pathfinder in the Southwest: The Itinerary of Lieutenant A. W. Whipple During His Explorations for a Railway Route from Fort Smith to Los Angeles in the Years 1853 & 1854* (Norman: University of Oklahoma Press, 1941), 62.

5. Ibid.

6. Ibid., 62 (footnote). The editor quotes from Mollhausen's diary: H. B. Mollhausen, *Diary of a Journey from the Mississippi to the Pacific*, vol. 1 (London: Longmans, Brown, Green, Longmans & Roberts, 1858), 109. See also Conrad Taylor Moore, "Man and Fire in the Central North American Grassland, 1535–1890: A Documentary Historical Geography" (Ph.D. diss., University of California–Los Angeles, 1972), 75, 87.

7. William H. Goetzmann, *Exploration and Empire* (New York: Alfred A. Knopf, 1966), xiii.

8. Ibid., xi.

9. Henry Y. Hind, *Narrative of the Canadian Red River Exploring Expedition of 1857 and the Assinniboine and Saskatchewan Exploring Expedition of 1858*, vol. 1 (New York: Greenwood Press, 1969), 292. Hind is quoted by Kenneth F. Higgins, "Interpretation and Compendium of Historical Fire Accounts in the Northern Great Plains," Resource Publication 161 (Washington D.C.: U.S. Department of the Interior, Fish and Wildlife Service, 1986), 22.

10. Comte de Trobriand (Philippe Regis Denis de Keredern de Trobriand), *Army Life in Dakota*, ed. by Milo Milton Quaife, trans. by George Francis Will (Chicago: The Lakeside Press, 1941), 339–340.

11. Don Juan de Oñate, "True Account of the Expedition Toward the East, 1601," in *Spanish Exploration in the Southwest, 1542–1706* (New York: Barnes and Noble, 1946), 259. Oñate is quoted by Moore, "Man and Fire," 72.

12. David Thompson, *David Thompson's Narrative of His Explorations in Western America* (Toronto: The Champlain Society, 1916), 248. Thompson is quoted by Higgins, "Interpretation and Compendium," 10–11.

13. Meriwether Lewis, *The Lewis and Clark Expedition* (Philadelphia: J. B. Lippincott Co., 1961), 26, 41, 60, 66, 70, 99, 106, 146, 152, 272–273, 743, 753–754, 876. Lewis is quoted by Higgins, "Interpretation and Compendium," 12–13.

14. John T. Irving, Jr., *Indian Sketches Taken During an Expedition to the Pawnee Tribes*, ed. by John McDermott (Norman: University of Oklahoma Press, 1955), 221–223. Irving is quoted by Higgins, "Interpretation and Compendium," 17.

15. Stella M. Drumm, ed., *Down the Santa Fe Trail and into Mexico: The Diary of Susan Shelby Magoffin, 1846–1847* (New Haven, Conn.: Yale University Press, 1926), 197; Josiah Gregg, *Commerce of the Prairies*, ed. by Max L. Moorhead (reprint, Norman: University of Oklahoma Press, 1954), 239.

16. Randolph B. Marcy, *The Prairie Traveler: The Bestselling Classic Handbook for America's Pioneers* (reprint, New York: Perigee Books, 1994), 137–138, 140.

17. Weather Records for Kansas, Fort Leavenworth, November 1848, Meteorological Register, T907 R176, National Archives, Washington, D.C.

18. Ibid., October 1851–March 1852.

19. Ibid., Fort Riley, Kansas Territory, November 1853–February 1866. Quotation from March 2, 1864, entry.

20. S. N. Carvalho, *Incidents of Travel and Adventure in the Far West; with Col. Fremont's Last Expedition Across the Rocky Mountains . . .* (New York: Derby & Jackson, 1859), 60.

21. George M. Grant, *Ocean to Ocean: Sanford Fleming's Expedition Through Canada in 1872* (London: S. Low, Marston, Low & Searle, 1873), 114. Grant is quoted by Moore, "Man and Fire," 32.

22. See, for example, Thomas J. Farnham, *Travels in the Great Western Prairies* (New York: Greeley & McElrath, 1843), 62. Farnham is quoted by Moore, "Man and Fire," 78.

23. Eugene F. Ware, *The Indian War of 1864* (Lincoln: University of Nebraska Press, 1994), 43. Ware's account was originally published in 1911 by Crane & Co.

24. Anonymous, *Travels from Ocean to Ocean, from the Lakes to the Gulf*, 4th ed. (Harrisburg, Penn.: Amos H. Gottschall, 1894), 82–83.

25. Richard Irving Dodge, *The Plains of the Great West and Their Inhabitants* (New York: G. P. Putnam's Sons, 1877), 78–79.

26. Oliver Clarkson McNary to "Pa," March 20, 1880[?], Camp Russell, Indian Territory, Oliver Clarkson McNary letters, MS 3128, Newberry Library, Chicago, Ill.

27. Elliot Coues, ed., *The Manuscript Journals of Alexander Henry and of David Thompson*, vol. 1 (New York: Francis P. Harper, 1897), 158–159.

28. McNary to "Pa," March 20, 1880[?].

29. Herman Lueg, "Across the Plains in '67: The Diary of a Pioneer," unpublished manuscript, SC 1166, North Dakota Institute for Regional Studies, North Dakota State University, Fargo, N.D., 18, 21.

30. Frank Collinson, "Jack Bickerdyke—Buffalo Hunter and Scout," unpublished manuscript, Panhandle Plains Historical Museum Research Center, Canyon, Tex., 3.

31. Irving, *Indian Sketches*, 53–54. Irving is quoted by Moore, "Man and Fire," 22. See also I. M. Spry, ed., *The Papers of the Palliser Expedition, 1857–1860* (Toronto: The Champlain Society, 1968), 157. Palliser is quoted by Higgins, "Interpretation and Compendium," 26–27.

32. John T. Kerr, "Diary Concerning the Colorado Gold Rush," November 3–4, 1859, Box 11, Folder 1, Western History Collections, University of Oklahoma, Norman, Okla.

33. J. Williams, "Narrative of a Trip from the State of Indiana to the Oregon Territory, in the Years 1841–42," *To the Rockies and Oregon, 1839–1842* (Glendale, Calif.: Arthur H. Clark Co., 1955), 281. Williams is quoted by Moore, "Man and Fire," 91. See also Howard Stansbury, *Exploration and Survey of the Valley of the Great Salt Lake of Utah, Including a Reconnaissance of a New Route Through the Rocky Mountains* (Philadelphia, Pa.: Lippincott, Grambo and Company, 1852), 32. Stansbury is cited by Moore, "Man and Fire," 36, 46.

34. Robert H. Becker, ed., *Thomas Christy's Road Across the Plains* (Denver, Colo.: Old West Publishing Company, 1969), May 5, 1850, entry.

35. Thompson, *David Thompson's Narrative*, March 11, 1798, 248. Thompson is quoted by Higgins, "Interpretation and Compendium," 10–11. For other writings on the absence of trees and the connection to fire, see E. Domenech, *Seven Years' Residence in the Great American Deserts of North America*, vol. 1 (London: Longman, 1860), 288. Domenech is quoted by Moore, "Man and Fire," 25.

36. H. M. Brackenridge, *Journal of a Voyage up the River Missouri; Performed in Eighteen Hundred Eleven*, in *Early Western Travels*, vol. 6, ed. by R. G. Thwaites (Glendale, Calif.: Arthur H. Clark Co., 1966), 52–53. Brackenridge is quoted by Higgins, "Interpretation and Compendium," 14. See also William H. Keating, *Narrative of an Expedition to the Source of St. Peter's River . . . under the Command of Stephen H. Long*, vol. 2 (Philadelphia, Pa.: H. C. Care & I. Lea, 1824), 40.

37. Gregg, *Commerce of the Prairies*, 240.

38. Gregory Thomas, "Fire and the Fur Trade: The Saskatchewan District, 1790–1840," *The Beaver* (Autumn 1977): 34; William H. Kilgore, *The Kilgore Journal of an Overland Journey to California in the Year 1850* (New York: Hastings House, 1949), 19.

39. Siegmund Rothhammer diary, Tuesday 10th [July 1863], Siegmund Rothhammer Papers, folder 5204B, Collection H92-34, South Dakota State Historical Society, Pierre, S.D., 11–12.

40. Rufus B. Sage, *Rufus B. Sage: His Letters and Papers, 1836–1847*, vol. 4 (Glendale, Calif.: Arthur H. Clark Co., 1956), 161.

41. Erastus F. Beadle, *Ham, Eggs & Corn Cake: A Nebraska Territory Diary* (Lincoln: University of Nebraska Press, 2001), 23–24. With such enthusiasm, it is not surprising that when he returned to New York in 1858, Erastus Beadle became the publisher of Beadle's Dime Novels. See Albert Johannsen, *The House of Beadle and Adams and Its Dime and Nickel Novels: The Story of a Vanished Literature* (Norman: University of Oklahoma Press, 1950).

42. Frederick Law Olmsted, *A Journey Through Texas; or, A Saddle-Trip on the Southwestern Frontier; with a Statistical Appendix* (New York: Dix, Edwards & Co., 1857), 215–216.

43. Ibid., 216–220.

44. Ibid, 220–221.

45. Trobriand, *Army Life in Dakota*, 342.

Chapter Four: "One First Grand Cause"

1. George M. Munger Vertical File, biographical summary, Kansas State University Special Collections, Manhattan, Kans.; Helen Bradford, "The Man Who Planted Trees," George M. Munger Vertical File, Kansas State University Special Collections, Manhattan, Kans.

2. George M. Munger Journals Collection, Box 1, April 5, 1887 entry, Kansas State University Special Collections, Manhattan, Kans.; ibid., March 17, 1890.

3. *Kanzas News* (Emporia), March 6, 1858; October 9, 1858.

4. *Colorado Springs Gazette*, October 23, 1875.

5. *Rocky Mountain News* (Denver, Colo.), June 30, 1874.

6. *Walnut Valley Times* (El Dorado, Kans.), January 13, 1871; March 3, 1871.

7. Ann Elizabeth Wright Anderson interview, Lilla Day Monroe Collection of Pioneer Stories, Collection 163, Manuscripts Division, Kansas State Historical Society (hereafter KSHS), Topeka, Kans.; Mrs. Alzada Baxter interview, ibid.

8. *Emporia News* (Kans.), October 8, 1859; Mrs. Cornelia Bayly interview, Lilla Day Monroe Collection of Pioneer Stories, Collection 163, Manuscripts Division, KSHS, Topeka, Kans.

9. *Walnut Valley Times* (El Dorado, Kans.), November 18, 1870.

10. Henry Inman, compiler, *Buffalo Jones' Forty Years of Adventure: A Volume of Facts Gathered from Experience by Hon. C. J. Jones . . .* (Topeka, Kans.: Crane & Company, 1899), 104; Merton Field, "By Many Trails," unpublished manuscript, North Dakota Institute for Regional Studies, folder 6, North Dakota State University (hereafter NDSU), Fargo, N.D., 71.

11. Jesse Kennedy Snell Collection, Manuscript Division, Collection 80, Box 1, KSHS, Topeka, Kans.

12. *Jamestown Alert* (Dakota Territory), November 25, 1881, quoting the *Vermillion Republican* (Dakota Territory).

13. John L. Finley, "The Effects of Prairie Fires on Vegetation," in *Report of the Kansas State Board of Agriculture* (Topeka: State of Kansas, 1894), 147.

14. "Reminiscences of Byron N. Stone, Sr.," in Byron N. Stone Collection SC 1486, North Dakota Institute for Regional Studies, NDSU, Fargo, N.D.

15. S. N. Carvalho, *Incidents of Travel and Adventure in the Far West* (New York: Derby & Jackson, 1859), 48.

16. George Crossman to T. J. Walker, October 9, 1894[?], George Hampton Crossman Papers, Collection No. 20189, North Dakota State Historical Society, Bismarck, N.D. The letter describes the construction of Fort Ransom and in-

cludes a section on the fire. An account of the Fort Ransom fire and Crossman's description is also in *Fort Ransom Community History: 1878–2003* (Gwinner, N.D.: J&M Companies, n.d.), 15–17. Just after the fire, in October 1867, a letter written by George Crossman was published in the Cleveland, Ohio, *Leader*; it detailed the events of the great prairie fire. The *Philadelphia Inquirer* picked up the story and published it in its October 29, 1867, issue. The Philadelphia version of Crossman's letter is reprinted in *Fort Ransom Community History*, 17.

17. James F. Hoy, ed., "A Window on Flint Hills Folklife, Part II: The Diary of Elisha Mardin," *Kansas History: A Journal of the Central Plains* 14 (Winter 1991–1992): 246, 252. Hoy noted the significance of Mardin's spring burn, and the influence of the Indian burns, in his introduction. See also Jim Hoy, ed., *A Window on Flint Hills Folklife: The Mardin Ranch Diaries 1862–1863* (Emporia, Kans.: Center for Great Plains Studies, 2009). For another story of burning continuity in the Kansas Flint Hills, see an article on the Sauble family's ranch in the *Wichita Eagle* (Kans.), June 21, 2004. The Sauble ranch had been passed from one generation to the next, starting in 1856 and continuing until at least 2004. "The Indians burned the prairie," ranch owner Pat Sauble noted in 2004. "The first ranchers learned from them and burned the prairie, too."

18. *Saguache Chronicle* (Colo.), April 13, 1878, paraphrasing the Evans (Colo.) *Journal*.

19. See James E. Sherow, "Workings of the Geodialectic: High Plains Indians and Their Horses in the Region of the Arkansas River Valley, 1800–1870," *Environmental History Review* 16 (Summer 1992): 61–84.

20. Elliott West, *The Contested Plains: Indians, Goldseekers & The Rush to Colorado* (Lawrence: University Press of Kansas, 1998), 37–38. West noted that during the wet 400 years between 800 and 1200 A.D., permanent villages flourished along streams and rivers in western Kansas and eastern Colorado.

21. Orland Eittreim Esval, *Prairie Tales: Adventures of Growing up on a Frontier* (Banner Elk, N.C.: Landmark House, 1979), 103.

22. See Dan Flores, "Bison Ecology and Bison Diplomacy: The Southern Plains from 1800 to 1850," *Journal of American History* 78 (September 1991): 465–485; West, *The Contested Plains*; Andrew C. Isenberg, *The Destruction of the Bison: An Environmental History, 1750–1920* (Cambridge: Cambridge University Press, 2000).

23. Flores, "Bison Ecology and Bison Diplomacy," 465, 471, 478–485.

24. Geoff Cunfer, *On the Great Plains: Agriculture and Environment* (College Station: Texas A&M Press, 2005), 48–49.

25. West, *The Contested Plains*, 90.

26. Flores, "Bison Ecology and Bison Diplomacy," 466.

27. Cunfer, *On the Great Plains*, 49.

28. Ibid., 50.

29. Dr. Robert Maxwell, interviewed March 25, 1940, by Maude Swanson, Works Progress Administration Interviews, Box 3, Folder 25, Nebraska State Historical Society (hereafter NSHS), Lincoln, Nebr.; Mrs. Nellie Thompson Halverson, interviewed January 3–4, 1940, by Frank A. Kiolbasa, Works Progress Administration Interviews, Box 14, Folder 113, NSHS, Lincoln, Nebr.

30. *Emporia News* (Kans.), November 2, 1861.

31. Theodore Binnema, *Common & Contested Ground: A Human and Environmental History of the Northwestern Plains* (Norman: University Press of Oklahoma, 2001), 33.

32. Ned Horsbuch [signature illegible] to J. E. Hodges, Esq., Secretary, Espuela Co., London, July 15, 1903, Box 4, Folder 6, Espuela Land and Cattle Company Records, Southwest Collection, Texas Tech University (hereafter TTU), Lubbock, Tex.

33. Unknown to J. E. Hodges, Esq., July 20, 1903, Espuela Land and Cattle Company Records, Box 4, Folder 6, Southwest Collection, TTU, Lubbock, Tex.

34. Alan Cheales Diary of a Hunting Trip into the Cherokee Outlet (Strip), November 8 [n.d], Division of Manuscripts Collection, Box 10, Folder 15, Western Collection, University of Oklahoma, Norman, Okla.

35. Howard A. Cox, "The Economic Effects of Prairie Fires on the Cattle Industry," unpublished manuscript, May 25, 1936, Panhandle Plains Historical Museum Research Center, Canyon, Tex.

36. [T. D. Hobart], Ranch Manager, to J. Earle Hodges, Esq., Secretary, Espuela Company, London, July 20, 1903, Espuela Land and Cattle Company Records, Box 4, Folder 1, Southwest Collection, TTU, Lubbock, Tex.

37. Unknown to J. E. Hodges, Secretary, July 20, 1903, Espuela Land and Cattle Company Records, Box 4, Folder 6, Southwest Collection, TTU, Lubbock, Tex.

38. J. Earle Hodges, Secretary, The Espuela Land & Cattle Company Limited, to [ranch manager], February 16, 1906, Espuela Land and Cattle Company Records, Box 4, Folder 2, Southwest Collection, TTU, Lubbock, Tex.

39. C. A. Jones to Messrs. S. M. Swenson & Sons, November 24, 1908, Espuela Land and Cattle Company Records, Box 4, Folder 8, Southwest Collection, TTU, Lubbock, Tex.

40. *Norman Transcript* (Okla.), August 29, 1891; September 5, 1891.

41. *Silverton Standard* (Colo.), September 23, 1893.

42. *Fort Scott Monitor* (Kans.), reprinted in *Walnut Valley Times* (El Dorado, Kans.), October 20, 1871.

43. *Bismarck Tribune* (Dakota), April 15, 1874.

44. Ibid., September 12, 1877.

45. *Smoky Hill and Republican Union* (Junction City, Kans.), February 27, 1862.

46. *Emporia News* (Kans.), March 10, 1860.

47. *Jamestown Alert* (Dakota), October 21, 1879.

48. *Smoky Hill and Republican Union* (Junction City, Kans.), October 17, 1863.

49. *Walnut Valley Times* (El Dorado, Kans.), October 25, 1872.

50. *Emporia News* (Kans.), March 26, 1864; November 10, 1866.

51. *Burr Oak Reveille* (Kans.), April 2, 1880. Clipping can be found in Jewell County Clippings, vol. 1, KSHS, Topeka, Kans., 67.

52. Charles Loomis, interviewed by Martha R. Blaine, November 14, 1967, Oklahoma Oral History Collection, Oklahoma State Historical Society (hereafter OSHS), Oklahoma City, Okla.

53. Rooks County Records Manuscript Collection, March 17, 1893, KSHS, Topeka, Kans. The manuscript is a typed copy of a newspaper article from Stockton, Kans.

54. *Watonga Republican* (Okla.), September 27, 1893. There is a slight chance that the two Tomlinsons survived the fire. The *Watonga Republican* reported that although the two were alive at press time, their deaths were imminent. No further information about the family's fate could be located. Occasionally people burned severely by prairie fires survived their ordeal, even after newspapers reported that there was no hope, but such events were rare. Most severely burned victims died within hours or days of the fire.

55. *Lincoln Register* (Kans.), January 9, 1880. Clipping can be found in Saline County Clippings, vol. 1, KSHS, Topeka, Kans., 37.

56. See West, *The Contested Plains*, 54–55.

57. I. M. Spry, ed., *The Papers of the Palliser Expedition 1857–1860* (Toronto: The Champlain Society, 1968), 157.

58. Inman, *Buffalo Jones' Years of Adventure*, 103, 108.

59. *Walnut Valley Times* (El Dorado, Kans.), October 20, 1871. The *Times* reprinted an article titled "Prairie Fire" that originally appeared in the *Fort Scott Monitor* (Kans.).

60. Ibid.

61. S. S. Judy and Will G. Robinson, "Sanborn County History," *South Dakota Historical Collections* 26 (1952): 31–33.

62. Wayne Fields, "The American Prairies and the Literary Aesthetic," in Joni L. Kinsey, ed., *Plain Pictures: Images of the American Prairie* (Washington D.C.: Smithsonian Institution Press, 1996), vii.

63. George Goff, interviewed by Maude Swanson, August 22, 1940, Box 2, Folder 17, Works Progress Administration Interviews, NSHS, Lincoln, Nebr.

64. Joseph W. Snell, ed., "Roughing It on Her Kansas Claim: The Diary of Abbie Bright, 1870–1871," *Kansas Historical Quarterly* 37 (Autumn 1971): 237.

65. *Emporia News* (Kans.), October 20, 1860.

66. Alex A. Liska to Don Westover, November 30, 1976, Early Nebraska Prairie Fire Accounts Collection, MS No. 18, Folder 26, University of Nebraska Special Collections, Lincoln, Nebr.

67. *Walnut Valley Times* (El Dorado, Kans.), March 4, 1870.

68. In 1907 the Espuela Land and Cattle Company in west Texas brought a case to county court accusing a local farmer of cutting trees on company land. "This gentleman was turned loose on the ground that the alleged tree was not a tree but merely a mesquite bush." Apparently on the open prairie some residents were more inclusive in identifying trees than others. "There is quite a difference of opinion as to what constitutes a tree," an Espuela man concluded. See Harlen H. Johnstone to Hon. J. W. Veale, February 22, 1907, Box 4, Folder 7, Espuela Land and Cattle Company Records, Southwest Collection, TTU, Lubbock, Tex.

69. *Emporia News* (Kans.), March 10, 1860.

70. Raymond J. Pool, "1953: Fifty Years on the Nebraska National Forest," unpublished manuscript, Box 5, Folder 12, Raymond J. Pool Papers, RG No. 12/07/12, University of Nebraska Special Collections, Lincoln, Nebr., 29–30.

71. *Walnut Valley Times* (El Dorado, Kans.), March 28, 1873.

72. *Kanzas News* (Emporia, Kans.), March 6, 1858.

73. *Emporia News* (Kans.), January 14, 1860.

74. George M. Munger Journals Collection, Box 1, April 1, 1886, entry, Kansas State University Special Collections, Manhattan, Kans.

75. *Aberdeen News* (Dakota Territory), April 24, 1885.

76. First, Second, and Third Annual Reports of the U.S. Geological Survey of the Territories for the Years 1867, 1868, and 1869, Under the Department of the Interior (Washington, D.C.: Government Printing Office, 1873), 14–15; Henry Nash Smith, "Rain Follows the Plow: The Notion of Increased Rainfall for the Great Plains, 1844–1880," *Huntington Library Quarterly* 10 (February 1947): 169–193; "The Fear of Prairie Fires," *Denver Field and Farm* (Colo.), reprinted in *Range Ledger* (Hugo, Colo.), September 16, 1905.

77. *Range Ledger* (Hugo, Colo.), September 16, 1905.

78. *Fort Scott Monitor* (Kans.), reprinted in *Walnut Valley Times* (El Dorado, Kans.), October 20, 1871.

79. Unidentified newspaper, ca. 1910–1913, Trees Clippings, Manuscripts Coll., vol. 1, KSHS, Topeka, Kans.

80. *Fort Scott Monitor* (Kans.), reprinted in *Walnut Valley Times* (El Dorado, Kans.), October 20, 1871.

81. Charles V. Riley, *The Locust Plague in the United States: Being More Particularly a Treatise on the Rocky Mountain Locust or So-Called Grasshopper . . .* (Chicago: Rand, McNally & Co., 1877), 209–210. For a fascinating history of Riley and the Rocky Mountain locust, see Jeffrey A. Lockwood, *Locust: The Devastating Rise and Mysterious Disappearance of the Insect That Shaped the American Frontier* (New York: Basic Books, 2004). Lockwood noted Riley's opinions about prairie fire on pages 112–113.

82. *Kansas Farmer*, "Effects of Prairie Fires," September 23, 1874, quoted by Riley, *The Locust Plague in the United States*, 210.

83. Riley, *The Locust Plague*, 210–212.

84. Emily Combes to "Dearest," May 5, 1871, Emily Isabelle Combes Collection, Spenser Library Kansas Collection, University of Kansas, Lawrence, Kans.

85. *Burrton Telephone* (Kans.), March 22, 1879. The clipping can be found in Harvey County Clippings, vol. 1, KSHS, Topeka, Kans., 22–23.

86. Eliza M. Crawford to Robbie (Robert Crawford), May 3, 1884, Box 1, Folder 12, Robert D. Crawford Papers, MSS 290, North Dakota Institute for Regional Studies, NDSU, Fargo, N.D.

87. *Kiowa Herald* (Kans.), October 7, 1886.

88. Nathanial M. Ayers, *Building a New Empire* (New York: Broadway Publishing Co., 1910), 141.

89. *Walnut Valley Times* (El Dorado, Kans.), October 20, 1871.

90. Ibid.

91. *The Journals, Detailed Reports, and Observations Relative to the Exploration by Captain Palliser of That Portion of British North America* . . . (London: George E. Eyre and William Spottiswoode, 1863), 89. Palliser's work is quoted by Conrad Taylor Moore, "Man and Fire in the Central North American Grasslands 1535–1890: A Documentary Historical Geography," (Ph.D. diss., University of California–Los Angeles, 1972), 13.

92. Edmund C. Bray and Martha Coleman Bray, eds. and trans., *Joseph N. Nicollet on the Plains and Prairies: The Expeditions of 1838–39 with Journals, Letters and Notes on the Dakota Indians* (St. Paul: Minnesota Historical Society Press, 1976), 92.

93. *Walnut Valley Times* (El Dorado, Kans.), October 20, 1871.

94. *Globe-Republican* (Dodge City, Kans.), January 19, 1894.

95. *Emporia News* (Kans.), November 10, 1866; October 29, 1869; *Globe-Republican* (Dodge City, Kans.), October 26, 1899.

96. *Platte Valley Independent* (Nebr.), October 26, 1878.

97. George Starkey, "Prairie Fires," in *Chase County Historical Sketches*, vol. 1 (Chase County, Kans.: Chase County Historical Society, 1940), 120.

98. *Hennessey Clipper* (Oklahoma Territory), April 23, 1896.

99. *Ness County Sentinel* (Kans.), reprinted in *Liberal News* (Kans.), April 20, 1893.

100. *Bismarck Tribune* (Dakota), April 15, 1874.

101. *Range Ledger* (Hugo, Colo.), September 14, 1907. The Lincoln County reward policy began in August 1907 and continued until at least January 1920.

102. "The Wants of Kansas Farmers," *Leavenworth Conservative* (Kans.), reprinted in *Emporia News* (Kans.), September 3, 1864.

103. The Kansas law was quoted in *Yankton Press* (Dakota), April 17, 1872.

104. *Jamestown Weekly Alert* (Dakota), August 19, 1886.

105. *Edmond Sun-Democrat* (Oklahoma Territory), March 13, 1896.

106. Margaret L. Barns, interview by Joe L. Todd, July 20, 1988, Tonkawa, Okla., Oklahoma Oral History Collection, OSHS, Oklahoma City, Okla.

107. *Colorado Transcript* (Golden, Colo.), January 20, 1875.

108. Wm. H. Greenwood, General Manager, Denver & Rio Grand R'y, to Wm. S. Jackson, Secretary and Treasurer, Denver & Rio Grand R'y, November 13, 1872. The letter was printed in *Out West* (Colorado Springs, Colo.), November 14, 1872.

109. Claire Strom, *Profiting from the Plains: The Great Northern Railway and Corporate Development of the American West* (Seattle: University of Washington Press, 2003), 8–11; Craig Miner, *Kansas: The History of the Sunflower State, 1854–2000* (Lawrence: University Press of Kansas, 2002), 130.

110. Frank Zimmerman, interviewed by J. M. Winchester, date unknown, Panhandle Plains Historical Museum Research Center, Canyon, Tex.

111. *Texas Live Stock Journal* (Fort Worth), April 19, 1884.

112. *The Union Pacific Railway Company v. Eli McCollum* No. 61, Court of Appeals of Kansas, Northern Department, Western Division, December 1895.

113. *Kinsley Graphic* (Kans.), March 15, 1895; October 25, 1895.

114. *Globe-Republican* (Dodge City, Kans.), February 6, 1896; February 20, 1896; April 9, 1896.

115. George M. Munger Journals Collection, Box 1, April 7 and 11, 1888, entry, Kansas State University Special Collections, Manhattan, Kans.

116. *Walnut Valley Times* (El Dorado, Kans.), March 19, 1875.

Chapter Five: "Fight Fire When Necessary, Fight Together, and Fight It Out"

1. *Lawton Weekly Enterprise* (Okla.), March 4, 1904.

2. *Durango Democrat* (Colo.), March 4, 1904.

3. *Lawton Weekly Enterprise* (Okla.), March 4, 1904.

4. Ibid., March 11, 1904.

5. Ibid.

6. Ibid., March 4, 1904.

7. *Oklahoman*, March 4, 1904.

8. *Lawton Weekly Enterprise* (Okla.), March 4, 1904.

9. Ibid., March 4, 1904; March 11, 1904.

10. Minnie Calhoun Splinter, "Calhoun Chronicles," Manuscript Coll. No. 37, Box 1, Nebraska State Historical Society (hereafter NSHS), Lincoln, Nebr., 182–183; Mittie Hill, "Early History of the Bar CC Ranch," manuscript, 1936, Panhandle Plains Historical Museum Research Center, Canyon, Tex., 4.

11. Splinter, "Calhoun Chronicles," Box 1, 182–183.

12. Unknown author, "Wheatheart of the Plains, an Early History of Ochiltree County," MS Int. File 1982-31/37, Panhandle Plains Historical Museum Research Center, Canyon, Tex.

13. *Globe-Republican* (Dodge City, Kans.), September 22, 1893.

14. Mary Lou Zimmerman, Clark County Writer's Project, Works Progress Administration Papers, MS 71-1, Box 3, Folder 7, Wichita State University Special Collections, Wichita, Kans.

15. Beatrice Moyer to parents in Indiana, March 1916, reprinted in *Garden City Telegram* (Kans.), January 8, 1969. A clipping is in Haskell County Clippings, vol. 1, Kansas State Historical Society (hereafter KSHS), Topeka, Kans., 75–76.

16. J. O. Rochat to "Brother Charley," April 3, 1879, Rochat Manuscript Collection, KSHS, Topeka, Kans.

17. *Webster Daily Journal* (S.D.), June 19, 1931, Vertical File "Fires," South Dakota State Historical Society (hereafter SDSHS), Pierre, S.D. The clipping tells the story of the April 7, 1898, fire near Webster, South Dakota.

18. Lovenna Barnes, Clara Blanche Staggs, and Margaret May Poteet (sisters), interviewed by Joe L. Todd, October 27, 1982, Oklahoma Oral History Collection, Oklahoma State Historical Society (hereafter OSHS), Oklahoma City, Okla.

19. Marie Torbenson Papers, Manuscript Coll. 599, Folder 1, University of North Dakota Special Collections, Grand Forks, N.D., 2–3.

20. Norton Family Diaries, July 19–21, 1886, and November 3–4, 1886, Manuscript Coll. 1190, KSHS, Topeka, Kans. The November 4, 1886, entry is mistakenly labeled "Oct.," but the context of the surrounding diary entries shows that November is correct.

21. Mrs. R. R. Johnson, interviewed by Maude Swanson, August 15, 1940, Works Progress Administration Interviews, RG 515, Box 2, Folder 22, NSHS, Lincoln, Nebr..

22. Joanna L. Stratton, *Pioneer Women: Voices from the Kansas Frontier* (New York: Simon and Schuster, 1981), 83–84.

23. Cordia Sloan Duke and Joe B. Frantz, *6000 Miles of Fence: Life on the XIT Ranch of Texas* (Austin: University of Texas Press, 1961), 45.

24. John R. Armstrong Papers, November 3, 1906, MS Coll. 1988-138/1, Folder 3, Panhandle Plains Historical Museum Research Center, Canyon, Tex.

25. *Colorado Clipper*, reprinted in *Texas Live Stock Journal* (Fort Worth), October 28, 1882.

26. James W. Byrkit, ed., *Letters from the Southwest: September 20, 1884–March 14, 1885* (Tucson: University of Arizona Press, 1989), 32.

27. J. E. Phelan, Superintendent, Northern Pacific Railroad Company, to J. S. Greene, Secretary/Treasurer, North Dakota Stockgrowers Association, Septem-

ber 4, 1890, John S. Greene Papers, Coll. A 19, Box 1, Folder 1, North Dakota State Historical Society (hereafter NDSHS), Bismarck, N.D.

28. J. E. Phelan, Superintendent, Northern Pacific Railroad Company, to J. S. Greene, Secretary/Treasurer, North Dakota Stockgrowers Association, May 28, 1891, John S. Greene Papers, Coll. A 19, Box 1, Folder "Correspondence, 18 April to 31 December, 1892," NDSHS, Bismarck, N.D.

29. *Globe-Republican* (Dodge City, Kans.), November 24, 1893.

30. *Kinsley Mercury* (Kans.), reprinted in *Globe-Republican* (Dodge City, Kans.), April 9, 1896.

31. *Smoky Hill and Republican Union* (Junction City, Kans.), February 27, 1862.

32. *Anthony Republican and Bulletin* (Kans.), Clippings, May 19, 1938, KSHS, Topeka, Kans., 94.

33. John A. Schoen to Don Westover, December 8, 1976, Early Nebraska Prairie Fire Accounts Coll., MS No. 18, Box 1, Folder 25, University of Nebraska Special Collections, Lincoln, Nebr.

34. Charley Becklam, interviewed by Maude Swanson, November 4, 1941, Works Progress Administration Interviews, RG 515, Box 2, Folder 11, NSHS, Lincoln, Nebr. Oral-history interviews are full of statements like Becklam's. For other examples, see, in the same collection, John Cross, Box 1, Folder 1; and Mrs. Otto Fisher, Box 2, Folder 16.

35. *Denver Field and Farm* (Colo.), April 1, 1893; Enid Bern Collection, "Our Hettinger County Heritage," unpublished manuscript (1973), Small Manuscript Coll. MSS 21000, Microfilm Roll 6, NDSHS, Bismarck, N.D., 160.

36. Orland Eittreim Esval, *Prairie Tales: Adventures of Growing up on a Frontier* (Banner Elk, N.C.: Landmark House, 1979), 100.

37. Stratton, *Pioneer Women*, 84.

38. Wallace Taylor Collection, "Biographical Sketch of an Early Settler," SC 713, North Dakota Institute for Regional Studies, North Dakota State University (hereafter NDSU), Fargo, N.D., 3; Mrs. Jenny Hill, interviewed by Maude Swanson, March 18, 1941, Works Progress Administration Interviews, Box 2, Folder 20, NSHS, Lincoln, Nebr.

39. Mrs. J. H. Pieper, interviewed by Maude Swanson, July 8, 1940, Works Progress Administration Interviews, Box 3, Folder 30, NSHS, Lincoln, Nebraska.

40. *Emporia News* (Kans.), November 8, 1867.

41. Robert D. Crawford to "Dear Cousins Hugh and Malcolm," Robert D. Crawford Papers, MSS 290, Folder 12, Box 1, North Dakota Institute for Regional Studies, NDSU, Fargo, N.D.; Henry Inman, compiler, *Buffalo Jones' Forty Years of Adventure: A Volume of Facts Gathered from Experience by Hon. C. J. Jones* (Topeka, Kans.: Crane & Company, 1899), 105.

42. *Fair Play* (Valley Falls, Kans.), August 18, 1888.

43. Merton Field, "By Many Trails," unpublished manuscript, Merton Field Papers, MSS 28, Box 1, Folder 6, North Dakota Institute for Regional Studies, NDSU, Fargo, N.D., 72; Mrs. A. H. Bergh, "Pioneer Daughters of Dakota," *South Dakota Historical Collections* 33 (1966): 56.

44. Arthur E. Towne, *Old Prairie Days* (Otsego, Mich.: The Otsego Union Press, 1941), 134.

45. David M. Bartholomew, ed., *Pioneer Naturalist on the Plains: The Diary of Elam Bartholomew, 1871 to 1934* (Manhattan, Kans.: Sunflower University Press, 1998), 76–77.

46. C. E. King, interviewed by Maude Swanson, January 2, 1942, Works Progress Administration Interviews, Box 2, Folder 22, NSHS, Lincoln, Nebr.; Mary Bickett, interviewed by Ruby E. Wilson, October 25, 1935, Library of Congress American Memory Project, www.memory.loc.gov.

47. Towne, *Old Prairie Days*, 135.

48. "From 1873 Developments of Sanborn County and Storms, Prairie Fires & Three County Seat Wars," SDSHS, Pierre, S.D., p. 206.

49. Mrs. Frank Blough, interviewed by Maude Swanson, June 3, 1941, Works Progress Administration Interviews, RG 515, Box 2, Folder 12, NSHS, Lincoln, Nebr.

50. Mr. Floyd Gilmer, interviewed by Maude Swanson, August 14, 1940, Works Progress Administration Interviews, RG 515, Box 2, Folder 17, NSHS, Lincoln, Nebr.; S. M. Warner, interviewed by Maude Swanson, February 26, 1941, Works Progress Administration Interviews, RG 515, Box 4, Folder 36, NSHS, Lincoln, Nebr.

51. S. S. Judy and Will G. Robinson, "Sanborn County History," *South Dakota Historical Collections* 26 (1952): 98–99.

52. Elwin E. Rogers, "Almost Scandinavia: Scandinavian Immigrant Experience in Grant County, 1877–1920," *South Dakota Historical Collections* 41 (1982): 296–297; S. M. Warner, interviewed by Maude Swanson, February 26, 1941, Works Progress Administration Interviews, RG 515, Box 4, Folder 36, NSHS, Lincoln, Nebr.

53. Field, "By Many Trails," 73.

54. Isaac B. Hammond, *Reminiscences of Frontier Life* (Portland: self-published, 1904), 26–30.

55. C. A. White, "Prairie Fires," *American Naturalist* 5 (April 1871): 69; Lynus A. Kibbe, "Early Recollections of the Son of a Pioneer Newspaper Man of South Dakota and Dakota Territory," *South Dakota Historical Collections* 25 (1950): 328.

56. White, "Prairie Fires," 69–70; Edith Eudora Kohl, *Land of the Burnt Thigh: A Lively Story of Women Homesteaders on the South Dakota Frontier* (St. Paul: Minnesota Historical Society Press, 1986), 241.

57. Angie Debo, ed., *The Cowman's Southwest: Being the Reminiscences of Oliver Nelson* (Glendale, Calif.: Arthur H. Clark Co., 1953), 175–176.

58. Stephen J. Pyne, *Fire in America: A Cultural History of Wildland and Rural Fire* (Seattle: University of Washington Press, 1982), 92; *Rocky Mountain News* (Denver, Colo.), April 17, 2008.

59. John Cross, interviewed by Frederick W. Kaul, April 1939, Works Progress Administration Interviews, RG 515, Box 1, Folder 1, NSHS, Lincoln, Nebr.

60. Barnes, Staggs, and Poteet interview.

61. Mrs. H. C. Osterhout to Don Westover, December 5, 1976, Early Nebraska Prairie Fire Accounts, MS Coll. 18, Box 1, Folder 15, University of Nebraska Special Collections, Lincoln, Nebr. Osterhout quotes from her father's diary (entries dating from 1898 to 1904) in the letter.

62. *Garden City Telegram* (Kans.), January 8, 1969, quoting a letter by Beatrice Moyer, March 1916. The clipping is found in Haskell County Clippings, vol. 1, KSHS, Topeka, Kans., 75–76.

63. Mr. and Mrs. Frank Ball, interviewed October 23, 1975, by Fred Carpenter, Southwest Collection, Texas Tech University (hereafter TTU), Lubbock, Tex.

64. Unidentified clipping in Early Nebraska Prairie Fire Accounts, MS Coll. 18, Box 1, Folder 27, University of Nebraska Special Collections, Lincoln, Nebr.

65. Eppie Barrier, July 30, 1958, interviewed by Jean Paul, Southwest Collection, TTU, Lubbock, Tex.

66. The town of Albian, Nebraska, for example, was destroyed in 1878. *Colorado Weekly Chieftain*, October 31, 1878; *Kansas City Daily Times*, March 21, 1879, clipping found in Mitchell County Clippings, vol. 1, KSHS, Topeka, Kans., 130–131.

67. *Yankton Weekly Press and Dakotian* (S.D.), November 27, 1873.

68. James Reed, n.d., interviewed by Effie Cowan, Library of Congress American Memory Project, www.memory.loc.gov.

69. *Summit County Journal* (Colo.), March 25, 1916; *Kansas News* (Emporia), November 13, 1858.

70. *Ness County News* (Kans.), November 4, 1893.

71. *Texas Live Stock Journal* (Fort Worth), November 11, 1882.

72. Frances Jacobs Alberts, ed., *Sod House Reminiscences* (Holdrege, Nebr.: Sod House Society, 1972), 162.

73. Venola Lewis Bivans, ed., "The Diary of Luna E. Warner, a Kansas Teenager of the Early 1870s," *Kansas Historical Quarterly* 35 (1969): 431.

74. Wayne Gard, "When Fire Seared the Prairies," *Cattleman* 36 (May 1950): 37; Archibald R. Adamson, *North Platte and Its Associations* (North Platte, Nebr.: The Evening Telegraph, 1910), 132.

75. Mary A. Schmidt, "History of the Seventh-Day Adventist Church at Swan Lake, South Dakota," *South Dakota Historical Collections* 14 (1928): 557.

76. A[be] L. Squires, Delmont, Dakota, to Hollis Skinner, East Fairfield, Vermont, April 1, 1889; letter is in the author's possession.

77. John Hamblin, interviewed by Marvin E. Griffith, February 19, 1940, Works Progress Administration Interviews, Box 2, Folder 19, NSHS, Lincoln,

Nebr.; *Topeka Capital* (Kans.), March 8, 1916, Ford County Clippings, vol. 1, KSHS, Topeka, Kans., 162; *Akron Weekly Pioneer Press* (Colo.), April 14, 1916.

78. Enid Bern Collection, "Our Hettinger County Heritage."

79. Charles Jones, "Incidents of the Pioneer Days in Sumners Township" (1907), Jesse Kennedy Snell Collection, Manuscript Coll. No. 80, Box 1, KSHS, Topeka, Kans.; Thomas M. Goddard Family Letters, April 21, 1889, Coll. H71.3, Folder 3, SDSHS, Pierre, S.D.

80. Emeline Durst, "Some of the Incidents of the Pioneer Days of McPherson Co.," Lilla Day Monroe Collection, Manuscript Coll. No. 163, KSHS, Topeka, Kans.

81. *Empire* (Kans.), March 21, 1879, Cloud County Clippings, vol. 1, KSHS, Manuscript Coll., 88–92.

82. Clara Joyce Hileman, interviewed by Edna B. Pearson, August 7, 1939, Works Progress Administration Interviews, Box 4, Folder 47, NSHS, Lincoln, Nebr.

83. *My Folks Came in a Covered Wagon: A Treasury of Stories Handed down in the Families of Capper's Weekly Readers* (Topeka, Kans.: Capper Publications, 1956), 26; Mrs. Clifford Jencks Letter, March 24, 1910, SDSHS, Pierre, S.D.

84. Donald Easton, "McNary Fire," clipping in "Fires" Vertical File, SDSHS, Pierre, S.D.; C. Kay Cohea, "Pioneer Women," Panhandle Plains Historical Museum Research Center, Canyon, Tex.; Everett Dick, *The Sod-House Frontier: 1854–189:; A Social History of the Northern Plains from the Creation of Kansas & Nebraska to the Admission of the Dakotas* (Lincoln, Nebr.: Johnsen Publishing Company, 1954), 217.

85. Anaonetta Mills, interviewed June 21, 1939, Works Progress Administration Interviews, Box 12, Folder 5, NSHS, Lincoln, Nebr.

86. Mrs. C. W. Fleek, interviewed by Maude Swanson, August 26, 1941, Works Progress Administration Interviews, Box 2, Folder 16, NSHS, Lincoln, Nebr.; Bergh, "Pioneer Daughters of Dakota," 88.

87. Nell F. Fotheringham, "The Memoirs of Mrs. Lilian Bell," Panhandle Plains Historical Museum Research Center, Canyon, Tex., 16–17; Lucy Tillotson Ralston, interviewed by Virginia McVay, Butler County, Kansas, Works Progress Administration Papers, WPA Coll. MS 71-1, Box 2, Folder 13, Wichita State University Special Collections, Wichita, Kans..

88. Edwin "Goose" Ramey, interviewed by Jeff Townsend, May 8, 1974, Southwest Collection, TTU, Lubbock, Tex.

89. "Article from Harley Tripp's Writings," Misc. Osborne County Manuscript Collection, KSHS, Topeka, Kans., 2.

90. Mrs. Clifford Jencks, Brushie, South Dakota, to "Maybel and all," March 24, 1910, SDSHS, Pierre, S.D.

91. Rogers, quoting Hattie Thompson Erikson in "Almost Scandinavia," 296–297.

92. Adamson, *North Platte and Its Associations*, 134–135.

93. Kohl, *Land of the Burnt Thigh*, 244; Alberts, *Sod House Reminiscences*, 95; Ruby Wilson and W. Kenneth McCandless, "Sioux Lookout Country" (1942), unpublished manuscript, Works Progress Administration, NSHS, Lincoln, Nebraska, p. 16.

94. "Fremont's Story 1838–1839," *South Dakota Historical Collections* 10 (1920): 71; "Robbie" to "Aunt Eliza," January 21, 1884, Robert D. Crawford Papers, MSS 290, Box 1, Folder 12, North Dakota Institute for Regional Studies, NDSU, Fargo, N.D.; Gard, "When Fire Seared the Prairies," 36.

95. Craig Miner, *West of Wichita: Settling the High Plains of Kansas, 1865–1890* (Lawrence: University Press of Kansas, 1988), 163; Harriet Pierce, interviewed by Maude Swanson, September 20, 1939, Works Progress Administration Interviews, Box 3, Folder 30, NSHS, Lincoln, Nebr.

96. Marshall County News clippings, n.d., KSHS, Topeka, Kans., 117–118; David A. Clary, ed., "'I Am Already Quite a Texan': Albert J. Myer's Letters from Texas, 1854–1856," *Southwestern Historical Quarterly* 82 (July 1978): 47.

97. Grant Foreman, ed., *A Pathfinder in the Southwest: The Itinerary of Lieutenant A. W. Whipple During His Explorations for a Railway Route from Fort Smith to Los Angeles in the Years 1853 & 1854* (Norman: University of Oklahoma Press, 1941), 62 (footnote).

98. *Republican Journal* (Kans.), n.d., Riley County Clippings, vol. 1, KSHS, Topeka, Kans., 4.

99. Kate Pelissier Manuscript Collection, MSS 20576, Microfilm Roll No. 12, NDSHS, Bismarck, N.D.

100. Towne, *Old Prairie Days*, 135; Frank Wisnewski Family Collection, SC 1928, North Dakota Institute for Regional Studies, NDSU, Fargo, N.D.

101. Ed Grantham, interviewed October 19, 1938, Library of Congress American Memory Project, www.memory.loc.gov.

102. Richard E. Jensen, ed., *Happy as a Big Sunflower: Adventures in the West, 1876–1880* (Lincoln: University of Nebraska Press, 2000), 118; *Fair Play* (Valley Falls, Kans.), August 18, 1888.

103. *Garden City Herald* (Kans.), April 4, 1896; unidentified newspaper, March 27, 1879, Harvey County Clippings, vol. 1, KSHS, Topeka, Kans., 24–25.

104. *Lincoln Register* (Kans.), January 9, 1880, Saline County Clippings, vol. 1, KSHS, Topeka, Kans., 37; *Arkansas Democrat Gazette*, January 8, 2006; Fanny Kelly, *Narrative of My Captivity Among the Sioux Indians*, ed. by Clark and Mary Lee Spence (New York: Konecky & Konecky, 1990), 153; Wilson and McCandless, "Sioux Lookout Country," 16; Catherine Green Yahna interview, n.d., Grand Forks County, Historical Data Project, WPA Microfilm, NDSHS, Bismarck, N.D.

105. Roscoe Logue, *Under Texas and Border Skies* (Amarillo, Tex.: Russell Stationary Co., 1935), 44.

106. Edwin Allen, interviewed by Maude Swanson, September 26, 1941, Works Progress Administration Interviews, Box 2, Folder 10, NSHS, Lincoln, Nebr.

107. Nick B. Schilz, interviewed by Stanley A. Kula, January 22–23, 1940, Works Progress Administration Interviews, Box 16, Folder 141, NSHS, Lincoln, Nebr.

108. Jennie Mille, interviewed by Maude Swanson, August 22, 1940, Works Progress Administration Interviews, Box 3, Folder 26, NSHS, Lincoln, Nebr.; Evelyn Wells Grandy, interviewed by Harold J. Moss, December 6, 1939, Works Progress Administration Interviews, Box 9, Folder 101, NSHS, Lincoln, Nebr.

109. Daisy Wright, "Kansas Prairie Fire," Hist. Native Sons and Daughters Collection, Manuscript Coll. 214, Folder 2, KSHS, Topeka, Kans.

110. Miner, *West of Wichita*, 163.

111. Ibid; "A Prairie Fire," *Daily National Intelligencer* (Washington, D.C.), November 25, 1858.

112. Everett Evan Evans, n.d., interviewed by Emily Hartman, Oklahoma Oral History Collection, Tape 594, OSHS, Oklahoma City, Okla.

113. Emily Combes to "my loved one," October 16, 1871, Emily Isabelle Combes Manuscript Coll., Spencer Library Kansas Coll., University of Kansas, Lawrence, Kans.; Jim Metzger, "Metzger Memories," unpublished manuscript in Metzger Manuscript Coll. 128, Box 1, Folder 1, University of Nebraska Special Collections, University of Nebraska, Lincoln, Nebr., 7; Kohl, *Land of the Burnt Thigh*, 241.

114. Esther Dellis, "Recollections of Joe Killough: An Interview with a Pioneer" (1941), Panhandle Plains Historical Museum Research Center, Canyon, Tex., 5; Logue, *Under Texas and Border Skies*, 44.

115. Lewis F. Crawford Papers, Coll. A 58, Box 1, "Notes on North Dakota History Interviews," NDSHS, Bismarck, N.D.; Ethel Gramkow, March 7, 1974, interviewed by Mary Wiley, Tape 597, OSHS, Oklahoma Oral History Collection, Oklahoma City, Okla..

116. Howard A. Cox, "The Economic Effects of Prairie Fires on the Cattle Industry," unpublished manuscript, May 25, 1936, Panhandle Plains Historical Museum Research Center, Canyon, Tex., 1.

117. *Kansas Farmer*, January 1, 1872.

118. E. C. Rice, "A Prairie Burner" (Mandan, N.D.: Times Print, 1889); Ezekial C. Rice Papers, Coll. A4, Folder 1, NDSHS, Bismarck, North Dakota; C. E. Mitchell, Commissioner of Patents, U.S. Patent Office, to Ezekial C. Rice, Ezekial C. Rice Papers, Coll. A4, Folder 1, NDSHS, Bismarck, N.D.

119. G. S. Cyne to E. C. Rice, October 3 [1889?], Ezekial C. Rice Papers, Coll. A4, Folder 1, NDSHS, Bismarck, N.D.

120. Jas. E. Reed to E. C. Rice, August 1, 1890, Ezekial C. Rice Papers, Coll. A4, Folder 3, NDSHS, Bismarck, North Dakota; ibid., October 15, 1890.

121. Judge W. D. Crump, January 6, 1937, interviewed by Ivey G. Warren, Library of Congress American Memory Project, www.memory.loc.gov.

122. Norton Family Diaries, April 7–8, 1878.

123. *Emporia News* (Kans.), October 29, 1859.

124. Kohl, *Land of the Burnt Thigh*, 257.

125. Adamson, *North Platte and Its Associations*, 133.

126. *Garden City Herald* (Kans.), April 22, 1899.

127. *Meade Globe* (Kans.), reprinted in *Liberal News* (Kans.), October 14, 1897.

128. Louise F. Day, November 13, 1975, interviewed by Byron Price, Southwest Collection, TTU, Lubbock, Tex.

129. Mrs. C. C. West, November 15, 1937, interviewed by Elizabeth Doyle, Library of Congress American Memory Project, www.memory.loc.gov; Martha L. Smith, *Going to God's Country* (Boston: The Christopher Publishing House, 1941), 94.

130. Daisy Wright, unpublished manuscript, Hist. Native Sons and Daughters, Manuscript Coll. 214, Folder 2, KSHS, Topeka, Kans.

131. Wilson and McCandless, "Sioux Lookout Country," 15.

132. Monica Strack, July 2, 2002, interviewed by Michael Pierce and Charles Nabholz, Arkansas Center for Oral and Visual History, University of Arkansas, Fayetteville, Ark., 22.

133. Javan Irvine to [son], April 8, 1874, Javan Bardley Irvine Papers, Box 1, Folder 6, SDSHS, Pierre, S.D.

134. John Fraser Hart, *The Rural Landscape* (Baltimore, Md.: The Johns Hopkins University Press, 1998), 149.

135. Geoff Cunfer, *On the Great Plains: Agriculture and Environment* (College Station: Texas A&M University Press, 2005), 18–19; Pamela Riney-Kehrberg, *Rooted in Dust: Surviving Drought and Depression in Southwestern Kansas* (Lawrence: University Press of Kansas, 1994), 90.

136. Pyne, *Fire in America*, 92; "Entire Oklahoma Town Flees as Fires Spread," http://www.cnn.com/2009/US/03/06/Oklahoma.town.fire/index.html. The people of Taloga, Oklahoma, had to evacuate because of a prairie fire in March 2009. Fire also threatened homes in Edmund, Oklahoma. In April 2011 officials evacuated residents of Satanta, a town in southwestern Kansas, because of a grass fire that eventually burned 1,000 acres. See "Residents of SW Kansas Town Return Home after Fire," *Wichita Eagle*, April 4, 2011.

137. *Norman Transcript* (Oklahoma Territory), April 11, 1891.

138. Arthur Harbottle, December 17, 1940, interviewed by Maude Swanson, Works Progress Administration Interviews, Box 2, Folder 19, NSHS, Lincoln, Nebr.

139. Dick Rice, June 2, 1973, interviewed by Frank Benede, Oklahoma Oral History Collection, OSHS, Oklahoma City, Okla.

140. John L. Finley, "The Effects of Prairie Fires on Vegetation," in "Report of the Kansas State Board of Agriculture for the Quarter Ending March 31, 1894" (Topeka, Kans., 1894), 147.

141. Frederick Law Olmsted, *A Journey Through Texas; or, A Saddle-Trip on the Southwestern Frontier; with a Statistical Appendix* (New York: Dix, Edwards & Co., 1857), 220–221.

142. *Elbert County Banner* (Colo.), November 9, 1906.

143. *Globe-Republican* (Dodge City, Kans.), November 14, 1895.

Chapter Six: "A Horrible World of Cinders and Blackness"

1. *Belfield Times* (N.D.), November 12, 1914; *Fryburg Pioneer* (N.D.), November 12, 1914.

2. *Fryburg Pioneer* (N.D.), November 5, 1914; November 12, 1914; *Belfield Times* (N.D.), November 5, 1914; November 12, 1914; Ray Erwin, compiler, "The Prairie Fire in North Dakota" (self-published, 1992), North Dakota State Historical Society (hereafter NDSHS), Bismarck, N.D. Erwin, a relative of two of the fire's victims, Francis Pike and Ruth Olson, compiled information about the event to be deposited in the state historical society archives.

3. *Fryburg Pioneer* (N.D.), November 12, 1914.

4. *Belfield Times* (N.D.), November 12, 1914.

5. *Fryburg Pioneer* (N.D.), November 12, 1914.

6. *Republican Journal* (Kans.), date unknown, Riley County Clippings, vol. 1, Kansas State Historical Society (hereafter KSHS), Topeka, Kans., 4.

7. J. D. Trine, letter dated March 17, 1940, in place of interview, Works Progress Administration Interviews, RG 515, Box 13, Folder 11, Nebraska State Historical Society (hereafter NSHS), Lincoln, Nebr.

8. Anna, Larimore, Dakota Territory, to Mrs. Maggie Clark, Emerson, Ohio, October 10, 1886, letter in the possession of the author; unidentified clipping, Mari Sandoz Collection, Box 38.2, Research Files, Folder 23, "Prairie Fires, 1878," University of Nebraska Special Collections, Lincoln, Nebr.; Jesse Kennedy Snell Collection No. 80, Manuscripts Division, Box 1, KSHS, Topeka, Kans.

9. Unidentified clipping, Mari Sandoz Collection, "Prairie Fires, 1878."

10. Joseph W. Snell, ed., "Roughing It on Her Kansas Claim: The Diary of Abbie Bright, 1870–1871," *Kansas Historical Quarterly* 37 (Autumn 1971): 417.

11. Merton Field Papers, MSS 28, Box 1, Folder 7, North Dakota Institute for Regional Studies, North Dakota State University (hereafter NDSU), Fargo, N.D., 77.

12. Charles Augustus Murray, *Travels in North America During the Years 1834, 1835, and 1836*, vol. 2 (New York: Da Capo Press, 1974), 128. Murray is quoted by Kenneth F. Higgins, "Interpretation and Compendium of Historical Fire Accounts in the Northern Great Plains," Resource Publication 161 (Washington D.C.: U.S. Department of the Interior, Fish and Wildlife Service, 1986), 19.

13. "From 1873 Developments of Sanborn County and Storms, Prairie Fires & 3 County Seat Wars," South Dakota State Historical Society (hereafter SDSHS), Pierre, South Dakota, 206. This volume is a typed manuscript compilation of largely unidentified newspaper articles. No compiler or date is noted.

14. Minnie Calhoun Splinter, "Calhoun Chronicles," Manuscript Collection No. 37, Box 1, NSHS, Lincoln, Nebr., 188.

15. Adela Elizabeth Richards Orpen, *Memories of the Old Emigrant Days in Kansas, 1862–1865* (Edinburgh: William Blackwood & Sons Ltd., 1926), 72–73. Orpen is quoted by Everett Dick, *The Sod House Frontier, 1854–1890: A Social History of the Northern Plains from the Creation of Kansas & Nebraska to the Admission of the Dakotas* (Lincoln: Johnsen Publishing Company, 1954), 219.

16. Candy Moulton, *Roadside History of Nebraska* (Missoula, Mont.: Mountain Press Publishing Company, 1997), 239; Division of Manuscripts Collection, unidentified diary, October 11, year unknown, Western History Collection, University of Oklahoma, Norman, Okla.

17. Merrill J. Mattes, *The Great Platte River Road* (Lincoln: University of Nebraska Press, 1987), 146.

18. Fanny Kelly, *Narrative of My Captivity Among the Sioux Indians*, ed. by Clark and Mary Lee Spence (New York: Konecky & Konecky, 1990), 155; Merton Field Papers, Box 1, Folder 7, 45.

19. Henry Inman, compiler, *Buffalo Jones' Forty Years of Adventure: A Volume of Facts Gathered from Experience by Hon. C. J. Jones . . .* (Topeka, Kans.: Crane & Company, 1899), 107.

20. Eleanor Cail-Penny to Don Westover, Early Nebraska Prairie Fire Accounts Collection, MS 18, Box 1, Folder 18, University of Nebraska Special Collections, Lincoln, Nebr.

21. *Jamestown Alert* (N.D.), October 23, 1884.

22. "Em" to "My Loved One," October 16, 1871, Emily Isabelle Combes Collection, Spencer Library Kansas Collection, University of Kansas, Lawrence, Kans.

23. Kelly, *Narrative of My Captivity*, 154.

24. Ruby Wilson and W. Kenneth McCandless, "Sioux Lookout Country" (1942), unpublished manuscript, Works Projects Administration, NSHS, Lincoln, Nebr., 8.

25. Elliott Coues, ed. *The Manuscript Journals of Alexander Henry and of David Thompson*, vol. 1 (New York: Francis P. Harper, 1897), 253–254.

26. Richard Irving Dodge, *The Plains of the Great West and Their Inhabitants* (New York: G. P. Putnam's Sons, 1877), 80–81.

27. Judge Charles E. Wolfe to Mrs. H. P. Pennington, July 8, 1922, Charles E. Wolfe Papers, Small Manuscript Collections Microfilm MS 21000, NDSHS, Bismarck, N.D.; *Jamestown Alert* (N.D.), October 14, 1879; *McPherson Daily Republi-*

can (Kans.), May 10, 1947, McPherson County Clippings, vol. 2, KSHS, Topeka, Kans., 225.

28. Anonymous, *Travels from Ocean to Ocean, from the Lakes to the Gulf*, 4th ed. (Harrisburg, Pa.: Amos H. Gottschall, 1894), 84.

29. *Americus Greeting* (Kans.), October 10, 1907, reprinted in *Emporia Gazette* (Kans.), January 14, 1956.

30. Emil Elmshaeuser to Don Westover, relating Mathews's printed account, Early Nebraska Prairie Fire Accounts Collection, MS No. 18.

31. Unidentified newspaper reprinting a 1931 article from *Eureka Herald* (Kans.), Greenwood County Clippings, vol. 1, KSHS, Topeka, Kans., 221–222.

32. Donald Easton, "McNary Fire," in "Fires" vertical file, SDSHS, Pierre, S.D.

33. Martha L. Smith, *Going to God's Country* (Boston: The Christopher Publishing House, 1941), 95; Mary Bickett, interview by Ruby E. Wilson, October 25, 1938, Library of Congress American Memory Project, www.memory.loc.gov.

34. Napoleon Provancha, interviewed by Edna B. Pearson, June 13, 1940, Works Progress Administration Interviews, RG 515, Box 5, Folder 52, NSHS, Lincoln, Nebr.

35. *Boston Transcript*, quoted in the *Saguache Chronicle* (Colo.), December 12, 1884; Hazel Shaw, interviewed by Michelle Andrews, May 31, 1977, Oklahoma Oral History Collection, Tape 833, side 2, Oklahoma State Historical Society, Oklahoma City, Okla.

36. Mrs. C. L. Mehuron, interview dated September 19, 1938, Works Progress Administration Interviews, Library of Congress American Memory Project, www.loc.memory.gov; John Burroughs, quoting a "lady on the prairie," "Notes from the Prairie," *Century* 32 (September 1886): 788.

37. *Wabunsee County Herald* (Kans.), November 4, 1869.

38. Beatrice Moyer, Haskell County, Kansas, to parents, March 1916, reprinted in *Garden City Telegram* (Kans.), January 8, 1969, Haskell County Clippings, vol. 1, KSHS, Topeka, Kans., 75–76; *Fair Play* (Valley Falls, Kans.), August 18, 1888.

39. Comte Philippe de Trobriand, *Army Life in Dakota*, ed. by Milo Milton Quaife (Chicago: The Lakeside Press, 1941), 346.

40. H. A. Boller, *Among the Indians: Four Years on the Upper Missouri, 1858–1862* (Lincoln: University of Nebraska Press, 1972), 320. Quoted by Higgins, "Interpretation and Compendium," 22.

41. J. B. Tyrrell, ed., *David Thompson's Narrative of His Explorations in Western America* (Toronto: The Champlain Society, 1916), 248. Thompson's journal is quoted extensively by Higgins, "Interpretation and Compendium," 10–11.

42. A. R. Turner, "Surveying the International Boundary: The Journal of George M. Dawson, 1873," *Saskatchewan History* 21 (1968): 3–5.

43. "Em" to "My Loved One," October 16, 1871; *Garden City Herald* (Kans.), April 4, 1896.

44. *Farmer* (Kans.), January 22, 1880, Osborne County Clippings, vol. 1, KSHS, Topeka, Kans., 246; *Nebraska Farmer*, December 8, 1934, Early Nebraska Prairie Fire Accounts Collection, MS No. 18, Box 1, Folder 2.

45. T. R. Miller to University of Nebraska Department of Forestry, January 17, 1977, Early Nebraska Prairie Fire Accounts Collection, MS No. 18, Box 1, Folder 27.

46. Splinter, "Calhoun Chronicles," 192–194; *Oklahoman* (Okla.), March 31, 1910. Cline's experience and survival shocked people and therefore turns up frequently in the historical record.

47. *Lawton Weekly Enterprise* (Okla.), March 11, 1904; *Durango Democrat* (Colo.), January 3, 1901; The "charred" quote is from an unidentified newspaper, March 21, 1879, Beloit, Kansas, Mitchell County Clippings, vol. 1, KSHS, Topeka, Kans., 127–129.

48. *Commonwealth* (Kans.), March 19, 1879, Cloud County Clippings, vol. 1, KSHS, Topeka, Kans., 82–87.

49. American Red Cross, *Community First Aid and Safety* (American Red Cross, 2002), 160–164.

50. "Brock Bugle," July 21, 1976, Early Nebraska Prairie Fire Accounts Collection, MS No. 18, Box 1, Folder 9; Myrtle D. Fesler, *Pioneers of Western Kansas* (New York: Carlton Press, 1962), 90–91; Rooks County Manuscript Collection, transcribed from the *Rooks County Record*, March 17, 1893, KSHS, Topeka, Kans.; *Mancos-Times* (Colo.), June 21, 1918.

51. Ed Grantham, interviewed October 19, 1938, Works Progress Administration Interviews, RG 515, Box 9, Folder 101, NSHS, Lincoln, Nebr.

52. *Republican Journal* (Kans.), date unknown, Riley County Clippings, vol. 1, KSHS, Topeka, Kans., 4.

53. *Morning Times* (Cripple Creek, Colo.), April 18, 1899.

54. "Terrible Prairie Fire," *Kansas City Times*, reprinted in *St. Louis Globe-Democrat* (Mo.), February 10, 1876.

55. *Commonwealth* (Kans.), March 19, 1879, Cloud County Clippings, vol. 1, KSHS, Topeka, Kans., 82–87.

56. Charles Crutchett, "Grand View Douglas County's Ghost Town," *South Dakota Historical Collections* 30 (1960): 417.

57. Unidentified newspaper, Mitchell County Clippings, March 21, 1879, KSHS, Topeka, Kans., 127–129; *St. Louis Globe-Democrat*, reprinted in *Saguache Chronicle* (Colo.), June 7, 1879.

58. Jim Metzger, "Metzger Memories," Metzger Manuscript Collection No. 128, Box 1, Folder 1, University of Nebraska Special Collections, Lincoln, Nebr.; *Akron Weekly Pioneer Press* (Colo.), October 27, 1911.

59. *Colorado Weekly Chieftain*, September 6, 1877.

60. *Daily Journal* (Telluride, Colo.), November 29, 1897.

61. Ed Wright, interviewed by Ruby E. Wilson, January 29, 1940, Works Progress Administration Interviews, RG 515, Box 13, Folder 4, NSHS, Lincoln, Nebr.

62. Norton Family Diaries (1876–1895), November 4 [1887], Manuscript Coll. 1190, KSHS, Topeka, Kans.

63. *Akron Weekly Pioneer Press* (Colo.), April 7, 1916.

64. *Texas Live Stock Journal* (Fort Worth), November 11, 1882.

65. Even when trying to be sympathetic to the range loss problem, some newspaper editors, particularly those who pushed for tree planting and hoped for climate change, revealed their bias. The Dodge City, Kansas, *Globe-Republican* (November 5, 1890) editor, for example, stated after a prairie fire that "we have not heard of any property being destroyed, but the loss of range will fall heavily upon parties who have been grazing large flocks of sheep on the south side."

66. Roscoe Logue, *Under Texas and Border Skies* (Amarillo, Tex.: Russell Stationary Co., 1935), 44.

67. *Jamestown Alert* (N.D.), October 8, 1885; H. H. Henricks, interviewed by Ruby E. Wilson, June 14, 1940, Works Progress Administration Interviews, RG 515, Box 12, Folder 2, NSHS, Lincoln, Nebr.; *Texas Live Stock Journal* (Fort Worth), November 25, 1882.

68. M. Huffman, Foreman, November 29, 1894, XIT Manuscript Collection, Ranch Foremen Reports, Spring Lake Division, Box 94, Panhandle Plains Historical Museum Research Center, Canyon, Tex.

69. Ibid., December 31, 1894.

70. Ibid., Escarhada[?] Division, J. P. McLaren, Foreman, December 31, 1894.

71. J. R. Armstrong to Mr. H. S. Boice, November 17, 1906, John R. Armstrong Papers, Accession No. 1988-138/1, Folder 3, Panhandle Plains Historical Museum Research Center, Canyon, Tex.

72. *Oklahoman*, March 10, 1904; *Durango Democrat* (Colo.), March 4, 1904.

73. Albert D. Herndon, unpublished manuscript, Early Nebraska Prairie Fire Accounts Collection, MS No. 18, Box 1, Folder 5.

74. C. E. King, interviewed by Maude Swanson, January 2, 1942, Works Progress Administration Interviews, RG 515, Box 2, Folder 22, NSHS, Lincoln, Nebr.; Mrs. Eppie Barrier, interviewed by Jean Paul, July 30, 1958, Tape 1, side 1, Southwest Collection, Texas Tech University, Lubbock, Tex.

75. *Emporia News* (Kans.), March 5, 1864.

76. Rooks County Manuscript Collection, Manuscripts Division, KSHS, Topeka, Kans. An article from the *Rooks County Record*, March 17, 1893, has been transcribed and placed in the manuscript collection.

77. *Brownville Advertiser* (Nebr.), November 20, 1873, located in Early Nebraska Prairie Fire Accounts Collection, MS No. 18, Box 1, Folder 3.

78. Mrs. Anton Matoush to W. J. Bailey, W. J. Bailey Governor's Papers, 27-06-01-07, Folder 15, KSHS, Topeka, Kans.

79. Secretary to Governor Arthur Capper to Mr. A. M. Hopper, April 20, 1916, Arthur Capper Governor's Papers, General Correspondence, 1916, Box 9, Item 214, KSHS, Topeka, Kans.

Chapter Seven: "Awfully Grand"

1. J. Palliser, *Solitary Rambles and Adventures of a Hunter in the Prairies* (Tokyo: Charles E. Tuttle Co., 1969), 89–95. Palliser is quoted by Kenneth F. Higgins, "Interpretation and Compendium of Historical Fire Accounts in the Northern Great Plains," Resource Publication 161 (Washington D.C.: U.S. Department of the Interior, Fish and Wildlife Service, 1986), 26.

2. Paul Wilhelm, Duke of Wuerttemberg, "First Journey to North America in the Years 1822 to 1824," trans. by Dr. Wm. G. Bek, in *South Dakota Historical Collections* 19 (1938): 443–444.

3. C. C. Andrews, *Minnesota and Dacotah: In Letters Descriptive of a Tour Through the North-west, in the Autumn of 1856,* 2nd ed. (Washington, D.C.: R. Farnham, 1857), 162, accessed through the Making of America Books web site, http:// quod.lib.umich.edu/m/moagrp/; W. W. H. Davis, *El Gringo: Or, New Mexico and Her People* (reprint, Santa Fe, N.M.: The Rydall Press, 1938), 10.

4. Rooks County Manuscript Collection, Kansas State Historical Society, Topeka, Kans., March 17, 1893 The small collection consists of a hand-typed reprint of the *Rooks County Record* (Kans.).

5. H. Y. Hind, *Narrative of the Canadian Red River Exploring Expedition of 1857 and the Assinniboine and Saskatchewan Exploring Expedition of 1858,* vol. 1 (reprint, New York: Greenwood Press, 1969), 337. Hind is quoted extensively by Higgins, "Interpretation and Compendium," 22.

6. *Emporia News* (Kans.), October 8, 1859.

7. Maximilian, Prince of Wied, *Travels in the Interior of America, 1832–1834,* vol. 1, ed. by R. G. Thwaites (Glendale, Calif.: Arthur H. Clark Co., 1966), 289–290.

8. Robert D. Crawford to "Dear Cousins Hugh and Malcolm," Robert D. Crawford Papers, MSS 290, Folder 12, Box 1, North Dakota Institute for Regional Studies, North Dakota State University (herafter NDSU), Fargo, N.D.

9. George Starkey, "Prairie Fires," in *Chase County Historical Sketches,* vol. 1 (Chase County Historical Society, 1940), 119; James P. Price, *Seven Years of Prairie Life* (reprint, Goff, Kans.: Great Plains Book Company, 1983), 25. Price's original volume was published in 1891.

10. There were numerous stories in mid- to late-nineteenth-century issues of *Harper's* that discussed prairie fire. See, for example, "Snake Stories," *Harper's Weekly,* March 2, 1861, 139; "On the Plains," *Harper's Weekly,* April 21, 1866, 249–250; "Running the Fire-Guard," *Harper's Weekly,* March 28, 1868, 196. See also James Fenimore Cooper, *The Prairie* (reprint, New York: Dodd, Mead &

Company, 1954), 282–285. Cooper originally published this novel in 1827. A journalist writing for the magazine *Youth's Companion* took it for granted that readers of the Leatherstocking Tales (presumably both Plains and non-Plains residents) would be familiar with prairie fire, at least through literary description. *Youth's Companion* (date unknown), reprinted in the *Summit County Journal* (Breckenridge, Colo.), May 14, 1892.

11. Maximilian, *Travels in the Interior of America*, 281. Maximilian is quoted by Higgins, "Interpretation and Compendium," 18.

12. Annie Heloise Abel, *Chardon's Journal at Fort Clark, 1834–1839* (Lincoln: University of Nebraska Press, 1997), 187. Chardon is quoted by Conrad Taylor Moore, "Man and Fire in the Central North American Grassland, 1535–1890: A Documentary Historical Geography" (Ph.D. diss., University of California–Los Angeles, 1972), 32.

13. Andrew Evans, trans., *A Trip to the Prairies and the Interior of North America, 1837–1838: Travel Notes by Count Francesco Arese* (New York: The Harbor Press, 1934), 118–119. Quoted by Moore, "Man and Fire," 28.

14. James H. Pratt to Louisa Field Pratt, April 7, 1871, Pratt/Magee Family Papers, WH 636, Box 3, FF 3, Western History Collections, Denver Public Library, Denver, Colo.

15. *Smoky Hill and Republican Union* (Junction City, Kans.), February 27, 1862.

16. "A Sea of Fire," *New York Press*, reprinted in *Globe-Republican* (Dodge City, Kans.), April 2, 1890.

17. Abbie Bright, "Roughing It on Her Kansas Claim: The Diary of Abbie Bright, 1870–1871," ed. by Joseph W. Snell, *Kansas Historical Quarterly* 37 (Autumn 1971): 418.

18. Mabel Hubbard to Alexander Graham Bell, December 1876, Alexander Graham Bell Papers, accessed at American Memory, Library of Congress, www.memory.loc.gov.

19. *Fair Play* (Valley Falls, Kans.), August 18, 1888.

20. *Emporia News* (Kans.), September 29, 1860; October 8, 1859.

21. A. R. Turner, "Surveying the International Boundary: The Journal of George M. Dawson, 1873," *Saskatchewan History* 21 (1968): 5, 17.

22. "Em" [Emily Isabelle Combes], Salina, Kansas, to "My loved one," [James Waddell Cherrington], West Virginia, October 16, 1871, Emily Isabelle Combes Collection, Spencer Library Kansas Collection, University of Kansas, Lawrence, Kans.

23. "Wild Waves of Fire," *Inter Ocean* (Chicago, Ill.), August 20, 1893, Thomas Hornsby Ferril Scrapbooks, WH1195, Box 39, Vol. 3, Western History Collection, Denver Public Library, Denver, Colo.; *Garden City Herald* (Kans.), March 9, 1916.

24. "By Many Trails," unpublished autobiography, Merton Field Papers, MSS 28, Box 1, Folder 6, North Dakota Institute for Regional Studies, NDSU, Fargo, N.D, 74.

25. Jim Metzger, "Metzger Memories," unpublished manuscript, Metzger Manuscript Collection No. 128, Box 1, Folder 1, University of Nebraska Special Collections, Lincoln, Nebr., 7.

26. H. B. Mollhausen journal, quoted in *Cattleman* 36 (May 1950): 36.

27. J. Russell Harper, ed., *Paul Kane's Frontier,* including Kane's *Wandering of an Artist Among the Indians of North America* (Austin: University of Texas Press, 1971), 83.

28. Minnie Calhoun Splinter, "Calhoun Chronicles," unpublished manuscript, Manuscript Collection No. 37, Box 1, Nebraska State Historical Society, Lincoln, Nebr., 188.

29. Reprinted in *Louisville Daily Journal* (Ky.), November 14, 1860.

30. *Emporia Gazette* (Kans.), January 14, 1956. The *Gazette* reprinted a story from *Americus Greeting* (Kans.), October 10, 1907, in which pioneers reminisced about the founding of the town.

31. *Oklahoman,* March 30, 1910.

32. George Hampton Crossman to T. J. Walker, New York, October 9, 1894, George Hampton Crossman Papers, Collection No. 20189, Microfilm 21000, Roll 4, North Dakota State Historical Society, Bismarck, N.D.; Robert H. Becker, ed., *Thomas Christy's Road Across the Plains* (Denver, Colo.: Old West Publishing Company, 1969), May 5, 1850 entry.

33. Division of Manuscripts Collection, Box 10, Folder 15, October 11 (year unknown), University of Oklahoma, Western History Collection, Norman, Okla.

34. "By Many Trails," Box 1, Folder 4, 11.

35. *Smoky Hill and Republican Union* (Junction City, Kans.), March 27, 1862.

36. Frederick E. Shearer, ed., *The Pacific Tourist; Adams & Bishop's Illustrated Trans-Continental Guide of Travel, from the Atlantic to the Pacific Ocean. . . . A Complete Traveler's Guide of the Union and Central Pacific Railroads . . .* (reprint, New York: Crown Publishers, Inc., 1970), 22. This book was originally published in 1884.

37. Joni L. Kinsey, *Plains Pictures: Images of the American Prairie* (Washington, D.C.: Smithsonian Institution Press, 1996), 5.

38. Frank A. Root and William Elsey Connelly, *The Overland Stage to California* (reprint, Columbus, Ohio: Long's College Book Co., 1950), 543. This book was originally published by the authors in Topeka, Kansas, 1901.

39. Cooper, *The Prairie,* 282–285.

40. George Pope Morris, "The Prairie on Fire," in *The Thought-Blossom: A Memento* (New York: Leavitt and Allen, 1854), 169–171.

41. "Captain Dan Henrie, His Adventure with the Wolves," *United States Democratic Review* 24 (January 1849): 39–41.

42. For wolves as a perceived threat in the West, see Jon T. Coleman, *Vicious: Wolves and Men in America* (New Haven, Conn.: Yale University Press, 2004).

43. *Harper's New Monthly Magazine* 48 (December 1873): 154.

44. "Picturesque Features of Kansas Farming," *Scribner's Monthly* 19 (November 1879): 137–140.

45. Periodical writers were also in a good position to educate people about the fires and the techniques that Indians and Euro-American settlers developed for living among them. In 1868 *Harper's Weekly* printed an illustration of a Plains farmer plowing a fireguard and explained in an accompanying story that the practice, "which will be new to most of our readers," was just one "peculiarity" of a "peculiar country." "Running the Fire-Guard," *Harper's Weekly*, March 28, 1868, 196 The following year the magazine reported that, curiously, where fires were suppressed trees were "spring[ing] up spontaneously, in what was before considered a treeless district." "The Union Pacific Railroad—a Prairie on Fire in Nebraska," *Harper's Weekly*, August 28, 1869, 557.

46. "A Strange Story," *Harper's Weekly*, January 11, 1862, 26–28; "A View of the Proper Judicial Treatment of the Female Lawbreaker," *Harper's Weekly*, September 9, 1911, 7–8; Mary Livermore, *The Story of My Life; or, The Sunshine and Shadow of Seventy Years* (Hartford, Conn.: A. D. Worthington & Co., 1897), 374; "What My Love Forgave," *Harper's Weekly*, April 26, 1884, 266–267.

47. "The Wars," *Harper's Weekly*, June 19, 1858, 387–389; "The Nation an Army," *Harper's Weekly*, July 4, 1863, 418–419.

48. *Daily Missouri Democrat* (St. Louis), December 2, 1857.

49. "People's campaign song, No. 2," Civil War Song Sheets, series 1, vol. 3, Library of Congress, Washington D.C., accessed at American Memory, Library of Congress, www.memory.loc.gov.

50. Hannibal Hamlin to Abraham Lincoln, September 11, 1860, Abraham Lincoln Papers, accessed at American Memory, Library of Congress, www.memory.loc.gov.

51. Lewis C. Lockwood to Abraham Lincoln, Edwin M. Stanton, and Henry W. Halleck, January 12, 1863, Abraham Lincoln Papers, accessed at American Memory, Library of Congress, www.memory.loc.gov.

52. *Inter Ocean* (Chicago, Ill.), August 20, 1893, Thomas Hornsby Ferril Scrapbooks, WH1195, Box 39, Denver Public Library, Denver, Colo., 139–141.

53. Tirzah Plaisted, *There Lived a Man: Mother's Story* (New York: self-published, 1914), 73–78.

54. S. S. Judy and Will G. Robinson, "Sanborn County History," *South Dakota Historical Collections* 26 (1952): 101; Henry C. Hitch, n.d., interviewed by Raymond Fields, Oklahoma Oral History Collection, Oklahoma State Historical Society, Oklahoma City, Okla.

55. David A. Clary, ed., "'I Am Already Quite a Texan:' Albert J. Myer's Letters from Texas, 1854–1854," *Southwestern Historical Quarterly* 82 (July 1978): 47.

56. "Mother," Neligh, Nebraska, to "My dear Boy," April 15, 1887. The letter is in the author's possession.

57. *Daily Journal* (Telluride, Colo.), July 14, 1904, quoting an unidentified Kansas paper.

58. "Wedded an Indian Maiden," *Durango Wage Earner* (Colo.), January 30, 1902.

59. "Plain Pete Becomes a Hero: Story of a Western Prairie Fire," *Oklahoman*, May 15, 1910.

60. *Daily Journal* (Telluride, Colo.), August 3, 1901.

61. Ceph Fortenberry and Mae Taylor, "Pioneer Life at Cedar Hill," Fortenberry Manuscript Collection, Panhandle Plains Historical Museum Research Center, Canyon, Tex.

62. "Invasion of the Thistle!" *Garden City Herald* (Kans.), February 4, 1909.

63. *Liberal News* (Kans.), October 5, 1905.

64. Elliott West, *The Way to the West: Essays on the Central Plains* (Albuquerque: University of New Mexico Press, 1995), 137.

65. *Fargo Express* (Dakota), August 16, 1873, reprinted in "Dirt," *Bismarck Tribune* (Dakota), August 27, 1873.

66. "Southern Kansas," *Walnut Valley Times* (El Dorado, Kans.), January 13, 1871.

67. "Em" to "Dearest," November 5, 1871, Emily Isabelle Combes Collection, Spencer Library Kansas Collection, University of Kansas, Lawrence, Kans.

68. Roscoe Logue, *Under Texas and Border Skies* (Amarillo, Tex.: Russell Stationary Co., 1935), 46.

69. Andrew Wilton and Tim Barringer, *American Sublime: Landscape Painting in the United States 1820–1880* (Princeton, N.J.: Princeton University Press, 2002), 13–14.

70. Hind, *Narrative of the Canadian Red River Exploring Expedition*, 337.

71. Kinsey, *Plain Pictures*, 40–43, 92–93.

72. *New York Press*, reprinted in *Globe-Republican* (Dodge City, Kans.), April 2, 1890.

73. Charles Leroy Edson, "Prairie Fire," in *Prairie Fire* (Charleston, S.C.: Southern Prt'g & Pub. Co., 1924), 5.

74. Plaisted, *There Lived a Man*, 75–76.

Chapter Eight: "Burn, Prairie, Burn"

1. *Highmore Herald*, September 11, 1947, "Fire, Prairie" Vertical File, South Dakota State Historical Society (hereafter SDSHS), Pierre, S.D.

2. *Denver Field and Farm* (Colo.), April 1, 1893.

3. *Topeka Journal* (Kans.), January 16, 1950, Graham County Clippings, vol. 1, Kansas State Historical Society (hereafter KSHS), Topeka, Kans., 138.

4. *McPherson Daily Republican* (Kans.), May 10, 1947, McPherson County Clippings, vol. 2, KSHS, Topeka, Kans., 225.

5. *Russell Daily News* (Kans.), November 27, 1976.

6. *Garnett Review* (Kans.), February 6, 1936, Anderson County Clippings, vol. 2, KSHS, Topeka, Kans., 61–66.

7. *Webster Daily Journal* (S.D.), June 19, 1931, "Fires" Vertical File, SDSHS, Pierre, S.D. For examples of remembrance stories, see also *Oklahoman* (Okla.), September 23, 1934; *Anthony Republican and Bulletin* (Kans.), May 19, 1938; and *Marysville Advocate* (Kans.), April 25, 1946.

8. Pamela Riney-Kehrberg, *Rooted in Dust: Surviving Drought and Depression in Southwestern Kansas* (Lawrence: University Press of Kansas, 1994), 1–2.

9. "Farmers Fooled: Trees Made to Grow in South Dakota Where Everyone Said There Wasn't a Chance . . . Shelterbelt Program a Success," *Sioux City Journal* (S.D.), June 22, 1941, "Trees" Vertical File, SDSHS, Pierre, S.D.

10. David Dary, "The Flint Hills—Where Grass Burning Is Winning Favor," *Kansas City Star* (Kans./Mo.), April 23, 1972, Kansas Description Clippings, vol. 4, KSHS, Topeka, Kans., 88.

11. "The Future of the Great Plains," Message from the President of the United States Transmitting the Report of the Great Plains Committee Under the Title "The Future of the Great Plains," House of Representatives Document No. 144, 75th Congress, 1st Session (1936), 1–2, 14, 16, 18.

12. Dary, "The Flint Hills."

13. Jim Hoy, *Cowboys and Kansas: Stories from the Tallgrass Prairie* (Norman: University of Oklahoma Press, 1995), 114–115.

14. Maxine Frost, retired owner of "Frost Grocery," Butler, County, Kansas, interviewed February 1, 2003, by the author, Augusta, Kans.

15. Dary, "The Flint Hills."

16. Hoy, *Cowboys and Kansas*, 115.

17. Jim Hoy, *Flint Hills Cowboys: Tales of the Tallgrass Prairie* (Lawrence: University Press of Kansas, 2006), 2; "A Burning Prairie Question," *Wichita Eagle* (Kans.), May 1, 2010.

18. Randy Rodgers, "New Answer to Burning Questions," *Kansas Wildlife and Parks* 64 (March–April 2007): 2.

19. "Fire Marks Rebirth of Flint Hills," *Wichita Eagle* (Kans.), April 11, 2005; Dary, "The Flint Hills."

20. Hoy, *Cowboys and Kansas*, 114; Jim Hoy, "Prairie Fires," *Kansas School Naturalist* 39 (March 1993): 3.

21. "A Burning Prairie Question," *Wichita Eagle* (Kans.), May 1, 2010; Hoy, *Cowboys and Kansas*, 116; Janet L. Gehring and Thomas B. Bragg, "Changes in Prairie Vegetation Under Eastern Red Cedar (*Juniperus virginiana L.*) in an Eastern Nebraska Bluestem Prairie," *American Midland Naturalist* 128 (October 1992): 209–217.

22. Hoy, "Prairie Fires," 6.

23. Ibid., 6–7.

24. Ibid., 7, 10. Hoy notes that usually only half matches are used because they fall down deep into the grass, where they can easily set the grass alight, whereas whole matches will land on top and not start a blaze as efficiently.

25. Joe Dromey, "South Dakota Had Prairie Fires Also," in *Eighth Annual West River History Conference* (Keystone, S.D., 2001), 156; Hoy, "Prairie Fires," 10–11.

26. Hoy, "Prairie Fires," 10.

27. "Corralling the Prairie's Flame—with More Houses Pushing Their Way into the Grasslands, the Regular Spring Burning in the Flint Hills Becomes a Touchier Business," *Wichita Eagle* (Kans.), April 11, 2000. For an essay on urban and suburban dwellers moving to grass country (and the prairie fires that some of them ignorantly set), see Linda M. Hasselstrom, "Dear John: How to Move to the Country," in *No Place Like Home: Notes from a Western Life* (Reno: University of Nevada Press, 2009), 32–39.

28. "Cedar Trees Gone Bad—Native Evergreen Threatens Ecosystem," *Wichita Eagle* (Kans.), February 10, 2007.

29. "Fire Marks Rebirth of Flint Hills," *Wichita Eagle* (Kans.), April 11, 2005; Kristyn Eastman, interviewed October 8, 2006, by the author, Olathe, Kans. Eastman traveled the Kansas Turnpike the day of the 1994 accident.

30. National Public Radio, *All Things Considered* transcript, May 3, 2004, accessed through EBSCOhost.

31. Phyllis Jacobs Griekspoor, "Fire Marks Rebirth of Flint Hills," *Wichita Eagle* (Kans.), April 11, 2005.

32. Hoy, "Prairie Fires," 5–6.

33. John Schlageck, "Prairie Fires a Part of the Kansas Culture," *El Dorado Times* (Kans.), May 18, 2005.

34. Rick Brunetti, Director, Bureau of Air, Kansas Department of Health and Environment, "Kansas Flint Hills Smoke Management Plan," September 9, 2010, Joint Committee on Energy and Environmental Policy, Topeka, Kans.. http://skyways.lib.ks.us/ksleg/KLRD/Resources/Testimony/EEP/9–09–10/14-KDHE-Bureau-of-Air-Brunetti-FlintHillsSmokeMgmt.pdf; "A Burning Prairie Question," *Wichita Eagle* (Kans.), May 1, 2010; Brian Obermeyer, Director, Flint Hills Initiative, Nature Conservancy, interviewed by the author, November 15, 2010, by telephone. See also "Smoke Plan Historic," *Wichita Eagle* (Kans.), December 19, 2010; "Flint Hills Plan Is a Smoke Screen," *Wichita Eagle* (Kans.), December 26, 2010; "KDHE Issues Burn Ban for April," *Wichita Eagle* (Kans.), March 10, 2011; "Plume over Wichita Spurs Review of Flint Hills Smoke Plan," *Wichita Eagle* (Kans.), April 4, 2011.

35. Samuel D. Fuhlendorf and David M. Engle, "Restoring Heterogeneity on Rangelands: Ecosystem Management Based on Evolutionary Grazing Pat-

terns," *BioScience* 51 (August 2001): 625–626, 628–630; Rodgers, "New Answers to Burning Questions," 8.

36. Stephen J. Pyne, *Fire: A Brief History* (Seattle: University of Washington Press, 2001), 59–60.

37. Rodgers, "New Answers to Burning Questions," 4, 6–7.

38. "Patch Burning May Be Part of the Solution," *Wichita Eagle* (Kans.), May 1, 2010.

39. Hoy, *Cowboys and Kansas*, 113.

40. Hoy, "Prairie Fires," 3; "Burning Maintains Flint Hills Ecology," *Wichita Eagle* (Kans.), April 20, 2009.

41. Schlageck, "Prairie Fires a Part of the Kansas Culture."

42. "At Home on the Range," *Wichita Eagle* (Kans.), May 4, 1997.

43. "Burn, Prairie, Burn: Tourists in Kansas Come to Torch Grass," *Wall Street Journal* (New York), May 9, 2005.

44. Prairie Fire Festival, http://www.prairiefirefestival.com; Hoy, *Flint Hills Cowboys*, 158.

45. Craig Miner, *Kansas: The History of the Sunflower State, 1854–2000* (Lawrence: University Press of Kansas, 2002), 9. For more on the Curry mural, see M. Sue Kendall, *Rethinking Regionalism: John Steuart Curry and the Kansas Mural Controversy* (Washington D.C.: Smithsonian Institution Press, 1986).

46. Wichita Art Museum, www.kansastravel.org/wichitaartmuseum.htm; Joni L. Kinsey, *Plain Pictures: Images of the American Prairie* (Washington, D.C.: Smithsonian Institution Press, 1996), 176.

47. Robert Scott, www.sharecom.ca/scott. For a biography of Bosin and information regarding his painting, see Mid-America All-Indian Center, http://www.theindiancenter.org/Museum/Artists.

48. "Kansas Photos Attract Smithsonian," *Wichita Eagle* (Kans.), January 5, 1992; Larry Schwarm, *On Fire* (Durham, N.C.: Duke University Press, 2003).

49. Kinsey, *Plain Pictures*, 173.

Conclusion: "A Prairie Fire Came upon the Place"

1. "Race Between a Locomotive and a Prairie Fire," *Milwaukee Daily Sentinel* (Wis.), January 21, 1867. For another, briefer account of a locomotive's "race" with a prairie fire, see *Topeka Capital* (Kans.), March 25, 1916, Ford County Clippings, vol. 1, Manuscript Collections, Kansas State Historical Society, Topeka, Kans., 163–164.

2. "Race Between a Locomotive and a Prairie Fire."

3. "A Prairie on Fire!" *Maryland Gazette* (Annapolis, Md.), April 27, 1837.

4. "Race Between a Locomotive and a Prairie Fire."

5. Jacob Ferris, *The States and Territories of the Great West* (Buffalo, N.Y.: E. F. Beadle, 1856), 208–210.

6. "An Exciting Scene," *Milwaukee Sentinel* (Milwaukee, Wis.), November 10, 1870, reprinted in *Sioux City Journal* (S.D.), November 4, 1870.

7. "Terrible Prairie Fire," about a fire that nearly destroyed the Kansas town of Cottonwood Falls, *St. Louis Globe-Democrat* (Mo.), February 10, 1876, reprinted in *Kansas City Times*. The prairie fire burned all around the spectacular courthouse that still stands in the town today.

8. Joseph W. Snell, ed., "Roughing It on Her Kansas Claim: The Diary of Abbie Bright, 1870–1871," *Kansas Historical Quarterly* 37 (Autumn 1971): 415.

Bibliography

Primary Sources

Archival
Denver Public Library, Denver, Colo.
    Ferril, Thomas Hornsby, Scrapbooks. WH1195, Western History Collection.
    Pratt/Magee Family Papers. Western History Collections.
In author's possession.
    Larimore, Anna, Letter, October 10, 1886.
    "Mother," Neligh, Nebraska, to "My dear Boy," April 15, 1887.
    Squires, Abe L., Letter, April 1, 1889.
Kansas State Historical Society, Topeka, Kans.
    Governor's Papers.
        Bailey, W. J.
        Capper, Arthur.
    Manuscript Collections.
        Hist. Native Sons and Daughters Collection. Manuscript Coll. 214.
        Norton Family Diaries. Manuscript Coll. 1190.
        Osborne County Manuscript Collection.
        Rochat, J. O. Manuscript Collection.
        Rooks County Records Manuscript Collection.
    Manuscripts Division.
        Anderson County Clippings.
        Cloud County Clippings.
        Ford County Clippings.
        Graham County Clippings.
        Greenwood County Clippings.
        Harvey County Clippings.
        Haskell County Clippings.

Kansas Description Clippings.
Marshall County News Clippings.
McPherson County Clippings.
Mitchell County Clippings.
Monroe, Lilla Day. Coll. No. 163.
Osborne County Clippings.
Riley County Clippings.
Snell, Jesse Kennedy. Coll. No. 80.
Saline County Clippings.
Trees Clippings.
Kansas State University, Manhattan.
Munger, George M., Collection. Kansas State University Special Collections.
Library of Congress.
Bell, Alexander Graham, Papers.
Civil War Song Sheets. Series I.
Lincoln, Abraham, Papers.
National Archives, Washington, D.C.
Weather Records for Kansas, Fort Leavenworth, Kans. Meteorological Register, T907 R176.
Nebraska State Historical Society, Lincoln.
Calhoun, Minnie. Manuscript Coll. No. 37.
Nebraska Works Progress Administration Oral History Interviews.
Wilson, Ruby, and Kenneth McCandless. "Sioux Lookout Country." Unpublished manuscript.
Newberry Library, Chicago, Ill.
McNary, Oliver Clarkson, Letters. MS 3128.
North Dakota Institute for Regional Studies, North Dakota State University, Fargo.
Crawford, Robert D., Papers. MSS 290.
Field, Merton, Collection.
Lueg, Herman, Collection. SC 1166.
Stone, Byron N. Collection SC 1486.
Taylor, Wallace, Collection. SC 713.
Wisnewski, Frank, Family Collection. SC 1928.
North Dakota State Historical Society, Bismarck.
Bern, Enid. Small Manuscript Coll. MSS 21000.
Crawford, Lewis F., Papers. Coll. A 58.
Crossman, George Hampton, Papers. Coll. No. 20189.
Erwin, Ray, compiler. "The Prairie Fire in North Dakota." Self-published, 1992.
North Dakota Stock Growers Association. Coll. A 19.
Pelissier, Kate, Manuscript Collection. MSS 20576.

Rice, Ezekial C., Papers. Collection A4.

Wolfe, Charles E., Papers. Small Manuscript Collections MS 21000.

Works Progress Administration Historical Data Project, Grand Forks County.

Oklahoma State Historical Society, Oklahoma City.

Oklahoma Oral History Collection.

Panhandle Plains Historical Museum Research Center, Canyon, Tex.

Anonymous. An incomplete history of the Perry family, living in the Texas panhandle. Unpublished manuscript. MS Int. File 1982-31/37.

Armstrong, John R., Collection. MS Coll. 1988-138/1.

Bickerdyke, Jack, Collection.

Cohea, C. Kay. "Pioneer Women." Unpublished manuscript.

Cox, Howard A. "The Economic Effects of Prairie Fires on the Cattle Industry." Unpublished manuscript.

Fortenberry, Ceph, Manuscript Collection.

Fotheringham, Nell F. "The Memoirs of Mr.s Lilian Bell." Unpublished manuscript.

Hill, Mittie. "Early History of the Bar CC Ranch." Unpublished manuscript.

Killough, Joe, Collection.

Winchester, J. M., Collection.

XIT Manuscript Collection.

South Dakota State Historical Society, Pierre.

Anonymous compiler. "From 1873 Developments of Sanborn County and Storms, Prairie Fires & Three County Seat Wars."

Goddard, Thomas M., Family Letters. Collection H71.3.

Irvine, Javan. Papers.

Jencks, Mrs. Clifford, Letter.

Rothhammer, Siegmund, Papers. Collection H92-34.

Vertical File, "Fire, Prairie."

Vertical File, "Fires."

Texas Tech University, Lubbock.

Espuela Land and Cattle Company Records. Southwest Collection.

Southwest Collection Oral History Interviews.

University of Arkansas, Fayetteville.

Arkansas Center for Oral and Visual History. Oral History Interviews.

University of Kansas, Lawrence.

Combes, Emily Isabelle, Collection. Spencer Library Kansas Collection.

University of Nebraska, Lincoln.

Early Nebraska Prairie Fire Accounts Collection. MS No. 18. University of Nebraska Special Collections.

Metzger, Jim. Coll. 128. University of Nebraska Special Collections.

Pool, Raymond J., Papers. RG No. 12/07/12.

Sandoz, Mari, Collection. University of Nebraska Special Collections.

University of New Mexico, Albuquerque.
> Bourke, John G., Diaries. Center for Southwest Research, Zimmerman Library.

University of North Dakota, Grand Forks.
> Torbenson, Marie, Papers. Manuscript Collection 599, University of North Dakota Special Collections.

University of Oklahoma, Norman.
> Division Manuscripts Collection. Western Collection.
> Kerr, John T., Diary. Western History Collections.
> Lillie, Gordon William, Manuscript Collection.

Wichita State University, Wichita, Kans.
> Isely Family Letters. MS 88-31, Wichita State University Special Collections.
> Works Progress Administration Papers. MS 71-1. Wichita State University Special Collections.

Government Documents

Great Plains Committee. "The Future of the Great Plains." U.S. House of Representatives, 75th Congress, 1st Session, 1936.

Higgins, Kenneth F. "Interpretation and Compendium of Historical Fire Accounts in the Northern Great Plains." Resource Publication 161. Washington, D.C.: U.S. Department of the Interior, Fish and Wildlife Service, 1986, 1–36.

The Union Pacific Railway Company v. Eli McCollum. No. 61, Court of Appeals of Kansas, Northern Department, Western Division, December 1895.

U.S. Department of the Interior. First, Second, and Third Annual Reports of the United States Geological Survey of the Territories for the Years 1867, 1868, and 1869, Washington, D.C.

Newspapers and Periodicals

Aberdeen News (S.D.)
Akron Weekly Pioneer Press (Colo.)
Americus Greeting (Kans.)
Anthony Republican and Bulletin (Kans.)
Arkansas Democrat Gazette
Augusta Daily Gazette (Kans.)
Belfield Times (N.D.)
Bismarck Tribune (N.D.)
Boston Transcript (Mass.)
Brownville Advertiser (Nebr.)
Burr Oak Reveille (Kans.)
Burrton Telephone (Kans.)
Colorado Clipper

Colorado Springs Gazette
Colorado Transcript
Colorado Weekly Chieftain
Commonwealth (Kans.)
Daily Journal (Colo.)
Daily Missouri Democrat
Denver Field and Farm (Colo.)
Durango Democrat (Colo.)
Durango Wage Earner (Colo.)
Edmond Sun-Democrat (Okla.)
Elbert County Banner (Colo.)
El Dorado Times (Kans.)
Empire (Kans.)
Emporia Gazette (Kans.)
Emporia News (Kans.)
Eureka Herald (Kans.)
Fair Play (Kans.)
Fargo Express (N.D.)
Farmer (Kans.)
Fort Scott Monitor (Kans.)
Fryburg Pioneer (N.D.)
Garden City Herald (Kans.)
Garden City Telegram (Kans.)
Garnett Review (Kans.)
Globe-Republican (Kans.)
Harper's New Monthly Magazine
Harper's Weekly
Hennessey Clipper (Okla.)
Highmore Herald (S.D.)
Inter Ocean (Ill.)
Jamestown Alert (N.D.)
Kansas City Daily Times (Kans./Mo.)
Kansas City Star (Kans./Mo.)
Kansas Farmer (Kans.)
Kanzas News (*Kansas News* after 1858) (Kans.)
Kinsley Graphic (Kans.)
Kinsley Mercury (Kans.)
Kiowa Herald (Kans.)
Lawton Weekly Enterprise (Okla.)
Leavenworth Conservative (Kans.)
Liberal News (Kans.)
Lincoln Register (Kans.)

Louisville Daily Journal (Ky.)
Mancos Times (Colo.)
Maryland Gazette
Marysville Advocate (Kans.)
McPherson Daily Republican (Kans.)
Meade Globe (Kans.)
Milwaukee Daily Sentinel (Wis.)
Morning Times (Colo.)
Nebraska Farmer
Ness County News (Kans.)
Ness County Sentinel (Kans.)
New York Herald
New York Press
Norman Transcript (Okla.)
Oklahoman
Out West (Colo.)
Platte Valley Independent (Nebr.)
Range Ledger (Colo.)
Republican Journal (Kans.)
Rocky Mountain News (Colo.)
Rooks County Record (Kans.)
Russell Daily News (Kans.)
Saguache Chronicle (Colo.)
Scribner's Monthly
Silverton Standard (Colo.)
Sioux City Journal (S.D.)
Smoky Hill and Republican Union (Kans.)
St. Louis Globe-Democrat (Mo.)
Summit County Journal (Colo.)
Texas Live Stock Journal
Topeka Capital (Kans.)
Topeka Journal (Kans.)
Vermillion Republican (S.D.)
Wall Street Journal (N.Y.)
Walnut Valley Times (Kans.)
Watonga Republican (Okla,)
Webster Daily Journal (S.D.)
Wichita Eagle (Kans.)
Yankton Press (S.D.)
Yankton Weekly Press and Dakotian (S.D.)
Youth's Companion

Published Primary

Abel, Annie Heloise. *Chardon's Journal at Fort Clark, 1834–1839*. Lincoln: University of Nebraska Press, 1997.

Andrews, C. C. *Minnesota and Dacotah: In Letters Descriptive of a Tour Through the North-west in the Autumn of 1856*, 2nd ed. Washington, D.C.: R. Farnham, 1857.

Anonymous. "Captain Dan Henrie, His Adventure with the Wolves." *United States Democratic Review* 24 (January 1849): 33–43.

Anonymous. *Travels from Ocean to Ocean, from the Lakes to the Gulf*, 4th ed. Harrisburg, Pa.: Amos H. Gottschall, 1894.

Bandel, Eugene. *Frontier Life in the Army, 1854–1861*. Glendale, Calif.: Arthur H. Clark Co., 1932.

Bartholomew, David M., ed. *Pioneer Naturalist on the Plains: The Diary of Elam Bartholomew, 1871 to 1934*. Manhattan, Kans.: Sunflower University Press, 1998.

Bates, James C. *A Texas Cavalry Officer's Civil War: The Diary and Letters of James C. Bates*, ed. by Richard Lowe. Baton Rouge: Louisiana State University Press, 1999.

Beadle, Erastus F. *Ham, Eggs & Corn Cake: A Nebraska Territory Diary*. Lincoln: University of Nebraska Press, 2001.

Becker, Robert H., ed. *Thomas Christy's Road Across the Plains*. Denver, Colo.: Old West Publishing Company, 1969.

Bessey, Charles E. "Are the Trees Advancing or Retreating upon the Nebraska Plains?" *Science* 10 (November 24, 1899): 768–770.

Bivans, Venola Lewis, ed. "The Diary of Luna E. Warner, a Kansas Teenager of the Early 1870s." *Kansas Historical Quarterly* 35 (1969): 411–441.

Boller, H. A. *Among the Indians: Four Years on the Upper Missouri, 1858–1862*. Lincoln: University of Nebraska Press, 1972.

Brackenridge, H. M. *Journal of a Voyage up the River Missouri; Performed in Eighteen Hundred Eleven, in Early Western Travels*, vol. 6., ed. by R. G. Thwaites. Glendale, Calif.: Arthur H. Clark Co., 1966.

Bray, Edmund C., and Martha Coleman Bray, eds. and trans. *Joseph N. Nicollet on the Plains and Prairies: The Expeditions of 1838–39 with Journals, Letters and Notes on the Dakota Indians*. St. Paul: Minnesota Historical Society Press, 1976.

Burroughs, John. "Notes from the Prairie." *Century* 32 (September 1886): 784–790.

Byrkit, James W., ed. *Letters from the Southwest: September 20, 1884–March 14, 1885*. Tucson: University of Arizona Press, 1989.

Carvalho, S. N. *Incidents of Travel and Adventure in the Far West; with Col. Fremont's Last Expedition Across the Rocky Mountains . . .* New York: Derby & Jackson, 1859.

Carver, J. *Travels Through the Interior Part of North America in the Years 1766, 1767, 1768*. Minneapolis, Minn.: Ross and Haines, 1956.

Charlevoix, P. F. X. *Journal of a Voyage to North America*, vol. 1. Chicago: The Caxton Club, 1923.

Clary, David A., ed. "'I Am Already Quite a Texan': Albert J. Myer's Letters from Texas, 1854–1856." *Southwestern Historical Quarterly* 82 (July 1978): 25–76.

Coues, Elliot, ed. *The Manuscript Journals of Alexander Henry and of David Thompson*, vol. 1. New York: Francis P. Harper, 1897.

———. *New Light on the Early History of the Greater Northwest: The Manuscript Journals of Alexander Henry*, vol. 2. New York: Francis P. Harper, 1897.

Davis, W. W. H. *El Gringo: Or, New Mexico and Her People*. Reprint, Santa Fe, N.M.: The Rydall Press, 1938.

Debo, Angie, ed. *The Cowman's Southwest: Being the Reminiscences of Oliver Nelson*. Glendale, Calif.: Arthur H. Clark Co., 1953.

Denig, Edwin Thomson. *Five Indian Tribes of the Upper Missouri*, ed. by J. E. Ewers. Norman: University of Oklahoma Press, 1961.

Dodge, Richard Irving. *Our Wild Indians: Thirty-Three Years' Personal Experience Among the Red Men of the Great West*. Hartford, Conn.: A. D. Worthington and Company, 1882.

———. *The Plains of the Great West and Their Inhabitants*. New York: G. P. Putnam's Sons, 1877.

Domenech, E. *Seven Years' Residence in the Great American Deserts of North America*. London: Longman, 1860.

Drumm, Stella M., ed. *Down the Santa Fe Trail and into Mexico: The Diary of Susan Shelby Magoffin, 1846–1847*. New Haven, Conn.: Yale University Press, 1926.

Edson, Charles Leroy. "Prairie Fire." In *Prairie Fire*. Charleston, S.C.: Southern Prt'g & Pub. Co., 1924.

Evans, Andrew, trans. *A Trip to the Prairies and the Interior of North America, 1837–1838: Travel Notes by Count Francesco Arese*. New York: The Harbor Press, 1934.

Farnham, Thomas J. *Travels in the Great Western Prairies*. New York: Greeley & McElrath, 1843.

Ferris, Jacob. *The States and Territories of the Great West*. Buffalo, N.Y.: E. F. Beadle, 1856.

Finley, John L. "The Effects of Prairie Fires on Vegetation." In *Report of the Kansas State Board of Agriculture*. Topeka: State of Kansas, 1894.

Foreman, Grant, ed. *A Pathfinder in the Southwest: The Itinerary of Lieutenant A.W. Whipple During His Explorations for a Railway Route from Fort Smith to Los Angeles in the Years 1853 & 1854*. Norman: University of Oklahoma Press, 1941.

Gordon, Mary McDougall, ed. *Through Indian Country to California: John P. Sherburne's Diary of the Whipple Expedition, 1853–1854*. Stanford, Calif.: Stanford University Press, 1988.

Grant, George M. *Ocean to Ocean: Sanford Fleming's Expedition Through Canada in 1872*. London: S. Low, Marston, Low & Searle, 1873.

Gray, A. B. *Survey of a Route on the 32nd Parallel for the Texas Western Railroad, 1854*. Los Angeles: Westernlore Press, 1963.

Gregg, Josiah. *Commerce of the Prairies*, ed. by Max L. Moorhead. Norman: University of Oklahoma Press, 1954.

Griscom, George L. *Fighting with Ross' Texas Cavalry Brigade: The Diary of George L. Griscom, Adjutant, Ninth Texas Cavalry Regiment*, ed. by Homer L. Kerr. Hillsboro, Tex.: Hill Junior College Press, 1976.

Harper, J. Russell, ed. *Paul Kane's Frontier*. Austin: University of Texas Press, 1971.

Heloise, Annie, ed. *Tabeau's Narrative of Loisel's Expedition to the Upper Missouri*. Norman: University of Oklahoma Press, 1939.

Hennepin, Louis. *A New Discovery of a Vast Country in America*. Chicago: A.C. McClurg & Co., 1903 [London 1698].

Hind, Henry Y. *Narrative of the Canadian Red River Exploring Expedition of 1857 and the Assinniboine and Saskatchewan Exploring Expedition of 1858*, vol. 1. New York: Greenwood Press, 1969.

Hoy, Jim, ed. *A Window on Flint Hills Folklife: The Mardin Ranch Diaries 1862–1863*. Emporia, Kans.: Center for Great Plains Studies, 2009.

———. "A Window on Flint Hills Folklife, Part II: The Diary of Elisha Mardin." *Kansas History: A Journal of the Central Plains* 14 (Winter 1991–1992): 246–269.

Hoyt, William D., Jr. "Rosser's Journal, Northern Pacific Railroad Survey, September 1871." *North Dakota Historical Quarterly* 10 (January 1943): 47–51.

Humfreville, J. L. *Twenty Years Among Our Hostile Indians*, 2nd ed. New York: Hunter and Company, 1903.

Inman, Henry, compiler. *Buffalo Jones' Forty Years of Adventure: A Volume of Facts Gathered from Experience by Hon. C. J. Jones . . .* Topeka, Kans.: Crane & Company, 1899.

Irving, John T. *Indian Sketches Taken During an Expedition to the Pawnee Tribes*, ed. by John McDermott. Norman: University of Oklahoma Press, 1955.

James, Edwin. *An Account of an Expedition from Pittsburgh to the Rocky Mountains, Performed in the Years 1819, 1820; under the Command of Major Stephen Long*, vol. 15. Cleveland, Ohio: Arthur H. Clark Co., 1905.

Jensen, Richard E., ed. *Happy as a Big Sunflower: Adventures in the West, 1876–1880*. Lincoln: University of Nebraska Press, 2000.

The Journals, Detailed Reports, and Observations Relative to the Exploration by Captain Palliser of that Portion of British North America . . . . London: George E. Eyre and William Spottiswoode, 1863.

Keating, W. H. *Narrative of an Expedition to the Source of St. Peter's River . . . under the Command of Stephen H. Long*, vol. 2. London: George B. Whittaker, 1825.

Kelly, Fanny. *Narrative of My Captivity Among the Sioux Indians*, ed. by Clark and Mary Lee Spence. New York: Konecky & Konecky, 1990.

Kilgore, William H. *The Kilgore Journal of an Overland Journey to California in the Year 1850*. New York: Hastings House, 1949.

Lewis, Meriwether. *The Lewis and Clark Expedition*. Philadelphia, Pa.: J. B. Lippincott Co., 1961.

Livermore, Mary. *The Story of My Life; or, The Sunshine and Shadow of Seventy Years*. Hartford, Conn.: A. D. Worthington & Co., 1897.

Lowe, P. G. *Five Years a Dragoon ('49 to '54) and Other Adventures on the Plains*. Kansas City, Mo.: The Franklin Hudson Publishing Company, 1906.

Mallery, Garrick. "Picture-Writing of the American Indians," in *Tenth Annual Report of the Bureau of Ethnology*. Washington, D.C.: Government Printing Office, 1889.

Marcy, Randolph B. *The Prairie Traveler: The Bestselling Classic Handbook for America's Pioneers*. Reprint, New York: Perigee Books, 1994.

McDermott, J. F., ed. *Tixier's Travels on the Osage Prairies*. Norman: University of Oklahoma Press, 1940.

Mollhausen, H. B. *Diary of a Journey from the Mississippi to the Pacific . . .* vol. 1. London: Longmans, Brown, Green, Longmans, & Roberts, 1858.

Morris, George Pope. "The Prairie on Fire." *The Thought-Blossom: A Memento*. New York: Leavitt and Allen, 1854.

Murray, Charles Augustus. *Travels in North America During the Years 1834, 1835, and 1836*, vol. 2. London: R. Bentley, 1839.

Olmsted, Frederick Law. *A Journey Through Texas; or, a Saddle-trip on the Southwestern Frontier; with a Statistical Appendix*. New York: Dix, Edwards & Co., 1857.

Oñate, D. J. "True Account of the Expedition Toward the East, 1601." In *Spanish Exploration in the Southwest, 1542–1706*. New York: Barnes and Noble, 1946.

Palliser, J. *Solitary Rambles and Adventures of a Hunter in the Prairies*. Tokyo: Charles E. Tuttle Co., 1969.

Perrot, N. "Memoir on the Manners, Customs, and Religion of the Savages of North America." In *The Indian Tribes of the Upper Mississippi Valley and Region of the Great Lakes*, vol. 1. Cleveland, Ohio: Arthur H. Clark Co., 1911.

Price, James P. *Seven Years of Prairie Life*. Reprint, Goff, Kans.: Great Plains Book Company, 1983.

Riley, Charles V. *The Locust Plague in the United States: Being More Particularly a Treatise on the Rocky Mountain Locust or So-Called Grasshopper . . . .* Chicago, Ill.: Rand, McNally & Co., 1877.

Ross, Alexander. *The Red River Settlement: Its Rise, Progress, and Present State.* Minneapolis, Minn.: Ross and Haines, 1957.

Sage, Rufus B. *Rufus B. Sage: His Letters and Papers, 1836–1847*, vol. 4. Glendale, Calif.: Arthur H. Clark Co., 1956.

Shearer, Frederick E., ed. *The Pacific Tourist; Adams & Bishop's Illustrated Trans-Continental Guide of Travel, from the Atlantic to the Pacific Ocean . . . . A Complete Traveler's Guide of the Union and Central Pacific Railroads . . .* Reprint, New York: Crown Publishers, 1970.

Snell, Joseph W., ed. "Roughing It on Her Kansas Claim: The Diary of Abbie Bright, 1870–1871." *Kansas Historical Quarterly* 37 (1971): 233–268, 394–428.

Spry, I. M., ed. *The Papers of the Palliser Expedition, 1857–1860.* Toronto: The Champlain Society, 1968.

Stansbury, Howard. *Exploration and Survey of the Valley of the Great Salt Lake of Utah, Including a Reconnaissance of a New Route Through the Rocky Mountains.* Philadelphia, Pa.: Lippincott, Grambo and Company, 1852.

Thompson, David. *David Thompson's Narrative of His Explorations in Western America.* Toronto: The Champlain Society, 1916.

Thwaites, Reuben G., ed. *Original Journals of the Lewis and Clark Expedition, 1804–1806*, vol. 1. New York: Arno Press, 1969.

Trobriand, Philippe Regis. *Army Life in Dakota*, ed. by Milo Milton Quaife, trans. by George Francis Will. Chicago, Ill.: The Lakeside Press, 1941.

———. *Military Life in Dakota*, ed. and trans. by L. M. Kane. St. Paul, Minn.: The Alvord Memorial Commission, 1951.

Turner, A. R. "Surveying the International Boundary: The Journal of George M. Dawson, 1873." *Saskatchewan History* 21 (1968): 1–23.

Ware, Eugene F. *The Indian War of 1864.* Lincoln: University of Nebraska Press, 1994.

Wied, Prinz Maximilian von. *Travels in the Interior of North America*, vol. 23. Cleveland, Ohio: Arthur H. Clark Co., 1906.

Wilhelm, Paul, Duke of Wurttemberg. *First Journey to North America in the Years 1822 to 1824*, trans. by Wm. G. Bek. *South Dakota Historical Collection* 19 (1938): 7–474.

Williams, J. "Narrative of a Trip from the State of Indiana to the Oregon Territory, in the Years 1841–42." In *To the Rockies and Oregon, 1839–1842.* Glendale, Calif.: Arthur H. Clark Co., 1955.

Secondary

Articles
Axelrod, Daniel I. "Rise of the Grassland Biome, Central North America." *Botanical Review* 51 (April–June 1985): 163–201.

Bergh, Mrs. A. H. "Pioneer Daughters of Dakota." *South Dakota Historical Collections* 33 (1966): 56–57.

Boyd, Matthew. "Identification of Anthropogenic Burning in the Paleoecological Record of the Northern Prairies: A New Approach." *Annals of the Association of American Geographers* 92 (2002): 471–487.

Briggs, John M., Alan K. Knapp, and Brent L. Brock. "Expansion of Woody Plants in Tallgrass Prairie: A Fifteen-Year Study of Fire and Fire-Grazing Interactions." *American Midland Naturalist* 147 (April 2002): 287–294.

Clark, James S., Eric C. Grimm, Jason Lynch, and Pietra G. Mueller. "Effects of Holocene Climate Change on the C4 Grassland/Woodland Boundary in the Northern Plains, USA." *Ecology* 82 (March 2001): 620–636.

Crutchett, Charles. "Grand View Douglas County's Ghost Town." *South Dakota Historical Collections* 30 (1960): 374–435.

Denevan, William M. "The Pristine Myth: The Landscape of the Americas in 1492." *Annals of the Association of American Geographers* 82 (September 1992): 369–385.

Drake, Brian Allen. "Waving 'A Bough of Challenge': Forestry on the Kansas Grasslands, 1868–1915." *Great Plains Quarterly* 23 (Winter 2003): 19–34.

Dromey, Joe. "South Dakota Had Prairie Fires Also." *Eighth Annual West River History Conference.* Keystone, S.D., 2001.

Flores, Dan. "Bison Ecology and Bison Diplomacy: The Southern Plains from 1800 to 1850." *Journal of American History* 78 (September 1991): 465–485.

"Fremont's Story 1838–1839." *South Dakota Historical Collections* 10 (1920): 71–97.

Fuhlendorf, Samuel D., and David M. Engle. "Restoring Heterogeneity on Rangelands: Ecosystem Management Based on Evolutionary Grazing Patters." *BioScience* 51 (August 2001): 625–632.

Gard, Wayne. "When Fire Seared the Prairies." *Cattleman* 36 (May 1950): 35–37.

Gehring, Janet L., and Thomas B. Bragg. "Changes in Prairie Vegetation Under Eastern Red Cedar (*Juniperus virginiana L.*) in an Eastern Nebraska Bluestem Prairie." *American Midland Naturalist* 128 (October 1992): 209–217.

Gibson, David J. and Lloyd C. Hulbert. "Effects of Fire, Topography and Year-to-Year Climatic Variation on Species Composition in Tallgrass Prairie." *Vegetatio* 72 (1987): 175–183.

Hamalainen, Pekka. "The Rise and Fall of Plains Indian Horse Cultures." *Journal of American History* 90 (December 2003): 833–862.

Heisler, Jana L., John M. Briggs, and Alan K. Knapp. "Long-Term Patterns of Shrub Expansion in a C4 Dominated Grassland: Fire Frequency and the Dynamics of Shrub Cover and Abundance." *American Journal of Botany* 90 (2003): 423–428.

Hensel, R. L. "Recent Studies on the Effect of Burning on Grassland Vegetation." *Ecology* 4 (April 1923): 183–188.

Higgins, Kenneth F. "Lightning Fires in North Dakota Grasslands and in Pine-Savanna Lands of South Dakota and Montana." *Journal of Range Management* 37 (March 1984): 100–103.

Hoy, Jim. "To Start a Fire." *Kansas School Naturalist* 39 (March 1993): 7–11.

———. "Prairie Fires." *Kansas School Naturalist* 39 (March 1993): 3–6.

Judy, S. S., and Will G. Robinson. "Sanborn County History." *South Dakota Historical Collections* 26 (1952): 1–180.

Kibbe, Lynus A. "Early Recollections of a Son of a Pioneer Newspaper Man of South Dakota and Dakota Territory." *South Dakota Historical Collections* 25 (1950): 316–349.

Mock, Cary J. "Rainfall in the Garden of the United States Great Plains, 1870–1889." *Climatic Change* 44 (2000): 173–195.

Nelson, J. G., and R. E. England. "Some Comments on the Causes and Effects of Fire in the Northern Grasslands Area of Canada and the Nearby United States, ca. 1750–1900." *Canadian Geographer* 15 (1971): 295–306.

Rannie, W. F. "'Awful Splendour': Historical Accounts of Prairie Fire in Southern Manitoba Prior to 1870." *Prairie Forum* 26 (April 1, 2001): 17–45.

Rodgers, Randy. "New Answer to Burning Questions." *Kansas Wildlife and Parks* 64 (March–April 2007): 2–8.

Rogers, Elwin E. "Almost Scandinavia: Scandinavian Immigrant Experience in Grant County, 1877–1920." *South Dakota Historical Collections* 41 (1982): 275–452.

Rowe, J. S. "Lightning Fires in Saskatchewan Grassland." *Canadian Field-Naturalist* 83 (Oct.–Dec. 1969): 317–324.

Sauer, Carl O. "Grassland Climax, Fire, and Man." *Journal of Range Management* 3 (January 1950): 16–21.

Schmidt, Mary A. "History of the Seventh-Day Adventist Church at Swan Lake, South Dakota." *South Dakota Historical Collections* 14 (1928): 553–562.

Sherow, James E. "Workings of the Geodialectic: High Plains Indians and Their Horses in the Region of the Arkansas River Valley, 1880–1870." *Environmental History Review* 16 (Summer 1992): 61–84.

Stewart, Omer. "Why the Great Plains Are Treeless." *Colorado Quarterly* 2 (Summer 1953): 40–50.

Thomas, Gregory. "Fire and the Fur Trade: The Saskatchewan District, 1790–1840." *Beaver* (Autumn 1977): 32–39.

Wells, P. V. "Scarp Woodlands, Transported Grassland Soils, and Concept of Grassland Climate in the Great Plains Region." *Science* 148 (April 9, 1965): 246–249.

White, C. A. "Prairie Fires." *American Naturalist* 5 (April 1871): 68–70.

White, Richard. "Discovering Nature in North America." *Journal of American History* 79 (December 1992): 874–891.

Books

Adamson, Archibald R. *North Platte and Its Associations*. North Platte, Nebr.: The Evening Telegraph, 1910.

Alberts, Frances Jacobs, ed. *Sod House Reminiscences*. Holdrege, Nebr.: Sod House Society, 1972.

Amato, Anthony J. "A Wet and Dry Landscape." In Anthony J. Amato, Janet Timmermanm and Joseph Anthony Amato, *Draining the Great Oasis: An Environmental History of Murray County, Minnesota*. Marshall, Minn.: Crossings Press, 2001.

American Red Cross. *Community First Aid and Safety*. The American Red Cross, 2002.

Anderson, Roger C. "The Historic Role of Fire in the North American Grassland." In Scott L. Collins and Linda Wallace, eds., *Fire in North American Tallgrass Prairies*. Norman: University of Oklahoma Press, 1990, 8–18.

Ayers, Nathanial M. *Building a New Empire*. New York: Broadway Publishing Co., 1910.

Bandelier, Fanny. *The Journey of Alvar Nuñez Cabeza de Vaca*. Chicago, Ill.: The Rio Grande Press, 1964.

Bardwell, Denver. *Prairie Fire, a Gunfire Western Novel*. New York: Doubleday, Doran & Co., 1940.

Binnema, Theodore. *Common and Contested Ground: A Human and Environmental History of the Northwestern Plains*. Norman: University of Oklahoma Press, 2001.

Birney, Betty G. *Tyrannosaurus Tex*. Boston: Houghton Mifflin Company, 1994.

Blue, Anthony Dias. *The Complete Book of Mixed Drinks*, rev. ed. New York: Quill, 2002.

Branson, Terri. *Prairie Fire*. Dragonfly Publishing, 2001.

Coldsmith, Don. *Trails of the Spanish Bit*. New York: Bantam Books, 1980.

Coleman, Jon T. *Vicious: Wolves and Men in America*. New Haven, Conn.: Yale University Press, 2004.

Cooper, James Fenimore. *The Prairie*. Reprint, New York: Dodd, Mead & Company, 1954.

Cronon, William. *Changes in the Land: Indians, Colonists, and the Ecology of New England*. New York: Hill and Wang, 1983.

Cunfer, Geoff. *On the Great Plains: Agriculture and Environment*. College Station: Texas A&M University Press, 2005.

Dick, Everett. *The Sod-House Frontier, 1854–1890; A Social History of the Northern Plains from the Creation of Kansas & Nebraska to the Admission of the Dakotas*. Lincoln, Nebr.: Johnsen Publishing Company, 1954.

Duke, Cordia Sloan, and Joe B. Frantz. *6000 Miles of Fence: Life on the XIT Ranch of Texas*. Austin: University of Texas Press, 1961.

Edwards, Whit. *"The Prairie Was on Fire": Eyewitness Accounts of the Civil War in the Indian Territory*. Oklahoma City: Oklahoma Historical Society, 2001.

Erdman, Loula Grace. *The Edge of Time*. New York: Dodd, Mead & Company, 1950.

Esval, Orland Eittreim. *Prairie Tales: Adventures of Growing up on a Frontier*. Banner Elk, N.C.: Landmark House, 1979.

Fesler, Myrtle D. *Pioneers of Western Kansas*. New York: Carlton Press, 1962.

Fields, Wayne. "The American Prairies and the Literary Aesthetic." In Joni L. Kinsey, *Plain Pictures: Images of the American Prairie*. Washington, D.C.: Smithsonian Institution Press, 1996.

Fort Ransom Community History: 1878–2003. Gwinner, N.D.: J&M Companies, n.d.

Goetzmann, William H. *Exploration and Empire*. New York: Alfred A. Knopf, 1966.

Goodman, Susan E. *Cora Frear: A True Story*. New York: Aladdin Paperbacks, 2002.

Goudsblom, Johan. *Fire and Civilization*. London: Penguin, 1992.

Gregory, Kristiana. *Prairie River: A Grateful Harvest*. New York: Scholastic, 2003.

Hammond, Isaac B. *Reminiscences of Frontier Life*. Portland, Oreg.: self-published, 1904.

Hart, John Fraser. *The Rural Landscape*. Baltimore, Md.: The Johns Hopkins University Press, 1998.

Hasselstrom, Linda M. *No Place Like Home: Notes from a Western Life*. Reno: University of Nevada Press, 2009.

Hoy, Jim. *Cowboys and Kansas: Stories from the Tallgrass Prairie*. Norman: University of Oklahoma Press, 1995.

———. *Flint Hills Cowboys: Tales of the Tallgrass Prairie*. Lawrence: University Press of Kansas, 2006.

Isenberg, Andrew C. *The Destruction of the Bison: An Environmental History, 1750– 1920*. Cambridge: Cambridge University Press, 2000.

Jackson, Wes. *Becoming Native to This Place*. Lexington: The University Press of Kentucky, 1994.

Johannsen, Albert. *The House of Beadle and Adams and Its Dime and Nickel Novels: The Story of a Vanished Literature*. Norman: University of Oklahoma Press, 1950.

Killdeer, John. *Fire on the Prairie*. New York: Domain, 1995.

Kinsey, Joni L. *Plain Pictures: Images of the American Prairie*. Washington, D.C.: Smithsonian Institution Press, 1996.

Kohl, Edith Eudora. *Land of the Burnt Thigh: A Lively Story of Women Homesteaders on the South Dakota Frontier*. St. Paul: Minnesota Historical Press, 1986.

Lewis, Henry T. "An Anthropological Critique." In Omer Stewart, *Forgotten Fires: Native Americans and the Transient Wilderness*, ed. by Henry T. Lewis and M. Kat Anderson. Norman: University of Oklahoma Press, 2002.

Licht, Daniel S. *Ecology and Economics of the Great Plains*. Lincoln: University of Nebraska Press, 1997.

Lockwood, Jeffrey A. *The Devastating Rise and Mysterious Disappearance of the Insect That Shaped the American Frontier*. New York: Basic Books, 2004.

Logue, Roscoe. *Under Texas Border Skies*. Amarillo, Tex.: Russell Stationary Co., 1935.

Maas, L. J. *Prairie Fire*. Nederland, Tex.: Yellow Rose Books, 2002.

Malin, James. *The Grassland of North America: Prolegomena to Its History with Addenda to Subhumid Geographical Environment*. Gloucester, Mass.: Peter Smith, 1967.

———. *Winter Wheat in the Golden Belt of Kansas: A Study in Adaptation to Subhumid Geographical Environment*. Lawrence: University of Kansas Press, 1944.

——— and Robert P. Swierenga, eds. *History and Ecology: Studies of the Grassland*. Lincoln: University of Nebraska Press, 1984.

Mattes, Merrill J. *The Great Platte River Road*. Lincoln: University of Nebraska Press, 1987.

McHugh, Tom, and Victoria Hobson. *The Time of the Buffalo*. Lincoln: University of Nebraska Press, 1972.

Miner, Craig. *Kansas: The History of the Sunflower State, 1854–2000*. Lawrence: University Press of Kansas, 2002.

———. *West of Wichita: Settling the High Plains of Kansas, 1865–1890*. Lawrence: University Press of Kansas, 1986.

Mitchum, Hank. *Red Buffalo*. Toronto: Bantam Books, 1989.

Moulton, Candy. *Roadside History of Nebraska*. Missoula, Mont.: Mountain Press Publishing Company, 1997.

My Folks Came in a Covered Wagon: A Treasury of Stories Handed down in the Families of Capper's Weekly Readers. Topeka, Kans.: Capper Publications, 1956.

Orpen, Adela Elizabeth Richards. *Memories of the Old Emigrant Days in Kansas, 1862–1865*. Edinburgh: William Blackwood & Sons Ltd., 1926.

Palmer, Catherine. *Prairie Fire*. Wheaton, Ill.: Tyndale House Publishers, 1998.

Pendleton, Don. *Mack Bolan; Prairie Fire*. Toronto: Worldwide, 1984.

Plaisted, Tirzah. *There Lived a Man: Mother's Story*. New York: self-published, 1914.

Pyne, Stephen J. *America's Fires: A Historical Context for Policy and Practice*. Durham, N.C.: Forest History Society, 2010.

———. *Awful Splendour: A Fire History of Canada*. Vancouver: University of British Columbia Press, 2007.

————. *Burning Bush: A Fire History of Australia*. New York: Henry Holt and Company, 1991.

————. *Fire: A Brief History*. Seattle: University of Washington Press, 2001.

————. *Fire in America: A Cultural History of Wildland and Rural Fire*. Seattle: University of Washington Press, 1982.

————. *World Fire: The Culture of Fire on Earth*. New York: Henry Holt and Company, 1995.

Resnick, Jane Parker. *The Everything Bartender's Book*. Holbrook, Mass.: Adams Media Corp., 1995.

Reynolds, Marilynn. *The Prairie Fire*. New York: Orca Book Publishers, 2001.

Riney-Kehrberg, Pamela. *Rooted in Dust: Surviving Drought and Depression in Southwestern Kansas*. Lawrence: University Press of Kansas, 1994.

Roberts, Jim. *Gene Autry and the Prairie Fire*. London: Adprint Limited, ca. 1956.

Root, Frank A., and William Elsey Connelly. *The Overland Stage to California*. Reprint, Columbus, Ohio: Long's College Book Co., 1950.

Savage, Candace. *Prairie: A Natural History*. Vancouver: Greystone Books, 2004.

Schwarm, Larry. *On Fire*. Durham, N.C.: Duke University Press, 2003.

Sherow, James E. *The Grasslands of the United States: An Environmental History*. Santa Barbara, Calif.: ABC-CLIO, 2007.

Smith, Martha L. *Going to God's Country*. Boston: The Christopher Publishing House, 1941.

Starkey, George. "Prairie Fires." In *Chase County Historical Sketches*. Chase County, Kans.: Chase County Historical Society, 1940.

Stewart, Omer. *Forgotten Fires: Native Americans and the Transient Wilderness*. Norman: University of Oklahoma Press, 2002.

Stratton, Joanna L. *Pioneer Women: Voices from the Kansas Frontier*. New York: Simon and Schuster, 1981.

Strom, Claire. *Profiting from the Plains: The Great Northern Railway and Corporate Development of the American West*. Seattle: University of Washington Press, 2003.

Towne, Arthur E. *Old Prairie Days*. Otsego, Mich.: The Otsego Union Press, 1941.

Vale, Thomas R., ed. *Fire, Native Peoples, and the Natural Land*. Washington, D.C.: Island Press, 2002.

Vogl, Richard J. "Effects of Fire on Grasslands." In T. T. Kozlowski and C. E. Ahlgren, eds., *Fire and Ecosystems*. New York: Academic Press, 1974, 139–149.

Warren, Louis S. *Buffalo Bill's America: William Cody and the Wild West Show*. New York: Alfred A. Knopf, 2005.

Webb, Walter Prescott. *The Great Plains*. Reprint, Lincoln: University of Nebraska Press, 1981.

Wedel, Waldo. "The Central North American Grassland: Man-Made or Natural." In *Studies in Human Ecology*. Washington, D.C.: Pan American Union, 1957.

Werner, Patricia. *Prairie Fire*. Toronto: Paperjacks, 1988.

West, Elliott. *The Contested Plains: Indians, Goldseekers, and the Rush to Colorado*. Lawrence: University Press of Kansas, 1998.

———. *The Way to the West: Essays on the Central Plains*. Albuquerque: University of New Mexico Press, 1995.

Wilder, Laura Ingalls. *Little House on the Prairie*. New York: Harper & Row, 1935.

Wilton, Andrew, and Tim Barringer. *American Sublime: Landscape Painting in the United States 1820–1880*. Princeton, N.J.: Princeton University Press, 2002.

Worster, Donald. *Dust Bowl: The Southern Plains in the 1930s*. New York: Oxford University Press, 1979.

Wright, Henry A., and Arthur W. Bailey. *Fire Ecology: United States and Southern Canada*. New York: John Wiley & Sons, 1982.

Dissertation

Moore, Conrad Taylor. "Man and Fire in the Central North American Grassland, 1535–1890: A Documentary Historical Geography." Ph.D. diss., University of California–Los Angeles, 1972.

Film, Music, and Television

Arnold, Elliot and Lou Vittes. "Prairie Fire." *Rawhide* script, produced by Bernard L. Kowalski and Bruce Geller.

"Little House on the Prairie." Pilot. Lions Gate DVD, 1974.

Robbins, Marty. *More Gunfighter Ballads and Trail Songs*. Sony Records, 1990.

The Texans. Universal Western Collection, 1938, Paramount Pictures Inc.

Interviews

Eastman, Kristyn. Interviewed October 8, 2006, by the author in Olathe, Kans.

Frost, Maxine. Interviewed February 1, 2003 by the author in Augusta, Kans.

National Public Radio. *All Things Considered* transcript, May 3, 2004. Accessed through EBSCOhost.

Obermeyer, Brian. Director, Flint Hills Initiative, Nature Conservancy. Interviewed November 15, 2010, by the author by telephone.

Memorabilia

Little House on the Prairie board game. Parker Brothers, 1978.

Web Sites

Brunetti, Rick. Director, Bureau of Air, Kansas Department of Health and Environment, "Kansas Flint Hills Smoke Management Plan," Joint Committee on Energy and Environmental Policy," Topeka, Kansas, September 9, 2010. http://skyways.lib.ks.us/ksleg/KLRD/Resources/Testimony/EEP/9-09-10/14-KDHE-Bureau-of-Air-Brunetti-FlintHillsSmokeMgmt.pdf.

Drummond, Ree. *The Pioneer Woman*, http://thepioneerwoman.com/blog/2010/11/theres-a-fire/.

"Entire Oklahoma Town Flees as Fires Spread," http://www.cnn.com/2009/US/03/06/Oklahoma.town.fire/index.html.

"Fire, Grazing, and the Prairie," Fire Management, Tallgrass Prairie National Preserve, National Park Service, http://www.npns.gov/archive/tapr/fire.htm.

Library of Congress American Memory Project, www.memory.loc.gov.

Mid-America All-Indian Center. http://www.theindiancenter.org/Museum/Artists/.

Prairie Fire Festival. http://wwwprairiefirefestival.com.

Scott, Robert. www.sharecom.ca/scott.

University of Virginia, Geospatial & Statistical Data Center, Historical Census Browser, http://fisher.lib.virginia.edu.

Wichita Art Museum. www.kansastravel.org/wichitaartmuseum.htm.

Index